EXPRESSIVE ACTS

Celebrations and Demonstrations in the
Streets of Victorian Toronto

IAN RADFORTH

Expressive Acts

Celebrations and Demonstrations in the Streets of Victorian Toronto

UNIVERSITY OF TORONTO PRESS
Toronto Buffalo London

© University of Toronto Press 2023
Toronto Buffalo London
utorontopress.com

ISBN 978-1-4875-4574-1 (cloth)   ISBN 978-1-4875-4592-5 (EPUB)
ISBN 978-1-4875-4577-2 (paper)   ISBN 978-1-4875-4579-6 (PDF)

Library and Archives Canada Cataloguing in Publication

Title: Expressive acts : celebrations and demonstrations in the streets of Victorian Toronto / Ian Radforth.
Names: Radforth, Ian Walter, 1952– author.
Description: Includes bibliographical references and index.
Identifiers: Canadiana (print) 20220420564 | Canadiana (ebook) 20220420602 | ISBN 9781487545772 (paper) | ISBN 9781487545741 (cloth) | ISBN 9781487545925 (EPUB) | ISBN 9781487545796 (PDF)
Subjects: LCSH: Demonstrations – Ontario – Toronto – History – 19th century. | LCSH: Toronto (Ont.) – Social conditions – 19th century.
Classification: LCC FC3097.4 .R33 2023 | DDC 971.3/541–dc23

We wish to acknowledge the land on which the University of Toronto Press operates. This land is the traditional territory of the Wendat, the Anishnaabeg, the Haudenosaunee, the Métis, and the Mississaugas of the Credit First Nation.

University of Toronto Press acknowledges the financial support of the Government of Canada, the Canada Council for the Arts, and the Ontario Arts Council, an agency of the Government of Ontario, for its publishing activities.

 Canada Council for the Arts / Conseil des Arts du Canada

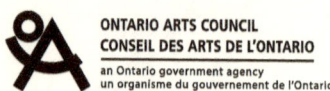 ONTARIO ARTS COUNCIL / CONSEIL DES ARTS DE L'ONTARIO
an Ontario government agency
un organisme du gouvernement de l'Ontario

Funded by the Government of Canada / Financé par le gouvernement du Canada

Contents

List of Maps and Illustrations vii

Acknowledgments ix

Introduction 3

1 Tory Rebels and a Viceregal Visit 15

2 The Press and Election Culture 38

3 A Prince in Town 62

4 Religious Processions and Disorder 85

5 Colonialism Triumphant: Celebrating the Suppression of the North-West Resistance of 1885 107

6 Boys, Young Men, and Disorder 134

7 Strikers and Their Supporters 152

Conclusion 177

Notes 183

Index 225

Maps and Illustrations

Map 1 Toronto Core, 1884 xi
Map 2 Toronto, 1884 xii

1.1 James Bruce, The Earl of Elgin and Kincardine 17
1.2 A Conservative journal lampoons the Rebellion Losses Bill 20
1.3 Mocking Lord Elgin's refusal to appear publicly 31
2.1 Torch-light procession given in honour of victorious George Brown 57
3.1 The prince, the governor general, and some members of his suite in Montreal 64
3.2 Toronto's Civic Arch on John Street 68
3.3 "Burning Cloud, Oronhyatekha" (1860) by Henry W. Acland 71
3.4 Strollers admiring the Orangemen's Arch, Toronto 80
4.1 Bishop John Joseph Lynch 88
4.2 Jubilee riot near Metropolitan Methodist Church 93
5.1 The Tenth Royals and Queen's Own Rifles marching out of the drill shed 114
5.2 "Take your discharge? – Certainly not!" 118
5.3 Queen's Own Rifles pose at the North Toronto Station, 23 July 1885 125
5.4 Toronto reception, 23 July 1885 127
5.5 The returned men of K (University) Company, Queen's Own Rifles 128
5.6 North-West Rebellion Monument, Queen's Park, Toronto 130
6.1 Young men and boys throwing stones during the Jubilee riots 138
7.1 Two-horse streetcar with driver and conductor, Toronto, ca 1892 155

Acknowledgments

I want to thank the anonymous readers who refereed the original writings that make up this book and those who refereed the book itself. It is better for their insights. Preparing this book has been an enjoyable pandemic activity. At University of Toronto Press, Len Husband enthusiastically supported the project from the start, Barbara Porter efficiently guided the manuscript through the production process, and Matthew Kudelka provided superb copy editing. Nate Wessel produced excellent maps. My friend Paul Eprile encouraged me throughout this project, and I appreciate his expertise in devising a title. As always, my partner Franca Iacovetta has been supportive of my historical writing. It was because of her urging that I took on the challenge of putting this book together.

I thank *Canadian Historical Review*, *Histoire sociale/Social History*, *Labour/Le Travail*, and the University of Toronto Press for permission to publish edited versions of the following:

Chapter 1: "Political Demonstrations and Spectacles during the Rebellion Losses Bill Controversy," *Canadian Historical Review* 92 (2011): 1–41.

Chapter 2: "Motley Crowds and Splendid Assemblies: Press Depictions of Election Culture in Mid-Victorian Toronto," *Histoire sociale/ Social History* 51/103 (2018): 1–25.

Chapter 3: *Royal Spectacle: The 1860 Visit of the Prince of Wales to Canada and the United States* (Toronto: University of Toronto Press, 2004).

Chapter 4: "Collective Rights, Liberal Discourse, and Public Order: The Clash over Catholic Processions in Mid-Victorian Toronto," *Canadian Historical Review* 95 (2014): 511–44.

Chapter 5: "Celebrating the Suppression of the North-West Resistance of 1885: The Toronto Press and the Militia Volunteers," *Histoire sociale/Social History*, 47/95 (2014): 601–39.

Chapter 6: "Boys, Young Men, and Disorder in Mid-Victorian Toronto," in *Violence, Order, and Unrest: A History of British North America, 1749–1876*, ed. Elizabeth Mancke, Jerry Bannister, Denis McKim, and Scott W. See (Toronto: University of Toronto Press, 2019).

Chapter 7: "Playful Crowds and the 1886 Toronto Street Railway Strikes," *Labour/Le Travail* 76 (2015): 133–64.

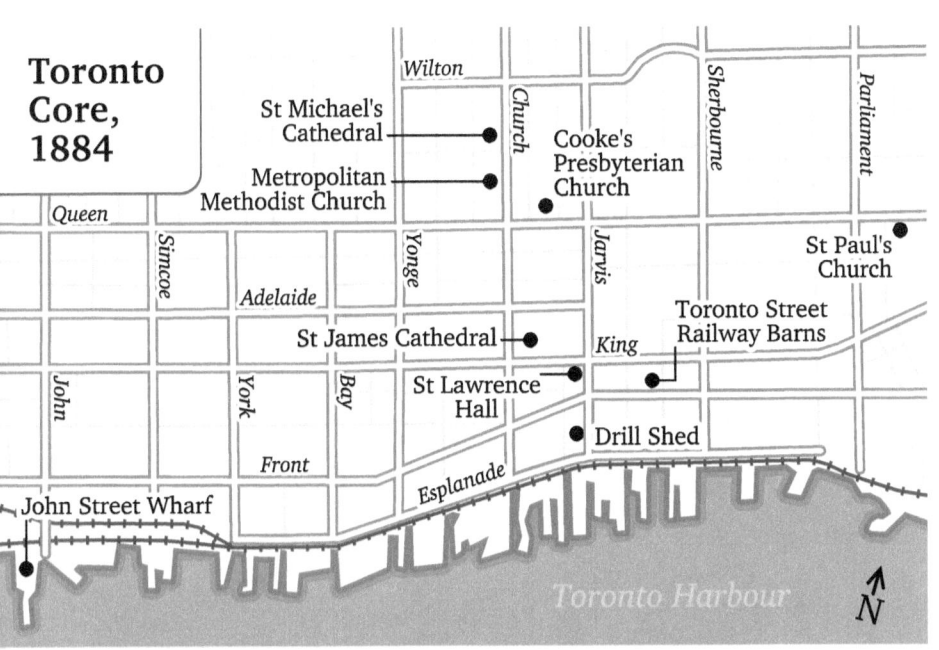

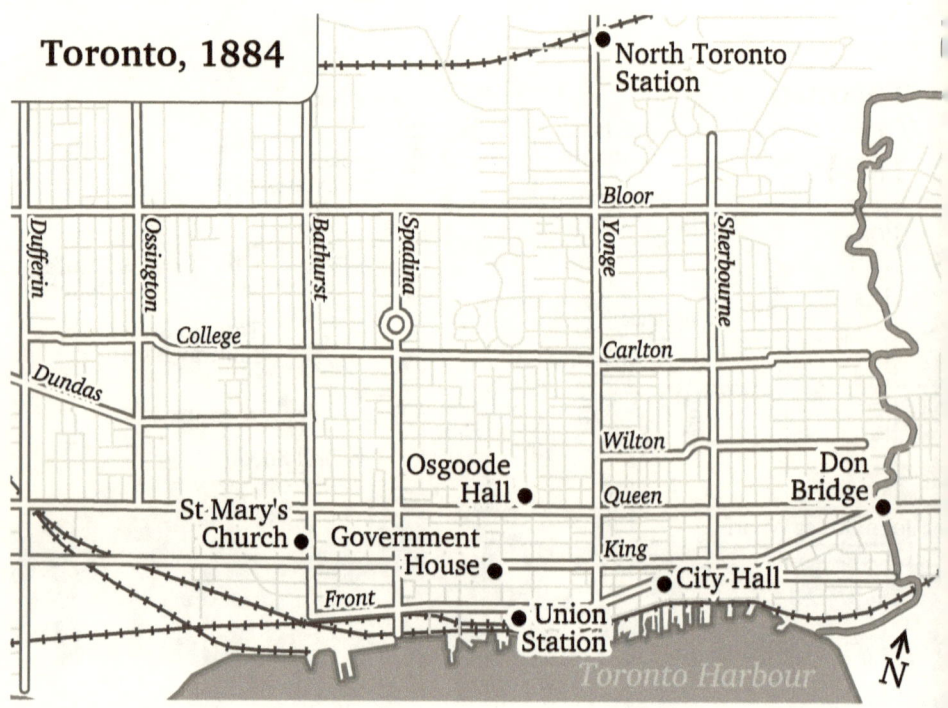

EXPRESSIVE ACTS

Introduction

"A disgraceful exhibition" took place in city streets on the evening of 4 May 1849, reported the Toronto *Globe*.[1] A crowd of men carrying sticks had assembled near a tavern on Queen Street. After dark, they formed a procession led by a fellow carrying a straw-and-tar effigy of Lord Elgin, Canada's governor general. At the time, many Tories throughout the province were incensed that Elgin had given royal assent to the Rebellion Losses bill, a measure introduced by the Reform government. Word had it that 2,000 Orangemen would march in Toronto and participate in the effigy-burning, but the crowd was no doubt smaller. Led by a city alderman mounted on a horse, the procession, according to the *Globe*, was composed of "ruffians," both "genteel and vulgar." At about 10:30, the march drew to a halt in a space opposite City Hall. On the steps of the hall, the mayor and other officials watched as some of the processionists raised a triangular structure on which they suspended the effigy. With a flaming torch, the protesters lit the stuffed representation of the governor, who blazed brightly in the night.

A few months later, Lord Elgin himself visited Toronto, a place on the itinerary of a tour of the province that he was making in the hope of demonstrating the widespread support for him. As he stepped from his steamer onto the Yonge Street wharf, the guns of Fort York boomed an official welcome. A popular salute came from the throats of an immense and enthusiastic crowd.[2] The mayor and civic officials greeted Elgin, after which he joined a procession in his honour that wound its way through city streets. Flags and banners flew from homes and shops along the route as throngs of people shouted "deafening acclamations."[3] The mayor read a formal address welcoming Elgin to the city and assuring him of the city's loyalty and deep regard for the British imperial connection.

In the space of just a few months, then, Toronto saw an angry demonstration and a joyous civic celebration, both focusing on the governor general. On the two occasions, people assembled in the streets and engaged in *expressive acts* that revealed the depth of the political divide between Tories and Reformers at mid-century, and how both parties used public space to advance their political positions.

This book examines instances of both celebration and protest, the focus being on special occasions when Torontonians took to the streets, putting their allegiances, politics, and values on display.[4] Celebrations and demonstrations in the streets of nineteenth-century Toronto reveal not just the city's vibrant public life but also intense social tensions and cultural differences within the city. Such moments illustrate what drove Torontonians to claim public spaces, where their passions lay, and how they gave expression to them. During these public performances, class identities gained shape and the conflicting ethno-religious identities so pervasive in Victorian Toronto manifested themselves. The essential source for this study is journalists' accounts in newspapers, which are also a subject of investigation to appreciate what meanings the writers attached to the events they discussed.

Contents

Expressive Acts brings together my research and published writings on celebrations and demonstrations in Victorian Toronto. In this volume, I have reworked some published pieces and lightly edited others. For instance, the chapter on the Rebellion Losses controversy now focuses on Toronto rather than being a province-wide study. The chapter on the 1860 royal visit brings together materials on Toronto that are scattered through my thematically organized monograph on the tour of the Prince of Wales through Canada and the United States. By bringing these writings together in one volume I show more clearly how certain matters recurred across time and event, such as the centrality of religious conflict in Victorian Toronto, the edge that partisan differences gave to social relations, and the importance of the press in giving shape to public events. These and other themes are discussed in the conclusion.

Chapter 1 of this book focuses on Toronto's involvement in the Rebellion Losses controversy of 1849. The Rebellion Losses bill, introduced by the province's Reform government, arranged for compensation for Lower Canadians who had suffered property damage in the rebellions of 1837–38. Tories believed the measure amounted to compensating traitors – French Canadian supporters of the insurrection whose property had been damaged by British troops. In Montreal, Tories torched the provincial parliament and egged the governor. Toronto Tories also demonstrated angrily in the streets, protesting the bill and Governor Elgin. Their illegal and riotous conduct was condemned by Reformers, who dubbed the protesters "Tory rebels." By contrast, when Elgin came to Toronto, many residents raised celebratory arches of welcome in the British tradition of viceregal and royal visits and cheered his procession through the streets. The chapter documents the heated language used by both Tories and Reformers during the controversy and analyses press and other reports of the street actions, both angry and joyous.

Chapter 2 examines the culture of provincial election campaigns as revealed in Toronto newspapers from the 1840s into the 1870s. Intensely contentious, election campaigns pitted political rivals and their supporters against each other. The press, deeply divided by partisan affiliations, represented the campaign activities of their favoured candidates as being above reproach and models of civil behaviour, while depicting their opponents as reliant on thuggery, intimidation at the polls, and corruption. Election meetings sometimes saw violence, as did many polling places. Victory celebrations that included parades through city streets were sometimes disrupted by disappointed supporters of defeated candidates. The chapter reconstructs election culture in mid-nineteenth-century Toronto, notes reforms of election procedures, and documents the vivid language of partisan politics.

The 1860 state visit to the city of Albert Edward, the eighteen-year-old Prince of Wales, is the topic of chapter 3. A grand public occasion, it entailed much planning as organizers worked out the program, as well as considerable expense as people busily decorated homes, businesses, and institutions in a style fit for a prince. Toronto put on an exceptionally fine display, but all did not go as planned. Trouble with Orangemen had plagued the prince's progress through Canada West, as it did in Toronto, where the Orange Order was a powerful presence and its members were long accustomed to claiming public space and attention. The royal visit had been intended to feature the city's loyalism and progress but ended up revealing much more: deeply ingrained political and social tensions.

Chapter 4 focuses on two instances of ethno-religious conflict triggered by Roman Catholic processions in mid-Victorian Toronto: the Corpus Christi celebration of 1864 and the Jubilee riots of 1875. On both occasions Church authorities chose to put their religious beliefs and practices on public display – a bold move in a city that was three-quarters Protestant and where militants of the Orange Order remained ever vigilant in constraining the power and place of the Catholic Church. Deepening the religious hostility was the history of religious conflict in Ireland, which was never far from the surface of Protestant–Catholic tensions in Toronto. Press reports of the 1870s documented the elaborate negotiations regarding the rights of Catholics as well as the riotous behaviour that resulted when militant Protestants and their supporters violently confronted the processionists, who then retaliated. The riots reveal the depth of feeling of those involved in the violence, conflicting understandings of appropriate religious expression in public, and the nature of rights talk in mid-Victorian Toronto.

Celebration is the focus of chapter 5. Torontonians took to the streets to honour the city's volunteer militiamen who had gone to the North-West to suppress the Riel resistance of 1885. As presented by the city's press, the public was wholly united behind the boys and their mission to put down Riel, a traitor leading an insurrection in defiance of the Queen's authority on the frontier. Newspapers portrayed the Toronto public as being enormously proud of the Volunteers' patriotism and readiness to risk their lives for Canada. Huge crowds of cheering, singing residents gathered at the railway depot to send off the boys in fine style, and a few months later, elaborate preparations marked the lead-up to the heroes' return. This chapter shows how the city organized the public display and how the press spun the story to highlight Toronto's undivided enthusiasm for the campaign. Colonialism triumphant was very much on display in 1885 Toronto.

Chapter 6 differs from the other chapters in that, rather than focusing on particular instances of public behaviour, it explores the role of a certain group of participants in street actions: boys and young men. Their "fooling around" often made them the instigators of violence perpetrated by older men. City authorities and newspaper editors roundly condemned the lads' troublesome behaviour. Portrayed variously as hooligans and reprobates, they emerged as a focus of concern about the need for public order and prompted a search for institutional means to discipline the lads, control their actions, and reform their morals. The chapter reveals the underside of the Victorian city and middle-class anxieties about that netherworld.

The final chapter deals with an aspect of industrializing Toronto: strikes of street railway workers in 1886. A prominent sign that the city was modernizing, streetcars provided mass transit in the burgeoning urban metropolis. Run by a private monopoly, the Toronto Street Railway was despised by the public, who depended on the service even while complaining that it was unreliable and overpriced. When a fledgling labour union among the street railway workers sought to challenge the company's labour policies, the bosses locked out the unionists, triggering two strikes. Initially, the public and the press appeared remarkably sympathetic both to the disciplined pickets and to the unruly crowds that disrupted a streetcar service run by strike-breakers. This chapter examines the growing class consciousness of workers in the industrializing city of the 1880s, the nature of the conflict that arose between workers and their employer, and the initial public sympathy shown the strikers. Unlike most studies of strikes, this chapter highlights how crowds could be both purposive and playful.

Sources

Without the newspapers, this book could not have been written. Many developments of enormous interest to the press were seldom discussed at any length in surviving diaries, memoirs, letters, and legal documents. There are exceptions, however. The 1860 visit of the Prince of Wales received enormous attention from the press and, furthermore, is well documented in politicians' private papers, the records of provincial and imperial government offices involved in making arrangements for the prince's tour, and the collection of the royal family. Other public occasions, including the Rebellion Losses controversy and the clashes between Protestants and Catholics in 1870s Toronto, are documented in sources such as politicians' papers, civic records, and the papers of religious leaders. Where available, these manuscript sources are made use of here.

Across Canada and the United States, a profusion of newspapers met the surge in readership that accompanied population growth and the spread of literacy during the nineteenth century. The low capital costs of publishing a newspaper boosted their proliferation, even though unreliable revenues made them dodgy enterprises. Driven less by the hope of profits than by the prospect of achieving influence, publishers in Victorian Canada established newspapers to advance the popularity of their own views or those of particular parties and politicians.[5] It was the era of political journalism and the political press.

In the mid-nineteenth century, every town in Canada West had at least one newspaper and Toronto had several. The Toronto *Globe* (1844–), the voice of its publisher George Brown and of Reform, was a mighty political force in Upper Canada.[6] An important rival of the *Globe* in the mid-nineteenth century, the Toronto *Leader* (1852–1878) provided a powerful conservative voice and became the province's leading Conservative Party organ in the 1860s.[7] Several other newspapers emerged and collapsed during the same period.[8] There were also newspapers that spoke for and to particular constituencies, including three for Irish Catholics and one for the Orange Order.[9] All of these journals featured Canadian politics and expressed spirited partisanship, but the style of their journalism was otherwise staid. Mid-century Toronto newspapers offered readers a few pages of cramped columns with tiny type and few, if any, illustrations.

Toward the end of our period, popular journalism emerged in Toronto. Newspapers appeared in the 1880s that were written in a lively style and featured stories of local interest, including coverage of crimes and the shenanigans of municipal politicians. "Penny dailies," such as the *News* (1881–1903) and the *World* (1880–1921), addressed a more popular or down-market audience than the political dailies.[10] In the case of the *News*, its distinctly "progressive journalism" embraced the expansion of the elective principle, support for organized labour, and a critique of the poverty and degradation accompanying industrialization.[11]

Illustrated newspapers, available to better-off Torontonians, provided readers with images of newsworthy developments in the form of woodcut etchings based on artists' drawings. Few illustrations appeared in the daily press during our period, and photographs were unknown as yet in city dailies.[12] For Canadian topics, the Toronto weekly *Canadian Illustrated News* (1869–83) had the richest selection of illustrations, and it pioneered the use of half-tone engravings.[13] At the time of the Riel resistance in 1885, the *Illustrated War News*, published in Toronto, brought the clashes in (what is now) Saskatchewan to life and showed Torontonians at home working to support and celebrate the Volunteers. Toronto readers could also subscribe to or purchase illustrated papers from London and New York, which sometimes included illustrations of Toronto events.[14] *Expressive Acts* provides examples of the artwork drawn from the illustrated press both to help readers understand certain street celebrations and confrontations and to show what images readers had before them.

Historiography

Several leading scholars laid the foundations on which *Expressive Acts* is built. In the 1960s, as historians gave greater attention to the dynamics of class formation, George Rudé, Charles Tilly, and Eric Hobsbawm saw the crowd as a worthy subject of analysis, one that helped them recover the long-neglected history of plebians.[15] E.P. Thompson's influential 1971 article, "The Moral Economy of the Crowd in the Eighteenth Century," makes a compelling case for seeing England's eighteenth-century bread riots not as irrational outbursts but as the purposeful response of common people angered by intrusions on what custom had taught them was right and just.[16] While these historians emphasized the economic context and motivation of crowds, Natalie Zemon Davis in her 1973 study of religious riots in early modern France showed how rioters were driven by religious convictions when they confronted people whom they saw as lacking doctrinal purity and defiling the community.[17] Rioters, who often included priests or pastors, had a sense that what they were doing was legitimate and would assist their cause.

The historical sociologist Charles Tilly similarly explored crowd actions, drawing attention to the performativity of the protagonists. In a 1977 article on local uprisings in seventeenth-century French villages, Tilly coined the term "contentious performances," which caught on among scholars.[18] Tilly used the metaphors "performance" and "repertoire" to draw attention to evidence indicating that crowds drew their claim-making performances from a limited repertoire. He and others have shown this to be true in a wide variety of contexts.[19]

In the 1980s, scholars began showing an interest in choreographed events such as celebrations and parades, where crowds are part of the story. In her influential 1989 essay, "The American Parade," Mary Ryan observes that the parade "reveals, in a particularly powerful, publicly sanctioned way, how contemporaries construed, displayed, and saw the social order."[20] A vast array of American studies, including two books by Ryan, documented public celebrations.[21] Historians of Canada have also contributed a great deal to the field by focusing on parades, commemorations, and national holidays.[22] The scholarship has shown, for instance, how elites organized public ceremonies and parades to articulate community identities in order to reinforce their own power and prominence.[23] Particular places and ordinary people, however, participated in events often for their own purposes, in the process contesting the organizers' goals.[24] At the same time, historical geographers have drawn attention to the use of public spaces and who gained access to them and how.[25]

Much of this literature on celebrations grapples with the nature of the public. For instance, Mary P. Ryan, in *Civic Wars*, demonstrates how in American cities during the 1820s and 1830s a vigorous popular sovereignty emerged in public spaces, although that public was limited to white men. Interest in the formation of publics gained traction with the translation of Jürgen Habermas's *The Structural Transformation of the Public Sphere* and the critiques it engendered.[26] Habermas argues that at the beginning of the nineteenth century in the West, there emerged an informed citizenry that participated in public life through their active voluntary associations, by reading newspapers and pamphlets, and by debating issues. Public opinion became a powerful force in governance. Jeffrey McNairn's *The Capacity to Judge* is a sophisticated Canadian study influenced by Habermas. It shows how democracy evolved in Upper Canada as an informed reading public debated political issues and public opinion came to be seen as a legitimate force in shaping how people were governed – or governed themselves, consent being seen as a by-product of deliberation.[27] *Expressive Acts* argues that there was another side to the making of democracy, involving combative politics that could spill into violence. This analysis fits with that of Mary P. Ryan, who argues that in the nineteenth-century United States, "American citizens enacted publicness in an active, raucous, contentious, and unbridled style of debate that defied literary standards of rational and critical discourse."[28]

A recent Canadian study that makes use of this sprawling body of scholarship is Dan Horner's *Taking to the Streets*.[29] Its topic is Montreal in the 1840s, a turbulent decade during which the streets of the city became what Horner calls "a politicized space." *Taking to the Streets* emphasizes the negotiation of community identities as the social vision of the city's liberal reformers clashed with the moral economy of the popular classes. As a caveat, Horner notes that the line between the two groups was sometimes blurred when reformers cast aside their ideal of restrained manliness to engage in rough street actions.

An extensive literature has documented the eruption of violence in many places in nineteenth-century Canada, the ideal of the "peaceable kingdom" notwithstanding.[30] Scott W. See has examined particular contexts in which disorder occurred, and he has recently reflected on the limitations of the aspirational phrase so much associated with Canadian nation-building: "peace, order and good government."[31]

Violence and overt social tensions in Victorian Toronto often stemmed from the troubled relations between the city's Protestants and Catholics, a theme developed in an extensive historical literature. In *The Sash Canada Wore*, historical geographers Cecil Houston and William Smyth documented the long reach of Orangeism throughout mid-nineteenth-century British North America and argued that Orangeism did not remain confined to the Irish but spread among Protestants of other backgrounds.[32] More recently, Smyth has explored Orangeism's central presence in Toronto history, one that involved endless sniping between Protestants and Catholics and where municipal governance showed the remarkable grip of the Orange Lodges for about one hundred years.[33] William Jenkins's book comparing the Irish in Buffalo and

Toronto documents not just the powerful presence of Irish Protestants in Toronto, which set the city apart from nearby Buffalo, but also the vitality of the Toronto's Irish Catholic minority.[34] That minority has been effectively studied for the mid-nineteenth century by Brian Clarke in his *Piety and Nationalism*. His subject is lay voluntary associations of Catholics, and he shows their proliferation and influence within the Church even at a time of ultramontanism, the top-down movement of clerical renewal that looked to Rome for authority.[35]

The celebrations and demonstrations examined in *Expressive Acts* overwhelmingly involved men, and thus masculine identities were very much on show. The substantial American, British, and Canadian scholarship on masculinity has helped me make sense of the various masculinities on display in Victorian Toronto, from genteel models of mature, reserved behaviour to the brutish explosions of boys and young men who disrupted the public peace, and many more besides.[36] Women and femininity figure much less prominently here. In the mid-nineteenth century, the planning of celebrations, their enactment, and reporting on them were very much the purview of men. Women appear in only a limited number of roles: as dancers at the balls, as spectators appreciating the manly processions, as helpers behind the scenes, and as figures in the iconography representing virtues like peace and justice.[37] Women's presence at demonstrations was even more circumscribed, at least in the texts created by male journalists. According to Victorian gender conventions, it was not respectable or appropriate for women to take part in street actions, and generally, journalistic conventions ensured that women disappeared from the scene. As we shall see, an important exception was the presence of girls and women walking in Catholic processions, demonstrating the Church's inclusion of them among the faithful and the dangers they were exposed to when processions were attacked.

Context

The period covered in *Expressive Acts* saw constitutional, political, demographic, and economic developments, an understanding of which is a helpful background to what follows. Our story begins in the 1840s, when Canadians were adjusting to the union of the Canadas and the coming of responsible government. Britain's parliament passed the Act of Union, 1840, which brought together Lower Canada and Upper Canada to create the United Province of Canada in February 1841. The one legislature had equal representation from each half of the province: Canada East, formerly Lower Canada, and Canada West, formerly Upper Canada. (During the Union period, the names prior to union remained much in use; the old and newer names are used interchangeably in this book.) The province's major political issue in the 1840s was responsible government, which became a reality in 1848. The coming of responsible government meant a transfer of some powers from the British-appointed governor to the Canadian executive council or cabinet made up of members of the party or groups that dominated in the elected legislative assembly. To hold power, a government now needed the confidence of a majority of members of the elected assembly. At the same time, Canada gained some autonomy within the empire because the imperial government no longer wished to intervene in matters relating strictly to Canada. Other constitutional developments came with Confederation in 1867, which saw the creation of a wider union with a federal structure.

Political parties changed considerably during our period. In the early 1840s, the dominant parties were the Conservatives (or Tories), who opposed responsible government, and the Reformers, who advocated it. Once responsible government came into being near the end of the decade, party formation became more complicated as new coalitions came into being. The old High Tories declined in significance and there emerged a new Liberal-Conservative party, often referred to simply as the Conservative Party. The Reformers regrouped, too, although they kept their name until the 1870s, when increasingly they became known as the Liberals. The parties differed over many issues, though not usually in ways that can be referred to as right and left. Both parties succeeded in forging alliances between English Canadians and French Canadians, although in our period the Conservative alliance of John A. Macdonald and George-Étienne Cartier was the sturdier one.[38]

The City of Toronto dates from 1834, but a population had lived near its lakeside site for a very long time. Indigenous people had been drawn to the area by the fish and game and by the Rouge, Don, Humber, and Credit Rivers, which facilitated travel into the hinterland and onwards to Georgian Bay. At various times, Anishinabeg and Iroquois peoples dwelled (often seasonally) on the shore of Lake Ontario where Toronto now stands. The Mississaugas had settled in significant numbers along the Credit River and were much in evidence when European newcomers arrived to claim the land and resources, first the French in tiny numbers and then, in much larger numbers, the British and British Americans.[39] In the mid-nineteenth century, residents ignored the Indigenous history of the place, preferring to recognize the city's founders as the Loyalists, people loyal to the Crown who arrived from the United States as a result of the American Revolution. In 1793, Upper

Canada's first lieutenant governor, John Graves Simcoe, founded the Town of York to the west of the mouth of the Don River. American settlers and then waves of immigrants from Great Britain transformed the wilderness outpost into a bustling commercial centre, renamed Toronto upon its incorporation as a city in 1834.[40]

Toronto lost its prized status as the capital of Upper Canada when the United Province of Canada came into being in 1841 with the city of Québec as its capital. After 1849, the provincial capital alternated between Québec and Toronto until in 1857 Queen Victoria chose Ottawa as the permanent capital of Canada. At Confederation, Ottawa became the capital of the Dominion of Canada, and Toronto resumed its capital status, now of the new Province of Ontario.

During our period, Toronto's population grew steadily and significantly. Its reported population in 1841 stood at just over 30,000; by 1861, it was about 56,000; and by 1881, about 86,000.[41] The Irish were the largest contingent and were split between the Protestant majority, mostly from Ulster, and the Roman Catholics, who by 1850 made up about one-quarter of the city's population as a result of the large influx who had come fleeing Ireland's Great Potato Famine of the 1840s.[42] The Catholic presence declined somewhat in later decades, but they were still about one-fifth of the city's population in the 1870s and 1880s.[43] Many Torontonians could trace their origins to England and Scotland, and large influxes of immigrants from those countries continued to reinforce the city's Britishness as the century wore on. In 1851, fully two thirds of Torontonians had been born abroad, but few were regarded as foreigners because so many of them had roots in the British Isles.[44] Non-British residents were few. Colonialism had pushed aside the local Indigenous people, most notably in 1848, when the Mississaugas along the Credit relocated to north of Lake Erie.[45] In the 1850s especially, men and women of African origin, both freeborn and former enslaved people, migrated north from the United States until they made up a small but significant component of the city.[46] A handful of people from the German states and Holland, Russia, Poland, Italy, and Greece added just a touch of ethnic diversity to the mid-century city.[47]

In the 1840s, Toronto was a commercial city that prospered from the buying and selling of goods and services. Imports came mainly from Britain and were distributed from Toronto to the burgeoning rural hinterland, which was peopled mainly by farm families. Wheat grown by those farmers and milled in the countryside or the city dominated Toronto's export trade. Manufacturing was small in scale and aimed at nearby consumers, but collectively it comprised a significant component of economic activity.[48]

Much changed in the 1850s, when Toronto's industrial revolution gained momentum. A dynamic manufacturing sector emerged and harnessed the power of the provincial state. The government of the Province of Canada adopted a vigorous policy of railway development that brought a huge infusion of capital, new opportunities for manufacturers, and increased trade. In the 1850s, Toronto manufacturers successfully pressured the Canadian government to adopt higher tariffs to nurture Canadian manufacturing – a vivid illustration of the growing power of industrialists. In the next decade, their support for Confederation promised both superior state finances and broader markets for Toronto's manufactured goods. Increasingly, the new bourgeoisie came to dominate the society and culture of Toronto, but not without contestation, mainly from a growing working class.[49]

Always stratified by class, the city became increasingly so with industrialization. In the 1840s, many men worked as labourers and carters and at the port. Somewhat above them stood the craftsmen, whose skills earned them better wages. All of these workers relied heavily on their wives to maintain the family economy. Employed women were nearly all young and single, working as servants, laundresses, and teachers. As time went on, men began to find jobs in factories and railway shops and on trains. In addition to employing men, factory bosses hired young, single women to perform specific tasks considered suitable for their gender. In the 1860s, many skilled workingmen leveraged their much-needed skills to challenge their bosses. They formed trade unions and engaged in strikes for improvements in pay and working conditions. By the 1880s, when unionism spread to less-skilled workers, "class warfare" had become a topic of growing public concern.

Early in our period, people of all classes resided near one another and there were only a few pockets distinguished by class, such as Stanley Street, where the Irish Catholic poor predominated. As the century wore on, distinct neighbourhoods developed that were stratified by class. People of the prosperous middle class often chose to live in Yorkville, for instance. Many wealthy families preferred the new, garden suburb of Rosedale. Cabbagetown was home to many Irish working-class families.[50]

So much for the context. The following chapters are arranged chronologically according to the topic of each. Together they give a vivid picture of Victorian Toronto on occasions when people put themselves on display, acting out their views, their feelings, and their politics.

1
Tory Rebels and a Viceregal Visit

A pivotal moment in Canadian political and constitutional history, the Rebellion Losses controversy of 1849 prompted members of Toronto's old Tory elite and others to take to the streets as they grappled with the coming of responsible government. Dubbed "Tory Rebels" by their opponents, these hotheads were sufficiently roused that their demonstrations sometimes broke the law, most notably when they burned effigies of the governor general, James Bruce, the Eighth Earl of Elgin. In response to these demonstrations, Toronto Reformers also took to the streets. They did so in celebration of the formal visit of Elgin to the city while he was touring the province to demonstrate the considerable approval he enjoyed for having given royal assent to the Rebellion Losses bill and for having respected the new regime of responsible government.

In 1849, the recently elected Reform government of Louis-Hippolyte LaFontaine and Robert Baldwin introduced the Rebellion Losses bill. Its purpose was to compensate people in Canada East for the financial losses they had suffered as a result of the destruction of property during the rebellion of 1837–38. The bill carried out a commitment made by Upper Canadian Reformers to their counterparts in Canada East who were aggrieved that a previous Tory government had compensated the people of Canada West but not those of Canada East. Upper Canadian Reformers made that commitment because it was needed to cement the alliance of Reformers from both sections of the province that had enabled Reformers to form a government in 1848. To the public, Reformers presented the measure as correcting an injustice. By contrast, their Tory opponents argued that the measure was nothing of the sort. Those compensated in Upper Canada had had their property damaged by insurrectionists during the rebellion, whereas the damage in Lower Canada had been done by British troops and other supporters of the regime as they suppressed the insurrectionists. Passage of the Rebellion Losses bill through parliament would amount to "compensating rebels." To make matters worse, whereas Canada West had earlier used its own revenues to compensate Upper Canadians, the bill would draw on the consolidated revenue fund of the United Province with the result that most of the compensation would come from taxes raised in the more commercially dynamic Canada West and go to French Canadians in Canada East.[1]

The controversy raged as the bill was debated in the parliament of the Province of Canada at Montreal, but thanks to the Reformers' dominance, it passed through both the upper and lower houses with solid majorities. Tory outrage grew deeper when Governor Elgin gave the bill royal assent. In doing so, he was following the new constitutional arrangement whereby Britain allowed the Canadian parliament autonomy over matters relating to Canada alone. By signing the bill, Elgin recognized the matter was of no moment to Britain and that the bill had majority support in the Canadian parliament. A ministry that enjoyed the confidence of the elected assembly thus got its way, confirming a basic tenet of responsible government.

On the evening that Elgin signed the bill, 25 April 1849, Tories hurled eggs and stones at the governor and his carriage. Later, defiant Tories stormed the legislature. Proceedings were disrupted, the mace was seized, and the building was torched. The legislative library was destroyed, and the parliament building was reduced to a shell. The rioting in Montreal, which continued intermittently into late August, saw physical assaults on LaFontaine and an attack on the boarding house of Robert Baldwin. In this context, many Conservatives, hitherto staunch loyalists of the Crown, joined the annexation movement, which sought the severance of Canada's British connection and union with the United States.[2]

Because the Canadian parliament met in Montreal and the governor resided there, it was the epicentre of the Tory demonstrations. Yet the political turmoil spread throughout the Province of Canada that year. Heated debates and demonstrations erupted in nearly every settlement in Canada West. Toronto being the largest and most influential city in Canada West, newspapers there hotly debated the rebellion loses controversy, modelling arguments for newspapers elsewhere. The city's streets became sites of political theatre as rival factions displayed their intense differences. The Tories' lawbreaking was extraordinary as they openly defied the government. Before 1849, the Tories had always been defenders of the colonial regime. It had been the Reformers who had had grievances with British authority, demanded constitutional change, and sometimes been sympathetic to the rebels of 1837. The tables had turned, however. Now it was the Tories who decried the policy of both the British authorities and the colonial government of the day.

James Bruce, The Earl of Elgin and Kincardine. This romantic and flattering photograph illustrates Elgin's rank and wealth at a time when few people were photographed.
Source: Library and Archives Canada, MIKAN 3644739.

The turbulence in the Province of Canada in 1849 arose in the context of the revolutions of 1848 in Europe, mass demonstrations by Chartists in the United Kingdom, and a sharp economic downturn that resulted in widespread business failures and unemployment, including throughout Canada.[3]

The mid-century decades in Upper Canadian history have come to be seen as the period when deliberative democracy triumphed. Historian Jeffrey McNairn has shown how public debate became increasingly central to political and constitutional practice as the mid-century approached.[4] Increasingly, those active in politics engaged in rational debate to shape public opinion and influence the course of change. The Rebellion Losses controversy, however, shows how, in addition to rational debate, political activists resorted to fiery rhetoric, street demonstrations, and violence to influence public opinion. I refer to such displays as examples of *muscular conservatism*. By this term I mean to signal that these expressions of popular conservatism were relatively unconstrained by the meeting hall's rules of order and that their robustness and even lawlessness derived from a construction of masculinity that validated public assertiveness and physicality. Muscular conservatism ran counter to the etiquette of deliberative democracy.

On their part, the governor and Reformers reinforced their own position on the Rebellion Losses bill and responsible government by making use of visual displays that were at least as theatrical as those of the Conservatives: public processions, addresses, and arch-building, all drawn from the repertoire of rituals associated with royal and viceregal visits.[5] By discussing both oppositional street demonstrations and patriotic displays rooted in royal celebrations – forms of political spectacle not usually treated together – I want to bring out the range of performative strategies that Upper Canadians pursued at a time of political crisis. Rational debate was the tidy, polite side of a political scene that was much messier and more impassioned. Democracy in Canada West involved deliberation but a whole lot more as well: demonstrations of physical force, violence, and dramatic spectacles that caught public attention, intensified political confrontation, and prompted reflections on what constituted legitimate means of political expression.

The Debates

Tories and Reformers certainly did engage in reasoned debate during the rebellion losses controversy, although they exceeded the boundaries of polite disagreement. Where Tories maintained that rebels were about to be compensated, Reformers argued that most of the claimants in Lower Canada had suffered property damage through no fault of their own, having been onlookers to the rebellion that swirled around them. An amendment to the bill made clear that no one convicted of treason or banished for treasonous behaviour would be compensated. Tories demanded that the British government intervene to disallow the act and prevent French Canadians from seizing power in a British province. Reformers countered that appeals to Britain must fall on deaf ears because the British government had approved the principle of responsible government. Tory calls for an election should be ignored, insisted the Reformers, because the election that had brought the Reformers to office had occurred only a year before, and the government had the confidence of parliament.

Reasoned arguments along these lines were a part of the controversy that erupted in 1849, but around them surged heated rhetoric that appealed to the passions rather than to reason. Polemicists sought to stir the populace with appeals to "race" and by treating Premier LaFontaine as the enemy of British interests. In an editorial titled "French Domination over Anglo-Saxon Canada," the Toronto *Patriot* declared: "The Rebellion claims which have roused, in every English breast, a feeling of strong antipathy against the French Canadian race, is but an affair of skirmishing, preparatory to the great battle for perpetual domination in Canada by the French Canadian race over those whom Mr. LaFontaine has styled their 'natural enemies.'" Writing immediately after the torching of parliament, the *Whig* said of LaFontaine: "Like Nero fiddling while Rome was burning, he inwardly rejoices at new triumphs to come ... to the time when Upper Canada will be taxed to make good the burning of Wednesday night." According to Tory polemicists, it was not too late to fight back. "A Letter from Gore" resolved: "We will have no more French domination, no French speeches, no French laws, no French men. This alien race and language must perish. It must pass away, naturally by amalgamation, or by the remorseless purification of the mind. It is not yet too late to amend."[6]

Blaming political situations on French Canadian domination was a rhetorical strategy often pursued by English-speaking Canadians in the pre-Confederation period because it worked: many Upper Canadians imagined their community as struggling under the yoke of external domination by French Canadians, a people foreign in language and religion. It was a perspective readily adopted by incoming waves of immigrants to Upper Canada, whose identity as Britons was anti-French and anti-Catholic.[7] By pushing this hot button and appealing to emotion, Tory journalists sought to mobilize opposition to the government and its measure. Unlike emotional appeals made in some other political contexts, such as

CANADA versus CALIFORNIA

Hiram. 'Say Zeb! I'm off right slick away for California. My wings is grew and my nails is mad for diggin!

Zeb. California be bust!—Canada's the washin for me; I guess I'll squat there, where Government pays for Rebellion and no questions axed!

A Conservative journal lampoons the Rebellion Losses Bill. Two hayseeds compare the returns of the California Gold Rush with the lucrative compensation from the Rebellion Losses Bill in Canada.
Source: *Punch in Canada*, 14 April 1849.

the American Revolution, however, in 1849 commentators offered no justifications for the appeals to emotion; they simply made them.[8]

In 1849 Tories also decried the villainy of Reform politicians from Canada West who, in a cynical bid for power, had made a pact with the devil – French Canadian Reformers – to create the Reform administration. When defending the bill in the assembly, the solicitor general for Canada West, William Hume Blake, had spoken for two days straight, and "this blathering bully" had shown no sympathy for the people who had been "murdered in cold blood, by the hands of traitors and assassins" or "whose houses were burned about their ears, by the rebels and invaders, on account of their known devotion in support of the Crown," yet he was "bursting with sympathy for the perpetrators of those atrocious deeds, and supplicating the House to compensate those who aided and abetted them in their wicked designs."[9] Once Elgin signed the bill, the Tories' ire focused on him. The day after Elgin made the indemnity bill a law, the *British Whig* fumed that he had given the Queen's assent to a "revolutionary measure, unprecedented in the history of civilized nations." True Britons in Canada grieved "this politically suicidal act of the Sovereign."[10]

Sometimes the Reform newspapers matched the white-hot rhetoric of the Tories. The Toronto *Mirror* justified the use of strong language when dealing with a party whose "very tenets are based upon the opposite to intellect, and its most liberal doctrine is strongly tainted with the poison of superstition and ignorance." "The cry of the minority and Library burners just now, is 'Exterminate the French ...' To a certain extent Reformers must parody the cry in its application to Toryism. We must work unremittingly until it becomes a moral nonentity, and is known no more in the land."[11]

In his long speech in the assembly on the bill, the solicitor general, Blake, got so carried away with his rhetoric that he soon regretted it deeply. Because he called Tories "rebels" and accused them of wanting to hang every Frenchman, he was challenged to a duel by the Conservative member from Kingston, John A. Macdonald. Unable to comply with the gentlemanly code, Blake did not show up at the appointed hour for the duel and had to live with the humiliation of being regarded as a coward.[12] Excessive rhetoric could be costly.

Public Meetings and Petitioning

The Upper Canadian press reported on public meetings called to debate the bill in towns across the province. It is now impossible to know what actually happened at such meetings because Reform newspapers claimed that meetings called by Reformers were heavily attended and models of civility, whereas Tory meetings were rowdy affairs where debate was drowned out. Tory newspapers similarly reported favourably on their own meetings and criticized those called by the Reformers. Physical assaults often occurred, though it is impossible from the politically biased reports to tell who initiated the violence. Bryan Palmer's assessment of the Upper Canadian political scene in the 1830s applies to the situation in 1849: "This was a public sphere as much of performance ... as it was of logical debate and articulate speech and it easily slipped into postures of extremism, in which both language and symbolic activity could veer toward the violent."[13]

The Reform press's coverage of a meeting in Toronto's old City Hall gives the flavour of such reports: "It was not a deliberative meeting, but an ebullition of faction and rage – All the blackguards and bullies in the City and neighbourhood were present." Whenever a Reformer tried to speak, "the bullies, adherents of those who had got up the meeting, set up a hideous yell, the most unearthly ever heard on earth, and not a word uttered by the speaker could be heard." An eyewitness charged that the meeting had been "hatched in the orange lodges, and might with the greatest propriety be called an *Orange Lodge Meeting!*" Given the situation, it was "absurd to call such a meeting an open meeting for public expression, where every thing was done by the yells of low Orangemen and violent party speeches of two Tory lawyers addressed not to the intelligence, but the drunken rowdy passions of ignorant persons."[14] It was characteristic of the Reform press to blame disorderly behaviour and intimidation on Orangemen, who were depicted as being the working-class muscle of Toryism in a city where both Conservatism and Orangeism were potent forces.[15]

The rhetoric used and reported on in newspapers derived almost entirely from the political elite – politicians in parliament and political journalists – but the meetings, petitioning, and street demonstrations drew participation from a much larger portion of the public, including many non-electors. Anyone could attend a public meeting, sign a petition, or join a demonstration. Literacy and access to the formal levers of power were unnecessary. Reform newspapers blamed the violence of their rivals on the involvement of the rabble.

After Elgin gave royal assent to the Rebellion Losses bill, Tories organized a mass petition demanding his recall. Having addressed the petition to the Queen, the Conservatives planned to send a deputation to England to present it to Her Majesty and plead their case to British politicians.[16] In so doing, they were resorting to a tactic formerly deployed by (Reform) oppositionists in Canada West – sometimes with success – during the period before the advent of responsible government.[17] Meantime, Upper Canadian Reformers under Robert Baldwin's direction organized meetings and petitions expressing the public's confidence in Elgin and responsible government – political occasions that resembled the many public meetings held a decade earlier when Reformers rallied to support the principal recommendations of Lord Durham's report: responsible government and the union of the Canadas.[18] In 1849 Baldwin personally financed the petition campaign in rural districts.[19] Reformers arranged for deputations to present the petitions directly to the governor. Public meetings got up to endorse one petition or the other brought another round of bombast and irregular behaviour.

Each side accused the other of false representation by padding the petitions with signatures unfairly gained. Representing himself as having local knowledge, a Reformer wrote that one Tory petition had "over 400 names: among them you will see little boys' names; names of persons who are out of the country, and have been for a long time; names obtained by misrepresentations; and names of persons whose consent had not been asked."[20] A Tory newspaper reported that virtually identical tricks were being played by the Reformers seeking names for their petitions supporting the governor: "In Upper Canada, the hawkers of Petitions go round secretly, and take the names of whole families; they represent to some people that it is a petition against the Rebellion Losses, to others that it is for the removal of the head of Government to Upper Canada, to others other lies, suiting them to the feelings of the men they happen to meet." The writer added: "Such disgraceful immorality is only to be expected as the natural result of the immoral act which Lord Elgin has sanctioned."[21] Comments such as these were hardly aimed at celebrating the involvement on a broad public in the democratic process; rather, the involvement of people other than male heads of households was labelled unfair and immoral.

Demonstrations and Effigy Burnings

Provoked by overblown rhetoric in the Tory press condemning the Reform government and Lord Elgin, and emboldened by reassurances from local authorities, some Conservatives turned from debate and bombast in the press to street demonstrations involving activities in defiance of the law, as they had frequently done in the past.[22] A wave of demonstrations that included effigy-burnings swept across Canada West in early May, following the governor's granting of royal assent to the Rebellion Losses bill.[23] But that activity was preceded by a riot in Toronto late in March, when the villain – or hero – of 1837, William Lyon Mackenzie, visited his hometown for the first time since he had led the Upper Canadian rebellion.

Tories argued that they were provoked into taking to the streets on the evening of 22 March because, as loyalists who had stood by the Crown in its moment of peril back in 1837, they were insulted by the reappearance of Mackenzie at the site of his treasonous activities. It was possible for him to return from exile in the United States because on assuming office the LaFontaine–Baldwin government had ensured that in 1849 a general amnesty was given to the rebels. That Mackenzie's return coincided with rising levels of Tory outrage prompted by the Rebellion Losses controversy added heat to the confrontation that ensued.

The Reform press charged that the Tories had grown so overwrought that they had actually *planned* to break the law and foment violence. The *Patriot* had tried "to incite that army of *Sans Culottes*, which the Tories of this city have constantly at command to commit open violence and personal injury, if not actual assassination."[24] Following a tradition of popular politics locally, protesters prepared in advance effigies of Mackenzie, William Hume Blake (the solicitor general), and Robert Baldwin (the attorney general for Canada West and co-premier).[25] Tar barrels for firing torches had been placed in the streets in the afternoon. Even bushels of stones had been brought from a distance and left near the house where Mackenzie was staying because the demonstrators knew that no stones could be "obtained from the street at the scene of the riot, where the mud was several inches deep."[26] Though premeditated, the demonstration was not officially authorized. The activists had not applied to the municipal council for a parade permit, as was the usual procedure in the case of processions.

On the evening of 22 March, emboldened by the mayor's announcement that he would be going to bed early that night, Conservatives brought the effigies into Yonge Street, where several hundred demonstrators had gathered. It was "an assemblage of unshaven, dirty looking, half-intoxicated men, and ragged boys," sniffed the *Examiner* in its dismissive account. As the Tory version had it, the demonstrators had raised three effigies on long poles and waved them "amid the cheers and exultations of the largest concourse of people beheld in Toronto since the election of Dunn and Buchanan."[27] The *Patriot* editorialized: "It would be impossible to describe the expressions of indignation and disgust on the part of the people towards the triumvirate [of effigies]." The demonstrators proceeded to Baldwin's house, where his effigy and that of the solicitor general were torched. From there the crowd set off for the temporary residence of Mackenzie, the Yonge Street house of John McIntosh.[28]

Demonstrators set ablaze tar barrels placed near the house and set off a fire alarm. Thousands of residents came out into the streets only to learn it was a false alarm, but many stayed on to see the action. In the *Examiner*'s critical account: "Horrid threats, hideous grimaces, and drunken imprecations, mingled in the street ... and, combined, made a horrible sound, comparable to nothing that we ever heard, but those horrible cries which escape the cells of violent lunatics. It soon became manifest that the fury of the mob might become uncontrollable."[29]

It is unclear exactly what happened once the marchers stopped outside Mackenzie's residence. According to the Reform account, the rioters armed themselves with their handy stones and began hurling them so hard at the windows of the house that not only were forty or fifty panes of glass broken but "part of the window frames were driven in." It was a shocking scene. "Mingled with the yells of the more violent and drunken, and the discharge of fire arms, were calls for McKenzie's [sic] life." By contrast, the Tory press maintained that the demonstrators had been provoked into stone-throwing by the actions of those inside the house. "Some person inside, with the most extraordinary folly, danced a doll at the window in evident ridicule and contempt of those outside. In one moment, mud, gravel and stones were hurled against the window, to the great dismay of its occupants." According to the *Patriot*, "Not a blow was struck, until one tall, dandified chap, who probably did not belong to any Temperance Society, hallowed out, 'Hurrah for McKenzie [sic].'" After spending their fury outside Mackenzie's residence, the crowd surged across the street and stoned a tavern owned by John Montgomery, the Radical tavern-owner convicted of treason in 1837–38. They then they proceeded to attack and stone the homes of Dr John Rolph, an associate of Mackenzie's in 1837, and George Brown, whose *Globe* newspaper had supported the Rebellion Losses bill.[30]

The Reform press made much of the fact that the riot had been allowed to continue for a few hours by partisan local authorities, who failed to do their duty and put a stop to it. According to a Reform account, the police presence was almost non-existent and the militia and military were not called out. "Shall we," the *Examiner* asked rhetorically, "excuse the non-interference of the Mayor from constitutional disposition to sleep so soundly that a brawling riot, which aroused the whole city, was insufficient to awake him?"[31] This failure of officials to apply the law against partisan friends was not at all unusual in Toronto and other British North American places in the mid-nineteenth century.[32] The day after the Mackenzie riot, local authorities took precautions, and the military came into view in an effort to prevent further outbreaks. The Tory papers grudgingly acknowledged the need for preventive action, coolly reporting that "a number of Special Constables were sworn in, and a strong detachment of the Canadian Rifles was stationed in the City Police Office."[33] As part of the process of shoring up deliberative democracy in the province, local government and professional police would become important partners "in controlling and maintaining politics as a sphere of rational, non-violent action." In 1849, however, that arrangement lay in the future and rioting still had some legitimacy as a form of political expression, though its legitimacy was being sharply contested.[34]

In the aftermath the Reformers had an opportunity to score points. "The violence exhibited by the Tories on Thursday night last," said the *Examiner*, "has covered them with an everlasting disgrace. The whole affair was dastardly, base and cowardly in the extreme." Tory loyalty had been exposed as a sham. By making Mackenzie's visit the occasion of a riot, the Tories had "emphatically condemned the just and humane course of Her Majesty [who had granted the amnesty], and done their best to trample the prerogative of mercy in the dust!"[35]

About a month after the Mackenzie riot, a round of Tory demonstrations swept the province, prompted by Elgin's signing of the Rebellion Losses bill. Press reports noted effigy burnings in many places, but specifically in Québec, Lévis, Brockville, Belleville, Toronto, and Whitby. The *Free Press* remarked on the similarity in the effigy-burning incidents across the province, quipping that "to Montreal belongs the infamous distinction of setting *the fashion* to the whole fraternity."[36] The difference was, of course, that Montreal's fiery display had been highly destructive, whereas an effigy-burning was a symbolic ritual that made use of fire but did no actual damage. The evidence, though sketchy, hints that the protests were encouraged and perhaps coordinated from the top by Conservative leaders who sent out "emissaries."[37] Certainly these incendiary events were locally arranged by party activists who mobilized large crowds, and they followed a common script: nighttime marches that climaxed with the hanging and burning of an effigy of Lord Elgin.

Why effigy-burnings? What meanings did they have for the people who witnessed them? Upper Canadians had burned effigies before 1849; Canadian Orangemen, for instance, ritually torched the Catholic traitor Guy Fawkes each November. And the practice had deep roots in British popular culture, where in the counter-revolutionary context of the early 1790s, for example, hundreds of thousands of people in England and Scotland had witnessed loyalist demonstrations that had burned effigies of the radical Tom Paine.[38] In 1849 Canada, however, the ritual may not have been familiar to everyone. When the Elgin-torching began, the *Globe* felt it necessary to describe the cultural form for the edification of readers: "The burning of an effigy is generally preceded by a procession, which attracts many idle and thoughtless [people] as lookers on. Publicity is the very object the parties have in view. The final act is often perpetrated at the house of the insulted party, whose friends are generally disposed to resent the insult."[39] The historical scholarship on effigy-burning indicates that it is a purging ritual, one that symbolically eliminates a threat posed by a political opponent. In its public theatricality – the marching, the hanging by rope, the setting ablaze, the singing and cheering – the effigy-burning emphatically condemns the individual under attack.[40] I would add that this spectacle does so in a way that no viewers, whatever the extent of their literacy, could mistake.

Always deliberate and never spontaneous, the demonstrations of 1849 were arranged by local activists, whatever their social position, but they drew crowds like magnets. Held in accessible public places but under the cover of darkness, effigy-burnings attracted curious onlookers intrigued by the revelry and the possibility of trouble, and made more willing to risk participation because their faces were obscured by the night. Spectators became actors, swelling crowds that, through sleight of hand, became impressive displays of political conviction in the reports of sympathetic journalists. A shouting crowd mobilized in a nocturnal setting, tramping through the heart of town with torches blazing, had a menacing aspect. Violence could erupt: that, after all, was part of the fascination for those on the scene and part of the ritual's political power. Unlike the targets of a related nocturnal community ritual widely practised in Canada West – the charivari – the targets in effigy-burnings were politicians or statesmen.[41]

In several places the effigy-burning demonstrations of 1849 went off without triggering violence, but in Toronto that was not the case. "We had a scandalous scene in Toronto on Wednesday evening," began the *Globe*'s hostile account of the events of 17 October.[42] "It had been known for several days, that the rowdies of the city were to try their hands at effigy-burning once more, and that the Governor General was to be the subject of their next disgraceful exhibition." Although rival newspapers reported that about 2,000 citizens joined the procession that night, the *Globe* reassured readers that there were only 100 to 200 young men, all of them Orangemen and "many of them lads." The "rowdies" included men "both genteel and vulgar." The procession, led by Tory alderman and deputy sheriff Robert Beard on horseback, passed through the streets. It was followed by "a considerable number of lookers on, and at length, about half past ten o'clock, it drew up opposite the City

Hall." The mayor and other officials watched as the protesters raised a scaffold, from which they suspended the tar-and-straw governor. He was then set alight.

The *Globe* explained that the whole demonstration had been got up by local Tory leaders – some of them civic officials – who wanted "the world to believe that *Toronto* have burnt Lord Elgin in effigy" because "the atrocious falsehood [would] aid their political purposes." In point of fact, maintained the *Globe*, only a tiny, irresponsible group had done the deed; opposition to the governor was much less extensive than the Tories made out.[43]

The Reform press made much of the fact that civic officials had both condoned the demonstrations and played a key part in counselling non-violence. Prior to the demonstration, Toronto's mayor had called a public meeting that intensified opposition to the governor and his Reform ministers. At the meeting, city magistrates had reassured the crowd by declaring that they had no objection to effigy-burning per se and that they would not sanction the swearing in of any special constables unless violence actually broke out. At the end of the meeting the mayor pleaded with the crowd "to commit no act of violence that would put the city authorities to the necessity of putting it down." Had violence erupted, the civic officials' position would have been untenable, after they had sanctioned the effigy-burning demonstration, and it would have created bad publicity for the Tory cause. The *Examiner* objected both to the authorities' tolerance for burning effigies of a statesman and to the civic authorities' failure to prepare for violence, which had put the community at risk.[44]

Confusion reigned as to the legality of effigy-burnings and thus the complicity of officials in condoning lawbreaking. In 1849 even Reform newspapers, which were quick to criticize the Tories for mounting such spectacles where the Queen's representative was burned, initially expressed uncertainty as to the legality of effigy-burnings. "The question has been canvassed," observed the *Globe*, "whether the burning of effigies be an illegal act. Although there is no special statute against it, there cannot be a doubt that it is so, as every other thing is which has an evident tendency to create a breach of the peace." The Chief Justice, Sir John Beverley Robinson, soon clarified the matter in a public statement on the matter:

> As the exhibitions are indecent and insulting, and have a tendency to lead to tumult, it is proper that it should be understood, that by the law of England, and the law of Upper Canada is the same, the burning or hanging of any person in effigy or puplicly [sic] even without a tumultuous

assemblage, is a misdemeanour, it is a kind of libel, and is so offensive in its character, that it has frequently been made the subject of prosecution where the party insulted has been a private individual[.] [W]here any one high in authority has been made the subject of such an exhibition, the offence is on that account more grievous, and where the object is to bring odium on the government and its measures, it becomes then SEDITIOUS in its character, and exposes those concerned in it to be punished for that offence.[45]

The Reformers were delighted that such a scion of the Tory establishment had in effect denounced the recent practices of local Conservatives. The Reformers were disappointed, however, when, after the burnings, the magistrates had shirked their duty, refusing to proceed against the effigy-burners. The *Examiner* said that "the majesty of the law ha[d] been insulted and trampled upon with impunity."[46]

The Governor's Tour

Even as the Reformers condemned the disorderly Tory spectacles in the streets, Reformers were laying plans for street spectacles in connection with a proposed tour of Canada West to be made by Governor Elgin. In the tradition of the royal tour, governors' tours aimed to buttress and enhance Crown authority and prestige through a series of local appearances where the people expressed their loyalty by turning out in large numbers to honour the monarchy and welcome the visitor to their festively decorated town. The visitor in turn honoured the people, showing his interest in them by condescending to come among them. The visit was a reminder of the mutual obligations between Crown and subject. In the far-flung colonies, royalism had its genuinely popular side, which was shown vividly during the local celebrations and reinforced by press coverage of visits elsewhere on a tour itinerary. Such tours had a ceremonial aspect that gave participants suitable roles to play, provided material for the press to cover, and added gravitas to the occasions. Formal entries, processions, triumphal arches, and levees were components that made the choreographed visits visually spectacular and aurally impressive.[47]

In 1849, Elgin had his own reasons for wanting to make a public tour. After being pelted by eggs and stones in Montreal, he had withdrawn to the safety of Monklands, the governor's well-protected estate to the west of the city. Initially concerned for his own safety and that of his family, he remained there, he said, because he did not want to provoke more outbursts by appearing publicly in the capital.[48] Seeing the governor holed up at Monklands, the Conservative press accused him of cowardice and charged that he dare not appear publicly anywhere in the province, so widespread and profound was his opposition. An editorial cartoon in *Punch in Canada* ridiculed Elgin by depicting him as a hermit. Tories could now redouble their demands for Elgin's recall on the ground that as a prisoner on the estate he could not carry out his duties.

For his part, Elgin grew determined to demonstrate that he could move freely, even triumphantly, throughout Canada West, where the great majority of English-speaking Canadians lived. It would be a direct appeal to the people.[49] A tour would put paid to Tory claims that the majority of Upper Canadians disapproved of his actions. He anticipated that his support for responsible government would be widely acclaimed in Canada West. His tour needed to be carefully timed, however. "I have been desirous to give full time for news [of Parliament's support for him] to come from England, for reason to resume its say, and for the manifestations [of support] from U. Canada to produce their effect."[50] Late summer appeared to be the optimal time for a tour of Canada West.

Reformers perceived the tour as a heaven-sent opportunity to gain prestige by being associated with the office of the governor, while the Tory press gasped in horror at the prospect, lashing out at the plans of the Reformers and the "Radical-visiting Governor."[51] Lord Elgin proposed to visit Canada West, charged the *British American*, "not as the Representative of her Majesty, but in an electioneering capacity, as the 'dignified' and recognized head of a faction whose hatred to every thing British is so proverbial."[52] The Tory commentators knew that the grandeur of viceregal visits could bring a backlash from taxpayers annoyed at the extravagance,[53] a pertinent concern because of the economic despair of 1849 and the fact that the controversy had originated with objections to the state's providing financial compensation. A Tory broadsheet exclaimed: "Britishers of Toronto! ... let your eggs be stale and your powder dry! *Down with Elgin! – Down with the Rebels!*"[54]

A placard, which Elgin believed Orange leader Ogle Gowan had prepared for Toronto streets, used equally strong language to stir people to action. Alleging that the Reformers were bringing in supporters from the countryside "to massacre the Loyal Inhabitants and to destroy their houses and property," it urged people to "perfect your Organization! ARM! ARM! ARM! Forward from the City – to protect your Wives and little ones from ELGIN and the Ruthless Assassins ... Hurrah, Britons! Strike Home! Now or Never!"[55]

In the United Province of Canada, sectional and urban rivalries ran strong, intensifying the politicking around the governor's tour. Robert

THE HERMIT

Lately discovered in the woods near Monklands; and now about to be forwarded to England by the Gentlemen of the British League, to whom this Portrait is respectfully dedicated.

Mocking Lord Elgin's refusal to appear publicly. J.B. (James Bruce) is portrayed in the woods as a hermit with an overgrown beard and rough clothes but a fashionable top hat.
Source: *Punch in Canada*, 15 August 1849.

Baldwin told a Toronto friend that he believed Montreal Tories were "making the most strenuous exertions" to discredit Upper Canadian cities in the hope of persuading the governor that there was no advantage in moving the capital from Montreal to a place in Canada West. "They are doing all they can," he wrote, "to get people in the west to play their game by insulting the Governor-General there, and are particularly anxious that he should be ill-received at Toronto, Kingston, and Bytown." Baldwin urged his Toronto colleagues to take whatever action they could to prevent a demonstration that would dash all hopes of the city's sharing "in metropolitan honours and advantages."[56] Prestige and patronage were at stake.

Much as Elgin had expected, his opponents lost some of their fire as time passed and the news sank in about the backing Great Britain gave the governor. Royal support for him became evident that summer when he was given a baronetcy and the Queen became the godparent of his newborn son. By late August several Conservative newspapers were criticizing the militant approach of some of their own partisans and "the language which has been made use of by certain violent newspapers." The Québec *Gazette*, after dubbing proposals to disrupt the tour "barbarous and unmanly," advised a low-key approach to the upcoming visits: "Let the Radicals *fete* him if they choose; Conservatives will best attain their own ends, preserve their dignity, and satisfy their consciences as gentlemen, by treating him and his suite with coldness and indifference."[57]

As it turned out, the towns of Canada West – even Tory ones – generally welcomed the governor correctly if not always warmly. Elgin had been shrewd. He had cautiously tested the waters by beginning his tour in the Niagara Peninsula and the southwestern part of the province, where Reform was strongest. He was encouraged by his reception there. Writing privately to Lord Grey from Niagara Falls, Elgin said he had been well-received with the exception of "the [Anglican] clergy who generally hang back, a certain portion of the magistracy, and a certain portion ... of the members of the orange lodges." As news spread both about his warm welcome in the southwestern region and about the way he had been backed up by Britain, Elgin grew confident enough to consider visiting Toronto, which he privately described as having not less than twenty-five Orange Lodges and being "the most Tory place in Canada."[58]

The governor came by steamer to Toronto, landing at the Yonge Street wharf, where he was correctly met by the (Conservative) mayor and corporation, the sheriff, and others. The military guard of honour from Fort York, and the royal salute from its guns, added a little splendour to the scene. The governor then got in his carriage and led a procession into the city centre. An admiring account described the dense crowds that filled the streets, the onlookers perched at every vantage point, the flags and banners flying on "most" houses, the colours hoisted on ships in the bay, the waving handkerchiefs, and the "deafening acclamations" shouted by people of all political persuasions – a scene "gratifying in the extreme." It was only slightly marred, the writer observed, by some of the spectators, who sounded "a few notes of disapprobation," and by "two miscreants, who, we are informed, ha[d] recently arrived from Montreal, threw each an egg at the carriage; the scoundrels were immediately taken into custody." (The British journal *Punch* referred to expressions of muscular conservatism when Elgin was egged as "getting a word in egg-wise.") A Tory report on the same reception presented a different picture entirely: "The cheers of the Radicals were drowned by the groans of their opponents; and Lord Elgin felt, during the whole time, that his presence was only tolerated, and only made sufferable by the high sense of duty of the public functionaries."[59]

Conservative accounts complained that most of the receptions gave the governor a distorted view of the real political situation because his Reform supporters had centre stage. Reformers by contrast represented the receptions as being inclusive and involving nearly everyone except Tory diehards. At Niagara, the *Mail* reported, "a vast concourse of people had assembled, and it would be in vain to think of forming anything like a correct estimate of their number. In point of respectability, it perhaps surpassed any former meeting in the neighbourhood, excepting the one for the reconstruction of Brock's monument." In Brantford the governor was met by the fire department in uniform, a large group of schoolchildren, and "the warriors of the Six Nations" accompanied by officials of the Indian Department. As true loyalists, "the Mohawk and Oneida vie with each other in their desire to do honour to their 'Great White Father.'" In Toronto some 300 gentlemen wished to be presented to the governor with the result that this phase of the reception ran to two hours. The city's St Andrews Society mounted their own parade with some 200 participants, who marched with flags and banners behind three pipers in Highland dress. They honoured the Scottish governor, who had been so shabbily treated by the St Andrews Society of Montreal, which had removed Elgin as honorary president after he signed the Rebellion Losses bill.

Addresses of welcome carefully crafted in advance by the groups that chose to participate were sent ahead to the governor so that his staff could draft suitable replies. In most places the addresses were complimentary, coming as they did from Reformers eager to commend the governor for following the principle of responsible government. Even the Toronto mayor, who a few months earlier had watched happily as the governor's effigy burned, swallowed his pride when he presented the city's address praising the British constitution and assuring Elgin of Toronto's "well-tried loyalism" that had always "distinguished this peaceful and flourishing city."[60]

The governor listened and replied to any address, whether fully complimentary or not, as long as it was respectfully phrased. At Woodstock, for instance, the Conservatives' address made plain that they differed from the governor as to the best course to be pursued in the case of the Rebellion Losses bill. "I rejoice," replied Elgin diplomatically, "to perceive that your dis-approbation of certain acts of the administration does not prevent you from receiving the Representative of Her Majesty when he comes among you with the consideration and good feeling enjoined by a sentiment of genuine loyalty."[61]

In several of the places visited by Elgin, the gloss of loyalty and respectability was marred by some incidents involving small numbers of Tories. In some cases, prominent individuals snubbed him. At Hamilton and Chippewa, the Anglican clergymen refused to pay the governor a call, even though Elgin had attended divine service in both places. The Tory leader and magistrate, Sir Allan MacNab, refused to recognize the governor's visit to his hometown, and he carried on with his high court duties, even though the jury petitioned him for an adjournment. When Elgin attended convocation at the University of Toronto, he told Grey privately that he found it "remarkable" that "in a Hall crowded to suffocation with Clergy of various denominations, professors of different colleges, members of the Bar etc. etc. & with the elite of the ladies of Toronto, the Bishop and the Chief Justice should have been absent."[62] (Note the rare reference to women being present, but of course this was a highly respectable occasion deemed suitable for "the elite of ladies" and one far removed from the tumult of the streets.)

Some skirmishes did occur during the governor's tour. In London, Tories on horseback rode through main streets knocking down the arches and other decorations of welcome, apparently with the approval of the mayor.[63] In Brantford, a man decorating a bridge was shot in the knee by someone trying to prevent a hearty welcome.[64] In Toronto, where Tory leaders counselled restraint, late in the evening of the day when Elgin arrived a few "rowdies who were obliged to practice self-restraint during the day," wandered into the Bay Street fire station and began ringing the fire alarm. This signal had often been used by the Orange-controlled fire companies to call out a crowd and prompt a demonstration, but in this case little happened. The bell ringers were quickly stopped and charged by the bailiff. Only "a dozen or two other stray animals" set out along King Street carrying torches and an effigy of Elgin. Soon "the police, after a desperate struggle, captured a number of the[m], including the leader." Reform newspapers represented these incidents as small blemishes in a remarkably smooth visit to the Tory stronghold of Toronto. The *Mirror* generously observed that "our good tory neighbours seemed to feel very proud of their good behaviour. We award them all credit for their improved demeanor, and all the more, because it cost them so great an effort."[65] The Montreal *Courier* railed at the inconsistency of Toronto Tories, who one day petitioned for the governor's recall, and the next received him with cheers. Their treachery was easily explained: they had sold their principles for the lucre that would flow from having the seat of government moved to Toronto. The pragmatic pursuit of self-interest would be another way of describing this behavioural shift.[66]

Uncharacteristically the authorities in Toronto pursued the Conservative demonstrators. The magistrates laid charges against thirteen men for riotous assembly and assault and against three others for ringing the fire bell in the absence of a fire. Thirteen of the men charged were tried and three convicted. Because these men were arrested – unlike the vast majority of demonstrators in 1849 – we know that they were mostly working-class and Orangemen. Their behaviour fit within a local tradition of plebeian political activities in the streets: political activity that diverged from the niceties of deliberative democracy.[67] The defendants, who enjoyed legal assistance from Orange aldermen, maintained that effigy-burning was not illegal and that they had merely acted in self-defence. "Here," remarks historian Gregory Kealey, "we have a defence of traditional plebeian political practice against the new constraints of a redefined public order."[68] Understandings of acceptable public behaviour were no doubt shifting, but it should be said, too, that the city officials' concern for Toronto's reputation was heightened at this moment because they hoped to curry the government's favour so that Toronto would become the provincial capital. As it turned out, the good behaviour probably paid off. Shortly afterwards it was announced that the seat of government would henceforth shift periodically between Québec and Toronto.[69]

Looking back toward the end of his tour, Elgin represented it to Lord Grey as a success. "I do not believe," he mused, "such enthusiasm was ever manifested towards any one in my situation in Canada as has been exhibited during my recent tour." He thought that he had restored his reputation for courage and his "moral influence." "Before I have traveled unattended through the Towns & villages of U. Canada & met 'the bhoys' as they are called, in all of them on their own ground, I think I shall have effected this object."[70]

Conclusion

The people of Toronto and Canada West dealt with a deeply divisive issue, then, through political theatre. The Rebellion Losses bill prompted political rivals to muster rational arguments in support of their positions, but both opponents of the bill and its supporters also *performed* their politics in public spectacles. Both sides called public meetings that engaged in deliberative democracy, but speakers' voices were frequently drowned out by the jeers of their critics, and debate gave way to brawls that were detailed in the press. Through shows of physical strength and numbers, as well as vivid displays got up by interests as diverse as the Orange Order and the governor's office, rivals sought to dominate the political moment. Such displays could reinforce positions articulated in public debate by mobilizing supporters and extending democratic participation beyond the wordsmiths of the legislature and editorial offices to involve members of a wider public that included more than just newspaper readers and propertied voters. Deliberative democracy built a public, but so too did muscular conservatism and monarchical display.

Participants in the "contentious performances" of 1849 engaged in a range of activities, all of them inextricably linked: press commentaries and invectives; public meetings intended to show broad support for particular positions usually detailed in formal resolutions; petitions endorsed by large numbers of people and addressed to authorities; marches through city streets; welcome ceremonies and addresses; menacing nighttime crowd actions that could include effigy-burnings; and brawls, stone throwing, and rioting that were sometimes countered variously by special constables, magistrates, and troops. This repertoire drew only on techniques previously deployed in the province. This is not surprising. A central contention of Charles Tilly's wide-ranging study of "contentious performances" is that "on the whole, when people make collective claims, they innovate within limits set by the repertoire already established for their place [and] time."[71]

The rebellion losses controversy raised crucial issues of political legitimacy. In 1849, Upper Canadian Conservatives forcefully questioned the legitimacy of a British colonial government dominated by French Canadians who, lacking proper respect for British political traditions, were leading the province toward political crisis and social and economic instability. When Conservatives failed in their multifaceted campaign to have the imperial authority intervene to correct the problem, they despaired for the future of the British imperial connection and monarchical institutions locally. However, the more adaptive of the Tories soon came to accept responsible government, in effect acknowledging the legitimacy of the new constitutional arrangements. In future they would find ways to cooperate with French Canadian Conservatives and regain office. Muscular conservatism had taken a beating in 1849. Disrupting meetings, bashing heads, rioting, and effigy-burning had not brought the desired results. Such tactics were widely deplored in the Reform press and by some Conservatives as well. Their legitimacy was called into question. Deliberative democracy came out the winner – although lively street confrontations would never disappear from the Canadian scene, especially at election time.

2
The Press and Election Culture

General elections in mid-nineteenth-century Toronto could not have been more different from recent ones. Mid-Victorian politicians heatedly debated issues and fought with opponents unrestrained by strict rules or many ethical constraints. Participation in the campaigns drew large numbers of men and boys into city streets to witness the campaign and cheer for their favoured candidates. On Election Day, partisanship grew so intense that violence often erupted at the polls. Thugs and bribes significantly affected the voting, which took place at a time when electors declared their choice openly. Studying the history of elections reminds us that "the past is a different country."

Toronto's lively, partisan journalism represented politics in the streets as being boisterous and combative, made so by aggressive masculine behaviour that could thwart the independent choices of electors. On many occasions newspapers noted the participation in electioneering of non-electors, men and boys who lacked the property qualifications for voting or were too young to vote, which points to the wide albeit gender-exclusive dimensions of electioneering. Newspapers that reported on election campaigns in mid-Victorian Toronto repeatedly deplored violence and urged decorous, restrained male behaviour. By giving so much attention to the bad behaviour of opponents' campaigns, however, newspapers ironically publicized models of masculinity that were anything but restrained.

This chapter explores how local newspapers depicted the election culture of parliamentary campaigns in mid-Victorian Toronto. By "election culture" I mean the practices, performances, and often ritualized behaviour of people in the public sphere who attended meetings and gathered in streets during and immediately after election campaigns. This political culture was structured by election law and its reform and expressed through a limited but rich repertoire of crowd behaviours.

By documenting how newspapers expressed partisanship we deepen knowledge of its meaning and role in elections.

The election campaigns studied are the parliamentary elections held during the period from 1841, when the first provincial contest was held in the new United Province of Canada, to the Dominion election of 1874, the last of the elections held under the voice-vote method and the year in which Canada introduced the secret ballot for Ontario and Dominion elections. This timeframe provides a substantial run of campaigns, twelve in total – enough to see practices frequently repeated and occasionally altered. Toronto's municipal elections are not included, except where their practices impinged on the parliamentary campaigns. Because municipal elections were annual, it is not possible here, given space constraints, to deal adequately with the thirty-three campaigns held during this period. Upper Canadian provincial elections prior to 1841, which have been studied by others, provide some points of comparison.[1] It is notable, for instance, that the scrappiness that characterized the contests of our period was evident in the 1834 and 1836 campaigns as well.

When the Act of Union (1840) created the new United Province of Canada, Toronto was a single riding with two seats. In the 1841 election, a pair of candidates stood as high Tories resistant to all reforms and another pair stood with the interventionist governor, Lord Sydenham, who took a moderate reform position.[2] Subsequently, newspapers identified pairs of candidates either as Conservatives or Reformers, although the odd individual asserted his independence. Party formation remained very much under way in the 1840s and 1850s, but journalists nevertheless generally represented candidates as being Reformers or Conservatives.[3] For the first time in the 1861 election, Toronto electors voted for one candidate in either the Eastern or Western Division, and soon after Confederation the Dominion parliament created a third division, Toronto Centre.[4] The increasing division of the city reflects its growth, yet throughout the period, it remained a sufficiently compact place for people to conveniently gather in its core. In the city, large crowds could congregate and create a volatile mass.

Throughout the mid-century period, Toronto election crowds performed in the streets and meeting halls in ritualized ways that gave expression to various masculinities. As we shall see, nomination meetings involved both addresses that conformed to a gentlemanly code of masculinity *and* aggressive heckling. Public meetings, held ostensibly for men to engage rationally in issues of public policy, were frequently disrupted by near riots. In the days of open voting, intimidation at the polls was routinized, however much it was deplored in the press. Post-election victors' processions were harassed by crowds lining the route. All such behaviour detailed in the press can be seen as contentious performances.[5] Moreover, because elections were often tight contests, some of the performances detailed in the press were not simply interesting rituals; they might well have determined electoral results.

The evidence for this chapter rests on the campaign coverage of all the surviving issues of Toronto newspapers of the period. The most useful newspaper for this study is George Brown's *Globe*, which had the financial resources to put reporters in the streets during election campaigns.[6] So did its main rival, the *Leader*, published in Toronto from 1852 by James Beaty, soon a staunch supporter of the Conservatives and later an elected Conservative politician.[7] Other newspapers provided less coverage of the campaigns in the streets and meeting halls, no doubt because of their more limited resources.[8] Although editors of such newspapers typically commented at length on the issues and candidates, they said little about how the campaign was proceeding, thus making these newspapers less rich for the purposes of this chapter. All editors presented a sharply partisan perspective on elections – a black-and-white view of candidates and issues – intended to pique readers' interest, confirm their preconceptions, create partisan communities, and engage them in the race to victory. As was typical of Victorian journalists' coverage of crowds, few if any individuals were ever identified beyond the candidates and those speaking at meetings. No on-the-street interviews were undertaken, and even characterizations of the make-up of crowds were few.

Regrettably, I have found no mention of women or girls in the city's election crowds. To be sure, political life was firmly gendered male in mid-Victorian Toronto, but women's absence from reports surely must have more to do with male journalists' erasures rather than with women's actual absence from the scene. After all, many women could be found daily in the streets going about their business, and it is hard to imagine that when electioneering brought excitement to the streets they disappeared entirely from the scene.[9]

For many years historians have been writing about Canadian elections, including ones in Toronto, yet remarkably little has been said about what happened during campaigns on the streets and in meeting halls.[10] A few local studies are exceptions. Scott See's "Polling Crowds and Patronage," which draws on an international literature on crowds, focuses on the highly contentious 1842–43 provincial election campaign in a rural New Brunswick riding where a distinctive geography and the dominance of two rival employers contributed to extraordinary levels of intimidation and violence.[11] In his study of crowd events in Montreal during the 1840s, Dan Horner undertakes a case study of the 1844 Montreal by-election that turned on the contentious issue of responsible government, sparked a riot, and prompted a lengthy debate in the press about election behaviour, mob rule, and democracy.[12] Colin Grittner has shown how persistent violence and intimidation in Montreal's municipal elections prompted vigorous attempts to rejig the franchise.[13] In his study of thirty-eight elections in Oxford County during the mid-nineteenth century, George Emery makes scattered references to election culture.[14] Duncan Koerber's study of the newspaper coverage of Upper Canadian elections prior to our period argues that newspapers, rather than focusing on issues or "substance," instead emphasized "style," that is, the individual candidates, their identities, and their relative success as public speakers.[15] In the course of developing this theme, Koerber touches briefly on features that continued to characterize Toronto election campaigns in the mid-nineteenth century: newspapers' pleas for supporters of favoured candidates to come out and vote, partisan heckling at public meetings, and street pageantry on the campaign trail and during victory celebrations.

Two studies of England and one of the United States focus on election culture and provide useful points of comparison with Toronto. Frank O'Gorman's work on England's election campaigns from 1780 to 1860 highlights their elaborate rituals, which he argues were an amalgam of official election processes and customary electioneering behaviour. The transfer of election laws and the migration of people from Britain to Canada meant that mid-Victorian parliamentary elections in Toronto displayed many similar processes and practices – nomination meetings, canvassing, and valedictory celebrations – but also that electioneering in Toronto lacked the more elaborate rituals of Hanoverian England. James Vernon's examination of mid-nineteenth-century English elections bolsters his broader point that disenfranchised men and women were nevertheless incorporated into the political nation, and as we will see, evidence from Toronto suggests this might have been true there, too. Similarly, Michael E. McGerr's study of nineteenth-century elections in the American North argues that the masses were spurred to public involvement, which he attributes both to partisan newspapers and spectacular campaign practices that included daily parades with floats and evening torchlight processions. Toronto's newspapers were also intensely partisan, but the city's election-time spectacles pale next to the elaborate, choreographed parading in the United States.[16]

Toronto's election campaigns resembled those in many places, but newspaper coverage of them shows that the partisan conflicts were extraordinarily intense. The city's leading newspapers, the *Globe* and the *Leader*, were fierce rivals that persistently framed all electioneering behaviour in partisan ways and frequently sparred with each other. Moreover, the combative election culture gained bite from the exceptional strength of Orangeism in the city. Toronto's municipal elections were hard fought by Orangemen determined to maintain their grip on the city administration, which gave them access to contracts, licences, and jobs.[17] Some Orangemen honed their skills as hecklers and intimidators in annual municipal elections and then lent their services to the parliamentary campaigns, generally of Tory candidates.

The chapter is organized to follow the process of election campaigns from the selection of candidates, through the rough and tumble of the campaigns, to polling and victory celebrations. This structure exposes the phases of campaigns and the cultural practices associated with each one.

The Campaign Gets Under Way

Toronto's election campaigns began, not with grand, formal entries to the constituencies as in Hanoverian England, but with public discussions of possible candidates. Even before the governor issued a writ for the election, individuals jockeyed for candidature in Toronto and elsewhere in the province.[18] Sometimes a man came forward to offer himself, but doing so opened him to criticism that he was thrusting himself on the electorate for personal gain. Things went more smoothly when a large group of men or a political party met to select a candidate.[19] Instead of holding meetings to select candidates, "friends," that is, supporters of a potential candidate, could get up a requisition – a petition with many signatures – urging the man to declare his candidacy. Press involvement came at every turn: in reporting on meetings, printing requisitions with their ever-growing lists of signatories, and commenting on the wisdom of selections.

In the 1857 campaign, the requisition got up by George Brown's friends and printed in the *Globe* was extraordinarily large and controversial. By mid-December, the petitioners numbered 1,716, thus making a powerful plea for Brown to run in the city and not just in the rural seat of North Oxford.[20] The requisition included many names of Orangemen, including masters of lodges. In his declaration, Brown acknowledged that it was a "pleasure to see the names of many who differed from me in the past," and to curry their favour he made a point of referring to "the entire subserviency of the Government to the Roman Hierarchy."[21] The *Leader*, which supported the Conservatives, charged that Brown's requisition included the names of many non-electors, that the *Globe* had "monstrously" exaggerated the number of Orangemen's names on the list, and that in any event these signatories were not sincere or authentic Orangemen. The *Globe*, of course, answered back. The *Leader*'s charge that non-electors signed the requisition, if it can be believed, raises the possibility that such people played a role in election campaigns even though they were barred from voting.[22]

By the 1870s, candidate selection meetings were often so large that the odds of unruliness and confrontations increased. This was the case, for instance, at the Reformers' Toronto East meeting in St Lawrence Hall that chose John O'Donohoe as candidate in 1874. The *Leader*'s coverage, printed with the headline "Rowdyism Rampant," claimed that when "a gentleman" tried to speak in favour of the Conservative candidate he was shoved off the platform and injured so badly he had to be carried home. The *Globe*'s version said that when the chairman asked the man to leave the platform he refused to do so until two or three from the audience persuaded him to make "a hasty flight."[23] Given that rival newspapers covered the incident, we can accept that some kind of confrontation arose, but we cannot be sure exactly what transpired.

Once a man became a candidate, he issued an address that local newspapers ran repeatedly throughout the campaign, whether the editor endorsed the candidate or not. Addresses conveyed a gentlemanly masculinity, with modesty being a key feature. In his 1847 address, Donald Bethune expressed himself with elaborate modesty by saying he hoped someone more qualified might be found, or that people would overlook his deficiencies, but then he thanked the people for having faith in him.[24]

Once in the running, candidates began their door-to-door canvass. In England, the candidate undertaking the canvass of electors was often accompanied by a large musical band and a retinue of notables compelled to submit to public mockery. In Toronto, candidates and their friends canvassed in a business-like way, knocking on doors and talking face to face with electors. Reports inevitably said that the canvass for a favoured candidate was going well. On George Brown's canvass in 1857, the *Globe* reported that "Mr. Brown's friends are pursuing their work vigorously, and at every step in their canvass meet with fresh encouragement." As for the rival candidate, he had been reduced to paying canvassers. "Mr. Robinson," the *Globe* reported, "has a good many hired canvassers, but they have up-hill work everywhere."[25] In 1861, in a virtually unique reference to women in connection with mid-century Toronto elections, the *Leader* reported that two women were taking an active role in the canvassing. Conforming to gender conventions of the time, the *Leader* admiringly, if patronizingly, commented that the wives of two of the Conservative candidates with their "winning ways made many electors warm up in the cause and work with redoubled zeal."[26] Reports on canvassing were consistently slanted for partisan purposes.

Nominations

In Hanoverian England, Nomination Day was a grand occasion, with colourful processions and an extravagant public breakfast. In Toronto, nomination day activity centred on the meeting, a civic spectacle that drew crowds as large as 6,000 people; celebrations and treating appeared on its fringes. Once the governor issued the writ and a returning officer was appointed for all ridings, returning officers were obliged to announce the exact time and place of the nomination meeting, which had to be held about midday in a prominent location. With the Crown footing the bill, hustings, which by law had to be "in the open air," were raised in advance so that the crowd could better see and hear the business of the meeting, and so that the returning officer could count hands when the time came to do so.[27] Moreover, as James Vernon has argued about similar requirements in England, the hustings crammed with officials and candidates helped the public associate the elevated leaders with political authority.[28]

As master of ceremonies of the nomination meeting, the returning officer ceremoniously read the election writ and then invited nominations. By convention, if the sitting member was up for nomination, his nominator went first. Nominators praised their candidates, and if present the nominee spoke to his own strengths. When there was more than one nomination (and in Toronto there always was), the returning officer asked for a show of hands. The officer then announced which candidate had won the election, and if no poll was demanded by a losing candidate, the victor took his seat in the legislature. While such elections occasionally took place in the province, in Toronto during the Union period defeated candidates always called for a poll, knowing that polling might overturn the show of hands. Unlike at the polls, at nomination meetings no attempt was made to determine whether the men who voted had the franchise. Newspapers contended when it came to rival candidates that many participants voted who were under twenty-one, lacked the property qualification, or had been brought from outside the riding to swell the vote. The show of hands provided an opportunity for non-voters to participate in the campaign and to feel part of the political process.[29] Notwithstanding the unreliability of the nomination vote, candidates wanted to win it because doing so signalled strength. Legislation in 1866 eliminated the show of hands as a method of election, and polling was required thereafter.[30] A justification for eliminating the show of hands was that it was "the cause of very great trouble" and gathered "together a large number of people, in reality only for eating, drinking and parading."[31] Public nominations continued without the show of hands, as did some of the unconstrained behaviour.

On nomination day, once it was determined that a poll would be required, the returning officer announced the location of polls and when polling would take place, by law within six to ten days. Further business required nominees to prove to the returning office that they met the property qualification for assemblymen.[32] Nomination day was not only about business, however. Free houses (where the candidates paid the bar bill) did a booming trade, and public drunkenness was prevalent. In this context, the gentlemanly tone of the public addresses gave way to far less restrained expressions of masculinity.

The 1840 Act of Union assigned the governor authority to select returning officers, which reformers believed disadvantaged them, so the Reform government introduced legislation in 1849 that gave sheriffs priority as returning officers.[33] In Toronto, William Botsford Jarvis, sheriff of the Home District (1827–56), often served in one of Toronto's ridings, as did Robert Stanton, collector of customs for the Port of Toronto. Sometimes newspapers commended the returning officer for conducting the nominations with authority, but complaints arose on occasion, too. The *Globe* alleged in 1861 that although a strong majority of those at the noon-hour nomination meeting in Toronto East raised their hands in support of George Brown, the returning officer decided for his opponent, John Crawford, which was scarcely surprising given that the returning officer had been the chairman of Crawford's central election committee.[34] The *Leader*, by contrast, reported that two thirds of the meeting had favoured Crawford, notwithstanding that Brown's friends had brought in several wagonloads of supporters from the countryside. Moreover, Crawford's dominance would have been far greater had the Reformers not spun out their speeches, knowing that many working-class Tories would have to return to work following their midday break.[35] It is impossible to sort out what actually occurred given the conflicting reports, but both the partisanship of the newspapers and the combativeness of the occasion are perfectly clear.

At these meetings, the nominator spoke of the candidate's admirable qualities – his business acumen, patrician status, unselfish motives, or Protestant militancy – as did the candidate in his own speech. Nomination meetings ran to a few hours and often grew tedious. The *Banner* judged candidate Donald Bethune's speech in December 1847 as "able and well delivered" but "too long for this cold weather." At the December 1851 nomination meeting, the crowd became restless listening to long speeches in wintery weather. The reporter for the *Examiner* wrote that he was unable to take notes on one speech because his hand was so cold. Eventually the audience refused to listen any longer and created a ruckus so that the meeting was adjourned.[36]

Nomination meetings were often enlivened by hecklers, who taunted the speakers. According to the *Globe*, when a speaker at an 1861 nomination meeting dismissed a candidate as "a mere cat's paw," "A Voice" called out, "He will give your man a good scratching anyhow!" At the Toronto East nomination meeting in 1874, the *Leader* reported that "the seething mass of non-electors who lent their aid for the occasion kept bellowing like a set of escaped lunatics." The *Globe* said that at one point a Conservative became so frustrated at hecklers that he lost his temper and, singling out a man, called him "a contemptible hound and a brute." While a reader might sympathize with the candidate's plight, the *Globe*'s point was that in terms of restrained masculinity, the candidate had fallen short.[37]

Some nomination meetings descended into turmoil. According to the *Globe*, when George Brown was about to be nominated in 1863, "rowdies hired for the occasion commenced to howl and scream their loudest," and the nominator could not be heard. Minutes later, Richard Reynolds, when denouncing Tory candidate John Crawford and calling him the pawn of the Roman Catholic bishop, raised a glass of water to his lips. The *Globe* reported that the Irish Catholic rowdies in front of the platform asked him to give them a drink. Reynolds dipped his finger in his glass and threw some drops of water toward them. Thinking he was mimicking "the act of the priest when sprinkling holy water," the Catholic "rascals" rushed the platform, and someone hurled an old boot on the end of a stick at the stage, hitting a journalist. Only with "strenuous exertions" was the returning officer able to restore some order.[38] Historian Frank O'Gorman refers both to the decorum characterizing nomination meetings in England and to the magnanimity nominees showed one another while addressing these meetings.[39] In Toronto's nomination meetings, by contrast, the gloves came off. These were indeed contentious performances where aggressive masculinity often prevailed.

Campaigning in Earnest

Once nominations were complete, the pace of the campaign quickened. Although the law did not require it, candidates held frequent public meetings. "It was important for candidates to be seen," comments James Vernon on electioneering in England.[40] In Toronto, as in other places, candidates appeared at meetings in the wards of their riding, generally at taverns where treating was convenient, and ideally the crowd spilled impressively into the street.[41] This grassroots, street-level politicking kept many electors involved and, it was hoped, loyal to the party, and for each meeting the newspapers carefully noted the chairmen and secretaries elected, giving ward bosses and activists their moment in the limelight. Treating had long been a widely practised ritual of male social bonding.[42] It took on particular meaning when ward bosses and candidates did the treating in the expectation that the drinkers would feel obliged to vote appropriately on polling day. At the ward meetings, the candidate's strategy was to engage with as many friends as possible, encourage them with partisan remarks, and build momentum both on the scene and more widely thanks to coverage in sympathetic newspapers. Such papers presented the meetings as impressive shows of the candidate's popularity, but newspapers backing rivals usually cast the same meetings in a starkly different light.

So contrary are press reports of many of the candidate meetings that it is impossible to tell what actually happened. In 1857, the *Leader* dismissed the meeting called by George Brown at the Temperance Hall, saying it came off like its predecessors as being "remarkable for the amount of noise and confusion which prevailed." Brown's own supporters, it alleged, had smashed the seats and pulled down stovepipes. Brown could only speak in "snatches as he got the opportunity in the abuse of the present Government and the Roman Catholic body, particularly the Clergy of that denomination, whom he always designated by the name of 'Petticoated Gentlemen.'" According to the *Globe*, a similar meeting called by Brown was yet "another triumphant meeting!" The large bowling alley in Terauley Street "was crammed by a respectable and intelligent assemblage" who heard Brown speak about government extravagance and high taxation, the Hudson's Bay Territory, "rep by pop," and sectarian schools.[43] In effect, the reports seesawed between depictions of aggressive masculinity and gentlemanly self-restraint.

Candidates were, of course, aware of what was being said by newspapers supporting their rivals. At one ward meeting in 1861, Crawford complained about "the gross misstatements in the *Globe* with reference to himself and his meetings."[44] Of course, journalists did not intend their reports to be accurate but rather to boost a candidate or party.

The newspapers touted the enormity and respectability of the crowd supporting their preferred candidate. According to the *Leader*, the Conservative candidates holding ward meetings in the city's two divisions in 1861 regularly drew crowds in the thousands – 3,000 in St David's Ward, 1,200 to 1,500 in St James, and the same in St Lawrence – but the *Globe* reported numbers much smaller at these same meetings, 300 to

500 at one, at another "four cabloads" (implying they had to be brought from outside the ward), and just 62 at one meeting in St James. Meanwhile, the *Globe* boasted that the Reform crowds were "immense" and "influential," whereas the *Leader* reported that at one of Brown's meetings, of the 200 to 300 present many were supporters of his rival, as indicated by the cheering.[45] The *Leader* also said that the hall at one of Brown's meetings had been packed with "young men and boys," implying that organizers, lacking sufficient support, had brought out immature lads lacking good judgment and the right to vote. If it were true that many in attendance were non-voters because they were underage, then such males had gained a significant role in elections, notwithstanding their official exclusion from polling.

Both parties often sent hecklers and bullies to their rivals' meetings. During the December 1851 election campaign, the *Examiner* reported that at a Reformers' meeting held at Darby's schoolhouse, "50 or 60 rowdies, retainers of the tory party," shouted so the speakers could not be heard, while others armed with clubs "put out the lights ... knocked down the stove-pipe and kicked it out of doors." (A lit woodstove without a stovepipe belched smoke into the room, further disrupting the meeting.) A second Reform meeting scheduled for later that evening near St Patrick's Market failed to come off because Tory enforcers arrived early and bullied all comers, including Clement Cape, a merchant, who was knocked down, kicked in the face, and injured so badly he was thought to be dead.[46] In the heat of the 1858 campaign, the *Globe* condemned the bullying methods of John Hillyard Cameron and the Conservatives. Particularly offensive was Cameron's own undignified conduct, "telling a man in a public meeting to keep quiet or he will make him, d___d quick, and offer to 'settle' any half-dozen in the room."[47] Cameron, a distinguished lawyer and blueblood, built a working-class following by such manly talk and by his adroit manoeuvring within the Orange Order.[48]

When Brown was riding the Protestant horse, the *Globe* characterized Catholics supporting his rivals by appealing to popular stereotypes, representing them as slovenly and all muscle, no brains.[49] "A more motley assembly was scarcely ever seen," began the 1857 *Globe* report of an Eastern Division meeting of 1,000 friends of the Conservative candidate. Close to the platform stood "about fifty of the unwashed *primed* and ready for any work their leaders might require of them ... Their tall forms, broad shoulders, heavy muscles and huge fists" made them "specimens of the 'animal' man."[50] On another occasion, the *Mirror*, as usual, leapt to the defence of Catholics, insisting that the Catholic voters of east Toronto were "not confined to the mean and vulgar class announced by the *Colonist* and *Globe*, and their numbers, their influence, their respectability would cast far into the shade the whole brood of their malignant revilers."⁵¹

In the 1857, 1858, 1861, and 1863 campaigns, both parties pursued the 400 or so votes of the city's African Canadians, whose numbers could tip the balance in a contest. Moreover, African Canadians took the initiative in convening public meetings and expressing their political preferences. According to the *Globe*, after the *Colonist* carried a statement by African Canadian electors supporting the Conservatives in 1857, African Canadian Reformers called a meeting in Bob Moodie's tavern and endorsed George Brown, who they declared had "helped the people of colour and stands for equality." Meanwhile, the *Leader* insisted that "all the leading and influential colored voters go against Brown because they are satisfied of his insincerity," attributing Brown's involvement in the Anti-Slavery Society of Canada to his cynical bid to get its printing contracts.⁵² In 1858, according to the *Globe*, a meeting of African Canadian Reformers was broken up by "a dozen of [Conservative candidate] Cameron's coloured rowdies" and a half-dozen "whisky-primed white roughs." A second meeting, however, endorsed Brown, noting his "long advocacy of the rights and liberties of all nations, and especially those of the down-trodden sons of Africa."⁵³ In their coverage of African Canadian involvement in the campaigns the newspapers thus represented Blacks as expressing, along with white men, both respectable and rowdy masculinity.

Politicians occasionally called all-candidates' meetings to challenge one another directly – at least that was the idea. The all-candidates' meeting held during the 1857 campaign was a fiasco. Reformers petitioned the mayor for a meeting to be held at City Hall, chaired by the mayor.⁵⁴ According to the *Globe*, the *Colonist*, championing as ever the Conservative cause, threatened "hot work" for Brown and the Reformers. More than 1,200 people turned up for the meeting, including a large and noisy contingent of Conservatives, who drowned out Brown, even as his supporters belted out his campaign song, "The People's Champion." As the *Globe* explained derisively, "the 'dogans' of St. Patrick's Ward were out in force, and even a much smaller number could have prevented any one from being heard." Because of the heckling, the mayor decided to dissolve the meeting. Amid uproar and confusion, Brown's supporters tried to carry him by chair out of the hall, but their way was blocked. Then, according to the *Leader*, "a regular fight ensued. Sticks and umbrellas were used on all sides." The police tried to rein in the crowd, but failed. Rioters smashed furnishings and people were trampled. Brown succeeded at last in exiting, and at that point a Conservative candidate managed to say a few words, boasting how he would beat Brown in the election and drive him out of town, words the *Leader* said got "tremendous cheering" and that the *Globe* said got "groans and hisses."[55] The 1861 campaign saw a replay of the event, except that this time Michael Murphy, the city's most prominent Irish nationalist, was charged with assault for clubbing Brown over the head from behind.[56] The repetition illustrates well that the participants drew from a repertoire of masculine behaviours in their contentious performances.

The press never condoned rowdy behaviour, however frequently it occurred and however helpful it might have been in winning elections. Particularly prominent in newspaper coverage were references to "Tory rowdies," said to be Orangemen close to the corporation, retainers of Tory politicians. The Orange Order provided a convenient institutional base for recruiting such men as well as a militant ideological position (ultra-loyal and militantly Protestant) that assisted mobilization. Moreover, the Tories of the corporation had patronage positions to dispense among grateful supporters, notably licensed cabmen, tavern owners, and carters, who might willingly reciprocate by providing service at elections. Reformers lacked an equivalent power base in municipal politics. Disappointed by the election of two High Tories in 1847, the *Banner* complained that "all the retainers and toadies of the Corporation were marched up at the word of command. The Reformers have no such discipline."[57]

In every election, tensions mounted as partisans made final demonstrations. "The eve of the election was marked with great excitement," reported the *Leader* in July 1861, "the streets being crowded with the electors of both parties up till a late hour." According to the *Leader*, 2,000 people in East Market Square cheered Crawford, the Tory candidate, drowning out the proceedings of Brown's meeting in St Lawrence Hall, where just 1,000 "young men and boys" had gathered to be "harangued" by Brown.[58]

On the eve of the 1872 vote in Toronto, local Conservatives staged a grand rally, the climax of its campaign to urge workingmen to vote for the Tories. Star attractions were Sir John A. Macdonald, party leader and prime minister, and Henry Buckham Witton, Parliament's "first working man," fresh from his electoral victory in Hamilton.[59] The *Leader* described an "immense crowd" of 10,000 people in front of City Hall and a torchlight procession headed by the band of the 10th Royals Regiment. Near the front of the procession, men carried a British ensign and a large transparency welcoming Witton to Toronto and urging Toronto workingmen to "Rally Round the Standard of Union and Progress," the party's slogan. When Sir John A.'s carriage arrived at City Hall, men carried him into the hall on their shoulders as the band played "For He's a Jolly Good Fellow." Partisan speeches dealt with workingmen's issues and touted Macdonald's labour policies. At the end of the meeting, about thirty men pulled Sir John A.'s carriage through the densely lined streets, past the *Leader* office, which was cheered, to the Queen's Hotel. Sir John was carried up the steps, from where he gave a speech, quipping to the appreciative crowd that he belonged to "the Cabinet-makers' union ... but he was no 'turner.'"[60] Supporters were now primed to get out the vote.

To the Polls

In 1841, polling took place at a single polling place in urban ridings and violence was extensive, so Reformer Robert Baldwin sought to promote order by introducing legislation in 1842 that required a polling station in each ward in cities, including in Toronto.[61] Thereafter, polling took place at locations selected and announced by the returning officer, with expenses paid by the Crown. In 1841, polling occurred over the course of six days, but the 1842 electoral reforms specified that subsequently in all ridings polls were to be open from 9:00 a.m. to 5:00 p.m. on two consecutive days.[62] (Two-day polls continued for a few weeks across the province following a schedule set by the administration in hope of a bandwagon effect triggered by victories in safe seats.)[63] Polling places, each under the charge of a deputy returning officer, were mostly located at taverns, until 1849 legislation aimed at discouraging treating pushed them out to shops, schools, the courthouse, and other locations.[64] Under the voice-vote system, an elector appeared before the deputy returning officer at the polling place and said his name, the location of the property that entitled him to vote, his occupation, and his favoured candidate's name. The poll clerk recorded these declarations in the poll book. In the mid-1850s, provincial legislation introduced the requirement of voters' lists based on municipal property assessments, but difficulties occurred in implementing the measure. From 1861, the use of voters' lists became standard practice, though manipulation of them occurred, perhaps frequently.[65]

Partisan newspapers urged supporters to arrive early for the polling in the hope that an early lead would encourage undecided electors to support the lead candidate. In 1857, the *Globe* advised supporters of Reform to "VOTE EARLY. One vote before noon on Monday is worth two afterwards." It conceded that there would be congestion, but opined, "Our friends must not mind a little squeezing. If they do, the enemy will be in before them."[66] Apparently, the advice was taken, because the *Leader* was soon complaining that Brown's supporters had rushed to the polls before nine o'clock and "took forcible possession of them and for a full hour hardly any votes could be polled for Robinson and Boulton." Conservatives were advised to arrive early the next day.[67] In this exchange, both sides used military metaphors (the "enemy" and "took forcible possession") that deepened the force of aggressive masculinity more generally in play.

Posters of all descriptions crowded the streets near the polling stations, entreating electors to vote in certain ways. Because each elector could vote for two candidates or "plump" for just one, possibilities were many. In 1851, the *Patriot* reported:

> The walls were placarded as usual with posters of all shapes and sizes, some calling on Conservatives to vote for Sherwood and Boulton – some advising Orangemen to desert Sherwood and vote for Boulton and Ridout – others invoking the aid of Reformers to settle the Clergy Reserve question by going unanimously to the polls for O'Neill and Capreol – and last and most absurd of all, huge bills advising Conservatives either to give plumpers for Ridout, or cast their second vote for a Reformer, rather than to Sherwood and Boulton.[68]

Many electors must have been puzzled about how best to proceed.

In Toronto, as elsewhere, friends of the weaker candidates took advantage of regulations to slow down the voting so that the results would not immediately affect ongoing tallies.[69] In 1857, St John's Ward was expected to vote strongly for Brown, and so, according to the *Globe*, Robinson's scrutineer sought to delay the result by asking "ridiculous and annoying questions of respectable citizens."[70] Four years later, the *Leader* charged that Brown's friends had exercised their right to challenge voters they knew to be Conservative with the result that a ward that was overwhelmingly Conservative was prevented from registering its preference promptly.[71]

Confusion and conflict often occurred at the polls as supporters of one candidate tried to press forward and vote early, while rivals tried to block them and push themselves ahead. According to the *Globe*, in 1857 Tories blocked Brown's voters' from accessing the St Patrick's Ward poll, beat some of them, destroyed placards bearing Brown's name, and assaulted drivers of vehicles bringing up his electors.[72] By contrast, the *Leader* contended that in various wards Brown's supporters blocking passageways so delayed Conservative electors that they had no opportunity to vote.[73] Newspapers always blamed opponents for the trouble.

Maintaining order at the poll was the responsibility of the returning officer and his deputies, police and special constables, and any justices of the peace asked by the returning officer to intervene. At least before Toronto's police reforms of 1859, the small police force was widely understood to be highly partisan, favouring Orange and Conservative candidates.[74] The 1842 Elections Act empowered returning officers to swear in special constables as needed to maintain the peace, and required them to do so on the written request of a candidate, his agent, or any two electors. The returning officer or deputy returning officers had the power to disarm people during the election and to ban any armed non-residents coming within two miles of polling places.[75] These arrangements notwithstanding, the state of peacefulness at the polls varied from campaign to campaign.

The 1841 election saw the most outrageous show of police bias and polling irregularities. According to the *Mirror*, the constables placed themselves at the head of the poll and voted for the Tory candidates, and then "secretly handed their staves to the Tory voters so that they might force their way to the hustings." In the morning some thirty or forty Tory electors filled the cellar of the building where the poll took place, and once the poll opened they were admitted through a trap door built so that they could vote early. Reformers were pleased when the returning officer blocked up the "Rat's Hole."[76]

In 1857, when the *Globe* charged that Conservative bullies rioted to prevent Brown's voters from reaching the polls in St Patrick's Ward, it maintained that "it is freely asserted that most of [the police], as well as their chief, sympathized with the rioters."[77] By contrast, the *Colonist* alleged that the special constables had been chosen by the mayor, a friend of Reform candidate George Brown. Calling this a "gross fabrication," the *Globe* retorted that the specials had been chosen by the chief of police, "no friend of Mr. Brown."[78]

In some years, such as 1847, 1851, 1858, and 1861, the police and specials maintained order effectively. At the end of the 1847 campaign, all the candidates praised the absence of violence, a development the *Banner* attributed to "the excellent Election Law of Mr. Baldwin, which divides the City into different wards." The *Leader* reported in 1861 that people were saying that there had never been such a peaceful election in Toronto (forgetting for the moment the earlier conflict at St Lawrence Hall). It was unusual that "no drunken men were seen in the streets; no parties of bludgeon men way-laying individual opponents as they left, or approached the polling booths; no racing of medical men hither and thither to repair the damages inflicted by sling-shot or axe-handles."[79] Peacefulness, or restrained masculine behaviour, thus got comment in the press, but battles for the polls and police shortcomings received more attention from newspapers eager both to denounce the electioneering of rival candidates and to enhance the excitement of the campaign.

Assessing the Results

Throughout the polling, throngs of people collected outside newspaper offices, where vote tallies were continually updated on bulletin boards.[80] In the days before the secret ballot, the moment the polls closed the tallies were known. Interest in elections can only have increased when candidates with opposing positions ran neck and neck, as they often did. In 1841, Governor Sydenham's two candidates beat the two Tories by just eighty-five votes. In 1854, the two Conservatives won by just ninety-five votes in total. George Brown edged out the leading Conservative in 1857 by a paltry fifty-one votes. Even in the post-Confederation elections, votes could still be excitingly close. In 1872, just twenty-eight votes separated the victorious Reformer from the Conservative in Toronto Centre, and the Reformer won by just ninety-seven votes in Toronto East.[81]

As soon as newspapers knew the results, they interpreted them in ways that denigrated their opponents. In 1841, the *Mirror* charged that the poll books proved that the Tories got the votes of people the corporation controlled through jobs or licences. "A vast majority of the tavern keepers and grog shop, and grocery and beer shop keepers, carters and labouring men," the *Mirror* claimed, "depend[] upon the corporation for their daily bread."[82] As for the opposing side, Governor Sydenham had threatened provincial government employees with dismissal if they voted for his opponents, and early in the campaign he fired one civil servant to set an example.[83] To reduce such intimidation, 1843 legislation disenfranchised various categories of provincial government employees.[84] According to the press, however, many electors were still unable to vote with their conscience. The *Globe* maintained in 1861 that Tory candidate John Crawford had won because the Roman Catholic clergy "exercised all their powerful influence on his behalf," every government official "was compelled to vote at the risk of losing his situation," and the Grand Trunk Railway intimidated its employees.[85] For Reformers, these sorts of infringements on the independence of the elector challenged the very basis of freedom and democracy.[86] Moreover, it was sometimes said that officials intentionally left names off the electoral lists to ensure a victory. In 1861, when municipal tax records first became the basis for the electors' lists, the *Leader* maintained that "at least 600 voters must have been disfranchised in the city by a scandalous manipulation of the election lists."[87] It was also possible for partisan or bribed municipal assessors to manipulate the property assessments to disfranchise some individuals.[88]

Bribery explained many results, or so newspapers on the losing side claimed both in Toronto and elsewhere in the province.[89] In 1844, Reformers complained that the Tories had triumphed thanks to bribery, a biased returning officer, and electors disqualified from voting.[90] In 1858, the *Leader* explained Brown's victory by claiming that near St David's poll, money funnelled from Montreal had been passed in handshakes from Brown's agents who "trafficked in votes as openly as men buy and sell vegetables in St Lawrence market." The *Leader* commented on the Reformers' 1863 victory, saying, "Elections in this city have almost reached the point when the man with the largest purse is sure to carry the day."[91] The *Globe* explained the Conservatives' 1864 victory thus: "Taverns and stores were opened all day, and liquor was circulated in great abundance. Few paid for it – the keepers of the shebeens saying the account was settled. Money circulated like water, and votes were purchased at from one to fifty dollars each."[92] Hard evidence of bribery in Toronto was seldom presented, however, thus making assessing the conflicting claims impossible.

Legislation, not well enforced, defined and outlawed unfair practices in elections, proscribing bribery, fraud, intimidation, and the treating of electors with food and drink. Later, prohibitions were tightened and penalties increased. The preamble to the province's Corrupt Practices Prevention Act (1860) justified tighter measures on the grounds that present laws were ineffective against "corrupt and demoralizing practices."[93] Afterwards, tolerance of illegal treating remained pervasive, probably because electors insisted they were owed this traditional reward. Supporters of defeated candidates who charged corrupt practices had the option of petitioning the legislature to void the result.[94] In Toronto, newspapers carried frequent threats to petition, but only in 1841 was a petition presented (and denied).[95] Hard evidence of corruption may have been difficult to obtain; moreover, it was widely believed that the legislature was reluctant to pursue corruption.[96] In 1857, the *Colonist* declared that "Parliament has become a sort of court for the acquittal of wrongdoers. Its majorities systematically sanctify rascality."[97]

Victory Processions

The moment the polls closed on the second day of voting, newspaper offices announced the unofficial results, which triggered victory celebrations. In England, after a formal declaration of the results, valedictory rituals included the victor's triumphal "chairing" and magnanimous speeches intended to heal and unite the community behind its elected member. Toronto had its victory processions, but the rivalry continued. In comparison with many other processions seen in Toronto and elsewhere, including in US election campaigns, the city's election parades were generally a simple ritual that involved little planning and preparation, but arrangements were occasionally more elaborate.[98] In June 1861, the *Leader* glowingly reported on the successful Tory candidates' "grand triumphal procession through the city, with British flags and bands of music." The victors gave speeches to their happy supporters. John Crawford headed for his committee rooms at the Masonic Hall, arriving nearly blinded by dust because he had come in an open carriage drawn not by horses but by men "whose hurrahs were absolutely deafening." Speaking from the hall's balcony, he thanked the electors and assured them in true partisan spirit that he had no personal agenda, but was "actuated by the single desire of serving my country by putting down forever Brownism and Clear Gritism in this city." The *Globe* downplayed and mocked the Tory victory celebrations that featured a boat perched on a wagon, saying that once the oars were shouldered, the horses lurched forward so that everyone aboard fell, much to the delight of the onlookers.[99]

In 1863, once again large and enthusiastic processions formed behind the victorious Reform candidates, one of whom said that he hoped the victory would not "be marred by an improper act." In fact, newspaper accounts differed as to whether there was violence. The *Leader* reported that a cab carrying John Mulvey, a ward boss in St Patrick's, was forced out of the procession by his "enraged Catholic brethren," but police intervened and prevented further trouble. By contrast, the *Globe* reported several skirmishes. The carriages carrying victorious candidates and their committees were decorated with Union Jacks, which supporters of the defeated candidates tried to remove as an insult and gesture of disapproval. Near the foot of Church Street, when "a miscreant" attempted to tear down a flag, a large crowd gathered and hurled stones at the processionists, hitting several people. A carriage carrying Mulvey and others from St Patrick's Ward, being "specially marked out for vengeance," was forced out of the procession and chased away by men "howling like so many demons."[100] At least some of the trouble was confirmed in a police court report concerning three men with the last name of Sheehan who were charged with disorderly conduct for throwing stones at the victory procession. Court testimony confirmed that attempts had been made to pull Union Jacks off the heads of horses in the procession.[101]

TORCH-LIGHT PROCESSION GIVEN IN HONOR OF THE HON. GEORGE BROWN, BY THE CITIZENS OF TORONTO.

Torchlight procession given in honour of victorious George Brown by citizens of Toronto. Supporters cheer the Reform politician as his handsome carriage drawn by white horses passes the office of the *Globe*, his newspaper, 1863.
Source: Library and Archives Canada, C-134199.

The 1874 sweep by the three Reform candidates occasioned both celebrations and angry demonstrations. Thousands of jubilant Reformers celebrated outside the *Globe* office at the close of the polls, and a procession appeared with men "bearing those emblems of complete victory – brooms." Shortly afterwards, 400 angry lads marched on victorious John O'Donohoe's committee rooms on King Street East, gave three cheers for the defeated Conservative candidate, demolished all the windows of the building, and repeated the protest at the Reformers' central committee rooms. The men then strode to the *Globe* office, where they smashed valuable plate-glass windows. Police finally arrived on the scene and dispersed the mob. The protesters returned later that evening to howl in the street, until baton-wielding police drove them away.[102]

Election results only became official a day or two after the polling, when the returning officer made a public declaration, mandated by law, usually to crowds that gathered in the street. In December 1851, Sheriff Jarvis formally declared from the steps of the courthouse that Ridout and Boulton were elected. Shifting to the warmer but crammed courtroom, the newly elected men were invited to speak, Ridout going first because he had gained the highest number of votes. He thanked his Conservative supporters, as well as those Reformers who had voted for him. Boulton spoke next and thanked especially the Orange Order, the *Patriot* quoting him as saying its members "were constantly stigmatized as Orange rowdies and Bullies, but they were the bone and sinew of Conservatism." The *British Colonist* had Boulton chortling at his victory despite what he called "the abuses of his character, the misrepresentation of him by the press, the opposition of the mercantile interests and the opposition of the lawyers." As depicted by the *Patriot*, a range of masculine behaviours were displayed by the losing candidates, who acknowledged their failures – Sherwood "gracefully" and O'Neill speaking bitterly of his friends' desertion.[103]

Toronto's most serious post-election disturbances occurred following the fraught campaign of 1841. Things began auspiciously as both parties marched through the streets immediately after the results were announced. "Great taste and profuse expenditure have been displayed in the various banners, devices, and ornamented vehicles," observed the *Patriot*. Yet violence was anticipated, and was carried out two days later in response to the victorious candidates' procession. Disappointed and angry Tory supporters, many of them Orangemen, first attacked a bagpiper wearing the victors' colours as he walked past Allan's Coleraine Tavern, a meeting place of Orangemen. Later they threw stones at the procession, but they were routed by the far larger numbers of their rivals and sought shelter in the Coleraine Tavern. When the procession reached the tavern, a riot erupted during which shots were fired from inside the tavern at the crowd outside. A bystander was killed, and three others injured, including a constable. Troops were called out to quell the riot.

Peter Way uses newspaper reports and the findings of a commission of inquiry into the riot to reconstruct the events and to argue that it was an example of combative street politics in which working men played an important but contested role, one attacked by middle-class reformers who sought firmer control over electoral behaviour and more peaceful electoral politics. Yet the class dynamics of election contests are exceedingly difficult to perceive, given the newspapers' propensity to represent their own supporters as respectable and opponents as the opposite. Tory supporters, many of them Orangemen, certainly demonstrated in a way that I have dubbed "muscular conservatism," engaging in rough, manly displays of directed violence.[104]

A provincial inquiry eventually laid the blame for the Toronto riot on the mayor, the corporation, and Orangeism. In response, municipal politicians and the Tory press charged that the inquiry was biased. Nevertheless, the report assisted Robert Baldwin when in 1842 he introduced legislation to discourage election riots by reducing crowding at the poll and by banning party colours, the carrying of weapons, bribery, and treating.[105] Baldwin and the Reformers also succeeded in passing legislation aimed at disabling Orangeism by banning its parades, although enforcing that measure proved elusive.[106]

Reforms that did change the electoral culture came in mid-1874, when the Liberal government brought in the secret ballot and eliminated the requirement for nomination meetings, those large gatherings of opponents where trouble often erupted.[107] The minister who introduced the bill observed that the government was both following recent initiatives on balloting in England and Australia and responding to the 1873 Pacific Scandal revelations of widespread bribery in the Dominion election of the previous year. With the secret ballot, the minister declared, a candidate would be less likely to bribe an elector because he could not know whether doing so actually resulted in a bought vote.[108] Opponents of the bill, including Toronto's J.H. Cameron, maintained the secret ballot would encourage dishonesty among electors (!), and, moreover, was "a sneaking, un-British mode of voting." During the first election after its introduction, the *Nation*, published in Toronto, observed that it made the campaign dull because "an early rush to the polls is incapable of producing any inspiring effect."[109] The introduction of the secret ballot significantly changed the rules of the game and moderated the conduct of elections, but it did not eliminate intense partisanship, dirty tricks, or the occasional violent confrontation in the streets.

Conclusion

Local newspapers portrayed election campaigns in mid-Victorian Toronto in highly partisan ways. Documenting their language illuminates how the press expressed partisanship. At every turn, newspapers, particularly the better financed ones, glowingly represented the campaigns of their preferred candidates while denigrating the illegitimate electioneering of rival candidates by relating stories of heckling, intimidation, dirty tricks, and violence. They describe a scrappy democracy in which participants drew from a repertoire of behaviours that we can call contentious performances.

The topic of electoral culture demonstrates better than any other topic covered in this book how the Canadian state made a concerted attempt to discipline the public. It was done to eradicate practices believed to cause trouble in the streets and distort democratic choices. Canada's Parliament provided an obvious place for debating and introducing top-down reforms in a sphere in which MPPs were so directly affected by the robust if often unfair practices of the streets. In the 1840s, Parliament was especially active in introducing reforms, which included requiring a polling station in each urban ward, establishing set hours for a two-day poll, empowering returning officers to swear in special constables, banning guns at polling places, and eliminating taverns as a place for polling stations. These measures were followed by further reforms, such as the clean-up attempted with the passage of the 1860 Corrupt Practices Prevention Act and the introduction in 1874 of the secret ballot.

From the stark partisan journalism, it is obvious that journalists wanted to provoke readers into supporting favoured candidates at public events and at the polls. McGerr's study of elections in the American North argues quite persuasively that partisan newspapers were crucial in mobilizing the public and getting out the vote.[110] For Toronto, however, it is impossible to say categorically how readers responded to newspaper messages. No systematic inquiries into voter behaviour were conducted, and the introduction of public opinion surveys was a century in the future. The impact of alternative influences, such as partisan placards and word-of-mouth networks – far more elusive sources for the historian – is even harder to assess. There are indications that the press probably had some effect on voter behaviour when, for example, electors were urged to vote early for certain candidates and rival newspapers reported they did so. Moreover, candidates who advertised their public meetings in the press, and newspapers that added their voices to pleas for public involvement, were behaving as though doing so mattered.

In representing electioneering, the mid-Victorian Toronto press depicted a masculine world where women were almost entirely absent but competing masculinities were very much in play. Newspapers endorsed masculine restraint. According to this ideal, cool heads should prevail even when the contest heated up. Somewhat reflecting upper-middle-class Victorian notions of sportsmanship, the campaign could be a vigorous contest but one in which conflicts stopped short of fisticuffs.[111] That ideal fit neatly with a commitment to deliberative democracy, a pursuit of best policies through rational debate among men with "the capacity to judge." It fit too with attempts by the legislature to reform election practices and provide a legal framework to enforce restrained behaviour. Yet the press simultaneously depicted the campaigns of rivals in ways that showed them falling far short of the ideal of restrained masculinity. Stories about persistent heckling that prevented views being heard, intimidation at the polls, vote-buying, and drunkenness reinforced a competing masculinity, one more muscular and passionate and less respectable. The press denigrated rivals who exhibited such behaviour during elections, calling them "rogues" and "rowdies," but gave little indication of who they actually were. Some of them may have been, as was sometimes asserted, non-electors too young to vote or unable to meet the property qualifications. Their participation seems to indicate that election campaigns were more broadly inclusive than the limited franchise would suggest.

Partisan journalism and scrappy electoral practices were characteristic of many places in mid-Victorian Canada, but Toronto politics had their own flavour. Because the city's population exceeded that of nearly all Canadian places, Toronto had sufficient people to assemble in large crowds and a population density that compressed them into compact spaces where the numbers looked impressive. Toronto stood out from many places, too, because of the strength of Orangeism. Orangemen, trained in the rough and tumble of the city's municipal elections, provided militant shock troops for the Conservatives. Moreover, Orangeism added a sectarian bite to many controversies, including, as we shall see, on the occasion of the 1860 royal visit to Toronto.

3
A Prince in Town

Sound the Trumpets! Beat the drums!
The Princely heir of England comes! ...
Write the Letters! Sweep the halls!
Erect the arches! Deck the Walls!
Charge all the guns! Subscribe for balls!
For hark, the trumpets! Hark, the drums!
The Princely Heir of England comes! ...

F.J. de Cordova, The Princes' Visit:
A Humorous Description (1861)

The grandest public occasion in Victorian Toronto was the 1860 state visit of Albert Edward, Prince of Wales, the eldest son of Queen Victoria and the man who would be king. That September, enormous crowds took to city streets to see the royal visitor, take in the grand procession through the elaborately decorated city, and join in the hoopla. Toronto's social and political elite spent months planning the best ways to showcase the city's progress, prosperity, and loyalty for the edification and enjoyment of the eighteen-year-old prince, as well as for the vast audience in Canada, Britain, and the United States who watched vicariously through press reports. On display as never before, the city competed with other places on the prince's itinerary to gain the admiration of the watching world.

In many respects, the Toronto organizers judged the spectacle they managed as a resounding success, but not everything went as planned. While hoping to put on display a happy, harmonious, and vital community, organizers, to their dismay, found that social and political divisions were also dramatically displayed for all to see. The 1860 visit revealed far more about Toronto than organizers had expected. A royal spectacle not only offered the city opportunities but also brought risks.

The visit occurred at a time when Canada's relations with the mother country were warm and stable. The rebellions of 1837 were a generation in the past. Victoria was a widely admired and loved monarch. Canadians celebrated the advance of self-government within the empire that had come under her rule, the divisiveness of 1849 now a thing of the past. Canadians realized that worries about Britain's removal in the 1840s of colonial trade preferences had not brought the economic disaster once predicted. The Province of Canada's commercial ties with Britain continued to strengthen, now supplemented by a growing trade with the United States. The royal visit of 1860 would not be a time, however, for enthusing about the prosperity derived from trade with the republic to the south. Indeed, references to the United States were few and often negative, whereas those to the United Kingdom were abundant and glowing.

The prince's visit to British North America grew from an 1859 invitation offered by the legislature of the Province of Canada to the Queen that had been forwarded by the governor general, Sir Edmund Head. Victoria had indicated that a royal visit might be possible. No one expected that she herself would venture so far from home, but protocol required that the invitation be made to her. In January 1860, the invitation was formally accepted with the understanding that it would be the Prince of Wales who would make a state visit that summer, the first state tour made by the young prince. The visit, declared the august London *Times*, "will illustrate not only the loyalty of these prosperous Provinces, but the immense extent of British dominion and the deep-laid foundation of British power."[1] The highlight of the tour was to be the prince's official opening of Montreal's Victoria Bridge, celebrated as a British engineering triumph over the ice floes of Canada's mighty St Lawrence River. The prince was to come with a small suite including his political adviser, the Fifth Duke of Newcastle, who was colonial secretary in Lord Melbourne's government, and Dr Henry Acland, the prince's physician. It was soon announced that the state visit would be extended to include stops in the Atlantic colonies, beginning with St John's, Newfoundland. And in June came the news that at the end of the state visit, the young man would make a private tour of the United States, including visits to Washington and New York.[2]

Newspapers and the illustrated press throughout British North America, Great Britain, and the United States featured the royal visit in countless news items and editorials. Well before the visitor arrived in town, local newspapers everywhere, including Toronto, covered the preparations being made and encouraged competition to determine what town would most distinguish itself. During the tour itself, leading dailies, including Toronto's *Globe* and *Leader*, contracted

The prince, the governor general, and some members of his suite in Montreal. From left to right: Sir Edmund Head, governor general; Major Christopher Teesdale, equerry; the Prince of Wales; General Robert Bruce, the prince's governor; the Duke of Newcastle, colonial secretary. Posing for photographs was at the time a tedious experience, and few were taken of the prince during his tour. William Notman, photographer.
Source: National Archives of Canada, C 181840.

with journalists on the spot to provide accounts of the visit. The great metropolitan dailies of London (the *Times*) and New York (the *Herald* and the *Tribune*) sent their own staff to travel alongside the prince and wire reports home and beyond. Nathaniel Woods of the *Times* enjoyed a special status granted by the Queen as he travelled with the prince and his suite. He obliged with a stream of commentary. After the tour concluded, his reports were gathered together and published in a substantial volume, as were those of some other reporters.[3] Respectful British and feisty American illustrated papers similarly featured the prince and his progress.[4] All this press attention generated interest in the tour, and it accounts in large part for the enormous crowds that greeted him in all the cities he visited. In the colonies, this eagerness to come into the streets and welcome the prince was hailed as a sure sign of respect for the monarchy and the loyalty of the people. Crowds were even bigger, however, in American cities, where the prince enjoyed status as a celebrity that fit oddly with republican values.

Toronto Prepares for the Prince

Toronto began planning for the September visit to the city on the first of June, when Mayor Adam Wilson called a public meeting at St Lawrence Hall, where the male elite of town took charge. The city's main ethnic groups – the English, Irish, and Scottish – were well represented, as were the churches – Anglican, Presbyterian, Methodist, and Roman Catholic. I have called the movers and shakers behind the local visit the "civic boosters." The meeting discussed aspects of a probable program: an official reception, an illumination, a levee, a dinner hosted by the bench and bar, and the formal opening of University (later Queen's) Park. The meeting agreed on the composition of the General Committee of Arrangements, which subsequently established several sub-committees to prepare each part of the program. The sub-committee on finances requested that to assist with preparations, the city allot $12,000 of public funds, an enormous budget for the time. In addition, subscription drives were expected to provide additional funds. The wider public engaged in the planning process by reading the details of the work of the committees reported in the press and by attending a meeting of all citizens called by the mayor at St Lawrence Hall at the end of June. That well-attended gathering endorsed the plans, which legitimized the use of public funds. On a motion of the Rev. Dr John McCaul, president of the University, the meeting resolved that the citizens "gladly avail themselves of the occasion ... to manifest their high appreciation of the distinguished honour thus conferred upon them by a reception suitable to the exalted station of his Royal Highness as Heir Apparent of the British Crown, and worthy of their city as the capital of Upper Canada."[5]

When designing a program for the reception of the Prince of Wales, Toronto's civic boosters demonstrated some awareness of the long tradition of royal entry ceremonies to cities, which always included a procession through city streets viewed by many spectators. Historians have shown how such occasions gave kings and subjects occasions to acknowledge their reciprocal obligations, thus strengthening monarchical power. Writing of royal entry ceremonies in seventeenth-century Dijon, France, Michael P. Breen remarks that for the notables who controlled municipal government, "royal entries were an opportunity to articulate a vision of the city's relationship with the crown, but also a chance to reaffirm the existing social order and to affirm vertical bonds of allegiance, deference, and community with the city's middling and popular classes."[6] In 1860, Toronto's civic boosters could easily have identified with this seventeenth-century strategy. Of course, their knowledge of the tradition came down to them haphazardly, through reading fiction and histories, attending the theatre, and seeing images of processions in illustrated newspapers.

In Toronto, much thought went into determining the route the prince's procession would take through the city and the order of those in the procession. The route had to be long enough that all the spectators could get a chance to see the prince, and it had to pass through the main streets of town to show off the character and grandeur of the town, such as it was. Sheriff William Jarvis, a patriarch of one of the city's grand old families, objected to the excessive length of the proposed route, saying, "It was too much like making an exhibition of His Royal Highness." He thought that it "savoured too much of the style of our neighbours across the lakes." The reception committee disagreed, declaring that only a long route would satisfy "the multitude."[7]

Suspense gripped the town as groups worried over who would take precedence in the procession. Would the shamrock top the thistle, or vice versa? It was well understood that municipal officials, fraternal orders, national societies, firemen's companies, and militia units would play a big part in the procession, the men of these organizations proudly strutting their stuff.[8] As in other places, participating groups represented their city in its component parts. On display were men who made a successful claim to what historian Mary Ryan has aptly called "ceremonial citizenship."[9] In Toronto the prince was placed almost at the end of the procession, so that the order rose climactically from the least important to the most important. The white organizers placed the Loyal United Colored Society first, which gained the group attention even as it relegated the African Canadians to the least prestigious place. Women were granted no places in the procession, just as they were excluded from participation in civic politics, national and fraternal orders, and the militia. Gender conventions cast walking on display in the streets as an inappropriate female activity, all the more so on such an auspicious occasion. The women were to admire the prince as enthusiastic participants among the spectators and embellish the scene with their pretty summer dresses. Elite women, "the ladies" dressed in hoop skirts, avoided mingling with the masses by perching at upper windows or on balconies, even if that meant paying for the privilege.

Like other centres throughout British North America, Toronto made improvements to city streets and the appearance of public buildings and gardens in anticipation of the visit. The civic boosters pressured private individuals with homes and businesses on the procession route to make repairs and improvements. Sprucing up included decorating homes, businesses, and public institutions with spruce boughs brought in from the country.

Arch-building became an obsession. The city, its fraternal orders, and businesses undertook to build arches – temporary structures of painted wood and plaster made to look like impressive granite structures. In doing so, they were following the example both of cities in Britain that had long been hosting royal visits and of triumphal arches erected in medieval and Renaissance Europe for ceremonial entries to cities, which in turn mimicked the grandeur of ancient Rome, where victories were marked and commemorated with triumphal arches.[10] Closer to home, it was customary in Canada to build at least one arch of welcome when the governor general made a formal visit to town – as we saw Torontonians do in 1849 when Lord Elgin visited.[11] In 1860 Canada, arch-building was simply *de rigueur*, so well understood that the need for building arches went unquestioned and unremarked.

Toronto built many arches, but a couple can be noted here. Toronto's Civic Arch stood on piers that had gilt, foliated capitals, and cornices with Roman mouldings. On either side of a portrait of the prince stood figures emblematical of the arts, science, literature, and commerce. Such detailing was meant to mark the sophistication of the place and add grandeur to the colonial city. By contrast, the city's Harvest Arch at King and York Streets was designed by civil engineer Sandford Fleming as a tribute to the agricultural production of the province. The main pillars were covered in bark to give a rustic effect. Smaller supports were thatched with oats, and from the corners sprung "tall, waving plants of Indian corn."[12] As newspapers described the local structures, cities vied to build the largest and most impressive arches. When the arches were nearing completion, attentive gazers gathered in the streets to assess them. "Crowds were assembled at the base of each arch criticizing each shield or flag as it was hoisted in its place," reported the *Globe*. In the evening "the ladies" turned out "in large numbers to admire the preparations."[13] Judgment was the right of the men; admiration the role of the women.

Another task undertaken before the prince's arrival in Toronto was the preparation of formal addresses to present to the prince in a ceremony. The municipality, churches, and fraternal orders eagerly took up their preparation. Again, in doing so colonial cities were following the example set long before by cities in Britain and Europe that hosted royal visitors.[14] In 1860, organizations wishing to present an address were instructed to prepare them well in advance so that Newcastle, the prince's adviser, could vet them and prepare appropriate replies from

Toronto's Civic Arch on John Street. Watercolour by the architect, William Storm. The image featuring the arch exaggerates the grandeur of the scene by making the people appear tiny.
Source: Archives of Ontario.

the prince. The addresses assumed a standard form. They expressed jubilation at the honour of the visit, loyalty and devotion to the Crown and British imperial connection, appreciation for the good government the Queen provided, and best wishes for the prince as he continued his tour. Although formulaic, they were elaborately formal and effusive statements beautifully penned on fine parchment. Altogether the prince on his tour would receive nearly 400 of them.

The Toronto addresses expressed unbounded admiration for Victoria as a model mother and monarch, deep pride in the British connection, a growing Canadian patriotism, and enthusiasm for the progress of the province. "This Synod," said the Presbyterian Church of Canada, "hails Your Royal Highness in your visit to these parts of the American continent, recognizing in you the representative of a Sovereign, who, no less by her example of domestic virtue than by her mild and prudent exercise of her queenly prerogative, has secured the hearty homage of her subjects and the universal respect of the civilized world."[15] Toronto's civic address emphasized progress, Indigenous people providing a foil for the industrious settlers:

> The generations which saw the settler's log-house succeeding to the red-man's wigwam on the site of little York, has not yet wholly passed away, and yet we venture to hope that your Royal Highness will look with satisfaction, on the evidence which our city presents – in our streets, railways, our private buildings, and our political institutions – of the successful results of industry and enterprise, fostered by constitutional liberty.

In many addresses, imperial pride mingled with Canadian patriotism. One penned by educator Egerton Ryerson on behalf of Upper Canada's Council for Public Instruction observed how "loyalty to the Queen and love of the mother Country are blended with the spirit of Canadian patriotism." Absent in the Toronto addresses was any reference to the French fact in the Province of Canada, which contrasted, not surprisingly, with the many loyal addresses presented in Canada East.[16]

The African Canadians of Canada West, who numbered about 21,000 in 1860, prepared several addresses to welcome the prince.[17] A Toronto "convention of colored people" wrote an address declaring that "as a free people escaped from slavery," it wanted "to show all classes in this noble Province that we will not be behind them incoming forward to show our Queen's Representative the prince of Wales, all the loyalty we can possibly bestow."[18] All such addresses praised the freedom enjoyed by people of African origins in Canada, and several contrasted that enjoyment with the situation in the United States, where, on the eve of the Civil War, slavery remained an institution in southern states. An address of the "Colored Inhabitants of this Province residing in Chatham, Oxford, Toronto, Galt" referred to themselves "as freeman many of whom have escaped from from a land of cruel injustice and oppression." Another alluded to all that had been done in the United States "to destroy our manhood" and "to obliterate our rights to liberty and the pursuit of happiness."[19]

Astonishingly, the official reply to each request by African Canadian groups to present an address was a refusal. One African Canadian group was told: "His Royal Highness learns with pleasure the expressions of loyalty contained your address. He is, however, desirous to recognize no distinctions of race among Her Majesty's subjects residing in Canada, and he is therefore advised to accept no address which owes its origin to such difference on these grounds."[20] No further explanation was offered, to the disappointment of excluded African Canadians. We can surmise, however, that Newcastle and other senior authorities were at pains to encourage goodwill between the United Kingdom and the United States and to ensure the success of the prince's imminent tour of America. The African Canadians' references to slavery in the United States would have been embarrassing. Their exclusion as a class was for them a setback that marred the royal visit. For most of the population, however, that exclusion went largely unremarked and unnoticed. African Canadians had very little power at the time, and any public response they might have made to the events was hindered by the lack of a Black newspaper, two such journals having recently folded for lack of funds.[21]

Canada West's Indigenous peoples gained almost no visibility in Toronto, although the city's press closely covered the occasions when First Nations took part in receptions in many other places. Almost no Indigenous people lived in Toronto in 1860, settler colonialism having pushed them aside, notably with the 1848 relocation of the Mississaugas from the Credit River Valley to lands north of Lake Erie on the Six Nations Reserve. Torontonians' understanding of their history honoured the Loyalist émigrés from the United States as the founders of the city and Canada West, completely erasing the history of Indigenous peoples' settlements. (Victoria Freeman has explored how this happened in the case of another spectacular celebration, Toronto's semi-centennial celebration of 1884.)[22]

Although First Nations had no public role in the prince's visit to Toronto, a few Indigenous people visited the city during the celebrations. One of them was Oronhyatekha ("Burning Cloud," or Peter Martin), a young Mohawk chief from the Six Nations Reserve near Brantford. Dr Henry Acland, the prince's physician, wrote home to his wife explaining that he had chanced to meet Oronhyatekha in a hotel corridor. Acland described him as "a young man, herculean, with a large ring in his nose and painted." An accomplished sketch artist, the physician asked the young Mohawk to pose for him. The two chatted as Acland sketched, the doctor learning that Oronhyatekha had obtained a superior education at Kenyon College in Ohio. The Oxford professor found the chief to be a man of "mental cultivation." Acland and Oronhyateka met a few days later in Niagara Falls and the two chatted about the past and future of the First Nations. Oronhyateka expressed great pride in them, as well as his confidence, contrary to the prevalent views of whites, that the First Nations and their cultures would survive.[23] So began a lifelong friendship, renewed when Oronhyateka travelled to Acland's Oxford home and sought his help in arranging to study medicine at the university. Oronhyateka later became a public figure in Ontario as leader of the Order of Foresters, a fraternal and insurance society in Canada.[24] Throughout his life, he remained a proud Mohawk.[25]

"Burning Cloud, Oronhyateka" (1860) by Henry W. Acland. The artist took care to represent Oronhyateka's clothing and nose ring.
Source: Library and Archives Canada, C–122434.

Toronto did have an indirect hand in the grand First Nations spectacle at Sarnia, where the representatives of the Anishinabeg and other peoples assembled to greet the prince. Toronto-based Richard Pennefather, the chief secretary of the Indian Department, as a white official of the state, oversaw the Sarnia display. He and his officers determined that the northern "Indians" would put on a spectacular display, dressed in their "traditional" clothing. "Our great object," explained one of his officers to a missionary, "is to show the Prince of Wales how the Indians dressed in their aboriginal state, and an artist will probably be there to take sketches of everything of note ... We want if possible to have a very grand affair."[26] And grand it was. Several representatives of First Nations – Anishinabeg, Ottawa, Mississauga, Munsee, Potawatomi, Delaware, Wyandot, and Oneida – travelled down to Sarnia to participate in the prince's reception and to hold a council meeting. They exchanged gifts with the Queen's eldest son, praised royalty, and took the opportunity to place their political grievances about the Indian Department before the visiting colonial secretary. Their appearance with painted faces, feathers, and buckskin clothing (in some cases prepared specially for the occasion) did indeed catch the attention of journalists and their readers. No headway was made, however, in gaining redress of the economic and political concerns.[27]

In many other places, too, Indigenous groups presented addresses of welcome to the prince, in sharp contrast with official policy regarding African Canadians. Newcastle very much wanted addresses of welcome and loyalty to come from "Indians." First Nations had long expressed their respect for and appreciation of British monarchs on important occasions, a practice rooted in past diplomatic relations between Indigenous groups and British military and colonial officials.[28] Here was an opportunity to continue a tradition, one that white officials perceived as having helped colonialism prosper.

Of much greater concern for Toronto's reception committee than an Indigenous presence was the proposal to have a general illumination of the city, another practice with deep roots.[29] Public buildings would be lit by specially placed gas lights, and businesses and homes with similar fittings or, if deemed too expensive, then by candles in windows. Illuminating a town marked the evening as special: a bright, playful gleam cut through the gloom that usually prevailed at night in the mid-Victorian city. Residents and businesses were eager to please the prince with all the brilliance, but they were even keener to compete with neighbours and rivals. As the gas lights went up on buildings, newspapers admired the work and encouraged others to match or best the effects.

Many illuminations formed mottoes or lit colourful transparencies. In Toronto, the preferred references were to "Our Glorious Empire." On Ridout's house were three transparencies, one depicting Canada by means of a female figure carrying a sickle and a handful of grain, another a figure of Britannia accompanied by ships and a railway, and the third depicting the heroic death of General Wolfe on the Plains of Abraham. On some transparencies, Canada was represented by an Indigenous woman, who signified the distinctiveness of Canada within the empire or its natural beauty. As in other places, illuminations were the work of men who for ceremonial occasions often appropriated idealized images of women to convey messages.[30]

At the outset, Toronto lawyers had proposed to host an exclusive dinner for the prince and the members of the Law Society of Upper Canada at elegant Osgoode Hall. However, after Toronto papers carried news of the prince's tour through the Atlantic colonies and it became known that the young prince loved to dance, the Toronto legal community decided to nix the dinner and instead host a ball. The male elite would be joined in their hall by their female partners, whose splendid gowns would display Torontonians at their finest. Donning its mantle as the voice of the people, the *Globe* objected strongly to such an exclusive affair for fear it would eclipse the much more socially inclusive ball that the municipality planned to hold – and pay for – at the Crystal Palace on the exhibition grounds. No fewer than five editorials focused on the matter.[31] "The lawyers will get the first glass of the bottle," said the *Globe*, "the citizens will be compelled to drink the dregs after the cork has been out some time." As it transpired, both dances were held, and were judged great successes. Surprisingly, a New York reporter found the lawyers' ball remarkably inclusive. It was not because of the class of the dancers but on account of the race of one attendee, the Jamaican-born Ontario barrister Robert Sutherland, a graduate of Queen's University who practised law in Walkerton, Ontario. Amazed at the presence of a Black man, the New York *Times* reported that "rigged out in full court costume," Sutherland "mingled freely with the *élite* of the city."[32]

During the lead-up to the visit, Toronto businesses appropriated the prince's name and image to sell products, snapping up opportunities to make a buck. John Nasmith advertised in the Toronto *Globe* a "new and delicious article," the "Prince of Wales Biscuit." Cut in the shape of the prince, it made a nice companion to others Nasmith offered, among them "Victoria and Albert, Sir Edmund Head, the Hon. J. A. Macdonald, and George Brown."[33] Publishers sold engravings of images of the prince and the royal family. Medals were struck and offered for sale. In addition, special services were dangled before the consuming public. High-priced cabins aboard the *Bowmanville* were made available for patrons who had the time and money to travel from Toronto to Gaspé to greet the prince upon his arrival in Canada. For just a dollar, the *Peerless* offered standing room to people wanting to spend part of the day of the prince's arrival in Toronto travelling alongside his steamboat as he approached the city.[34]

By all accounts the welcome Toronto gave the prince upon his landing was as splendid as the civic boosters had hoped. When the prince leapt ashore from his steamboat onto the wharf at the foot of John Street, he was greeted by the roar of a crowd of 50,000 people, many having come in from the countryside. "From that moment, there was such a wild, enthusiastic, joyous, uncontrolled excitement in the grand multitude as few shall ever again see," wrote an American journalist.[35] As the prince approached the platform, rounds of applause rang out again and again. "The vast multitude rose from their seats, the ladies waving handkerchiefs, the men their hats, in uncontrolled enthusiasm," reported the *Globe*. The ceremonies took place at sunset in front of the enormous, specially built amphitheatre – "a Canadian Coliseum" – where 3,000 schoolchildren stood to sing "God Save the Queen." Woods of the London *Times* commented on "the effect of the whole scene – the cheering of the crowd outside ... the flags on arches, and the dim illuminations of the city in the distance, along the streets of which crowds were running with a great rush by thousands, all of which no description, however vivid, can recall."[36]

Private assessments by the visitors were equally positive. "The enthusiasm of the people really knew no bounds," wrote Newcastle shortly afterwards in a formal letter to the Queen. "Both as an artistic display and as a popular demonstration it was the finest thing He has yet seen, and He likens it to be unsurpassed by any similar spectacle on the continent of Europe or elsewhere." Another member of the prince's suite called the display "magnificent," adding that "the enthusiasm as well as all the preparations for H.R.H.'s reception were very gratifying." Writing to his mother, the prince declared the Toronto welcome to be "one of the finest sights of the sort I have ever seen."[37]

Very soon after the triumphal royal entry to Toronto, however, trouble appeared in Toronto, as it had earlier at some other places along the Lake Ontario shore.

Arch Rivals

The near catastrophe of the tour pitted the militant Protestants from Upper Canada's Orange Lodges against, initially, the Roman Catholics of the province, and, ultimately, the prince's adviser, the Duke of Newcastle. At the heart of the dispute were different understandings regarding the right to demonstrate of a so-called party organization: the Orange Order. Fiercely committed to the British Crown (when worn by Protestants), the Orangemen presented themselves as the prince's staunchest supporters. In Toronto and other places, they built arches of welcome emblazoned with the talismanic dates and slogans of their brotherhood, and they made arrangements to march in the processions, dressed in their colourful regalia, with banners held high. However, the Roman Catholics of the province took strong exception to these plans, fiercely objecting to royalty's recognition of a rancorous party that had caused so much strife in Ireland and that threatened Catholic rights in Canada. A fierce confrontation, dubbed by the press "the Orange difficulty," ensued over access to public space, official recognition of the Order, and acceptable forms of public ritual.

The Orange Order and the Roman Catholic Church were both powerful institutions in Victorian Toronto. About 15 per cent of the city's adult male Protestants belonged to the Order. Although its roots were in Ireland and it commemorated Irish events, the Toronto membership included many Canadian-born men, as well as others with roots beyond Ireland, all of whom were attracted to the fraternal good cheer of lodge meetings, the secret rituals, the colourful banners and marching tradition, and the possibility of patronage appointments at the disposal of City Hall, where the Orange presence was considerable.[38] Their strength led Orangemen to make claims on public space, especially on the Glorious Twelfth (12 July), when their huge annual parade dominated city streets.[39] Orangemen liked to say they marched in the streets to display pride in their Order, which stood for loyalty and liberty, but for Catholics, Orange marches had always had threatening connotations – indeed, they could be outright dangerous.[40] Like the Orangemen, the Catholics of Toronto believed that as a substantial religious minority in the city, they had a right and duty to claim public space and recognition, especially annually on St Patrick's Day (17 March), when they celebrated the patron saint of Ireland. The festivities originally were organized by Catholic priests and focused on a Mass, but from 1857, with the blessing of Toronto's Bishop Charbonnel, the lay elite took charge of the celebration, which became secular and more popular.[41]

In 1860, reports of the Glorious Twelfth festivities in Toronto noted that the Orangemen planned a grand "blow out" when the prince came to town. Two years before, when visiting Sarnia, Governor Head had taken the unusual step of allowing Orangemen to escort him through town, and he had accepted and replied to their address. Orangemen were hoping that a similar policy would be adopted during the royal visit. However, this time a proposal that the Orangemen present addresses to the prince was scotched by Head. As the visit approached, newspapers reported on the Orangemen's plans to build arches of welcome; as well, the reception committee had assigned them a place in the civic procession.[42]

News of the plans enraged Catholics throughout Canada West. A delegation of prominent Catholics visited the Toronto program committee to express their objections to an Orange display, pointing out that it would prevent Catholics from joining in the welcome. In good conscience, they could never walk under an Orange arch, a symbol of the subjugation of Catholics. One of the delegates said that, personally, "sooner than walk under such an arch, he would rather be scalped any day!"[43] When construction began of the Orangemen's arch, Catholic lay leaders approached Mayor Adam Wilson, asking him to put a stop to it. A sympathetic Wilson, who unusually for a Toronto mayor was not an Orangemen, complied and ordered the construction to stop. Orange leaders immediately turned to the city's Board of Works, which had issued the building permit. The Orange-dominated board overrode the mayor's order, and work resumed.[44]

Catholics organized a mass meeting presided over by the Reverend Father John Walsh, rector of St Michael's Cathedral. Walsh blasted Orangemen for intending that the Catholics of the city "should walk beneath their yoke in token of their bondage and slavery," to which voices in the crowd shouted "Never!" Walsh reminded the crowd of 1,000 that "the soil of their native country [Ireland] had been repeatedly reddened by the blood of their martyred fathers in their struggle with traitors." The priest told the crowd that a delegation must go to the Duke of Newcastle, asking for his assistance, which he would certainly provide, given that his government was just then passing a law against Orange demonstrations in Ireland. (The Melbourne government was indeed presenting such a bill in the Commons.) The meeting passed resolutions that condemned the actions of the Orangemen and declared that Catholics would refuse to take part in the celebrations if the Orangemen persisted in their plans.[45]

These developments occurred alongside the *Globe*'s all-out attack on the province's Conservative government for what the newspaper saw as its biased, pro-Catholic guidance of the prince's visit to Lower Canada. *Globe* editor and Reformer George Brown sought to fire the British nationalism and Protestant sentiments of many Upper Canadians so as to undermine support for the government of George-Étienne Cartier and John A. Macdonald. When the prince arrived at Québec, declared the *Globe*, the governor general and his ministers had been shunted aside and Hector-Louis Langevin, the Québec mayor, had been permitted to present the address of welcome – in French, no less! What kind of a welcome was that to a British colony?! According to the *Globe*, during various ceremonies the Roman Catholic bishops had got too much attention and had been granted precedence over the leaders of the non-conforming Protestant churches. The prince had been guided through Catholic institutions, including Laval University and the Ursuline Convent, and in the latter, he had been made to praise convent education! The government had done nothing to suppress the flying throughout Lower Canada of the tricolour flag of France. By attempting to rouse all Protestants, even those who held themselves aloof from the Orange Lodges, Brown was creating an incendiary political situation in Toronto.[46]

People wondered how the prince's adviser would handle the conflict, given that the Crown had an ambivalent relationship with Orangemen in Ireland. The Crown sometimes encouraged the ultra-loyalism of Orangemen, relying on them to put down Catholic disturbances, whereas at other times the Crown and Parliament suppressed Orangemen as troublemakers.[47] Very soon after the Catholic delegation left Toronto to visit Newcastle and Head in Ottawa, the news broke that in response to the Orangemen's plans, Newcastle had announced his policy. The duke declared that because an Orange display was "likely to lead to religious feud and breach of the peace," he saw it as his "duty to prevent ... the exposure of the Prince ... [to] a scene so much to be deprecated and so alien to the spirit in which he visits Canada." He made clear his "terms": the prince would walk under no arch, nor would he visit any town where Orangemen persisted in demonstrating in their regalia. In a covering letter accompanying Newcastle's statement, Governor Head asked the mayors of Toronto and Kingston to inform him whether there was any doubt about compliance with the duke's wishes. He reiterated that there could be no "attempt to connect with His Royal Highness's reception, the public and open recognition of the Orangemen."[48]

Upon the announcement of Newcastle's terms, outrage spread throughout much of Canada West, especially among Orangemen. When the royal party was at Brockville, before reaching Kingston, a delegation led by the mayor of Kingston met with Newcastle to urge him to allow an Orange display, but the duke shot down every argument made. John A. Macdonald attended the meeting as both premier and a very interested politician who represented Kingston in the legislature. Macdonald urged that the visit to Kingston, however decorated, be allowed to take place. He explained that Upper Canadians felt that the Catholics "had had it all their own way in Lower Canada," which "made the dispute with Orangemen peculiarly difficult to deal with as it was difficult to understand why after the course pursued in Quebec such particularity as to banners etc. was to be observed in Upper Canada."[49] Macdonald was taking a political risk by backing the Orangemen; he was also taking on Newcastle, a man at the apex of the British aristocracy who was accustomed to being shown deference. Newcastle firmly rejected Macdonald's advice as well as the validity of any comparison drawn between the banners of the Catholic Church, "which were emblematical of a faith," and those of the Orangemen, "which were those of a rancorous party." There matters stood for the moment.[50]

On the sunny afternoon of Tuesday, 4 September, as the Prince of Wales sailed into Kingston harbour aboard the *Kingston*, Orangemen from fifty-four lodges lined the shore where the prince was to land. Dressed in colourful costumes and carrying a formidable array of banners, the men were defiant, as was emphasized the by militant Orange tunes blasting from a brass band. Just as the prince's steamboat was about to dock, she veered back into the middle of the harbour and anchored. Many people in Kingston were aghast that the visit, so long anticipated, would be cancelled.

Mayor Strange visited Newcastle aboard the *Kingston*, where he urged the duke to permit the prince to enter town by detouring around the Orangemen and avoiding the town's twelve Orange arches. Given that the Orangemen had so purposefully defied his terms, Newcastle refused to back down. The royal party remained aboard the *Kingston* for the night. Meantime, city council met to debate how to proceed, and in the end announced their support for the Orangemen, the position taken by public opinion in Kingston. American reporters on the scene thought they were observing a revolution in the making, but Orangemen insisted they were staunch loyalists who were protecting the rights of British freemen.[51]

At four in the afternoon of the second day, the *Kingston* weighed anchor and proceeded on her journey, without the prince having set foot in town. Premier John A. Macdonald, who had accompanied the prince throughout Canada, remained behind with the people of his riding.[52] In a private letter penned at the time, Newcastle explained his position to the Queen. "How would it look," he asked rhetorically, "if the duke countenanced the Orangemen's display in Kingston and then visited the north of Ireland, where he could not be a party to such an exhibition, without violating the laws of his country?"[53] Imperial concerns were his priority. The fact that Orange displays were legal in Canada did not make it appropriate for the prince to witness them and give them royal recognition.

The following morning the prince was scheduled to visit Belleville as he moved westward along the Ontario shore. Before he landed, however, scouts from his party found that overnight many Orangemen had arrived by train from Kingston, bent upon making a stand in Belleville. Newcastle decreed that the prince would not land. The *Kingston* proceeded farther west to Cobourg, where there was no Orange display.

Authorities had arranged for the train carrying the Cobourg-bound Orangemen to break down midway in a place where no alternative transportation was available. The prince got a warm reception in Cobourg, where he at last had accommodations on shore and an opportunity to dance. He told his mother that it was "a very pretty ball."[54]

Toronto had news of these developments to the east. Everyone wondered whether Newcastle would permit the visit to Toronto, which was meant to be the high point of his tour through Canada West. Would the Orangemen insist on making a display that would prevent the visit? They had certainly prepared an Orange display. At the heart of the city, in front of St James (Anglican) Cathedral, they had built an imposing arch crowned by a watchtower that soared sixty feet. It was said to be "a correct representation of the celebrated Bishop's Gate of Derry," a hallowed place for Orangemen in Ulster.[55] The arch was decorated with twenty-two transparencies, some of which were mottoes of the Order, such as the open Bible and the Crown. At the top of the watchtower appeared a picture of King William III (William of Orange) on his grey charger, the pride of all Orangemen.

A public meeting at St Lawrence Hall debated how to proceed. One commentator declared that feeling in Toronto was stronger than at any time since the rebellion of 1837. At their own, closed meeting, the Orange Lodges of the city met to consider what to do. After much disagreement, the lodges resolved to march on the morning of the visit *before* the arrival of the prince, and then to doff their regalia and join in the celebrations as citizens. Orangemen would refrain from interfering with the procession. "Orange Difficulty at an End," announced the *Globe*.[56]

On the evening of Friday, 7 September, Toronto breathed a sigh of relief: the prince made his landing on the John Street wharf, and the procession wound its way to Government House. It appeared that the grand reception had come off flawlessly.

That was not, however, the view of Newcastle. Shortly after the procession ended, he called Mayor Wilson to Government House. Intensely angry, the duke accused the mayor of decoying him into the city by assuring him, falsely, that Toronto had met his terms. The duke explained that when the procession passed under the arch at King and Church Streets, he had spotted atop it a transparency of King William III, an Orange symbol. The mayor withdrew, consulted his council, and eventually composed a letter to Newcastle explaining that, after he had written him saying all was clear, the Orangemen had reversed themselves and decided to leave the transparency of King William on their otherwise stripped arch. The mayor had consulted leading

Strollers admiring the Orangemen's Arch, Toronto. The portrait of mounted King Billy is clearly visible atop the arch.
Source: *Illustrated London News*, 3 November 1860.

Catholics and, desperate for the visit to proceed, they had agreed to look upon the transparency as being not that of an Orange hero, but "the representation of a good sovereign." Mayor Wilson said he accepted any blame for what happened. The tone of the letter was conciliatory – indeed many Torontonians saw it as spineless – but that is not how the duke saw it.[57] According to Dr Acland, who was on the scene when Newcastle read Wilson's reply, the duke "swore roundly that the mayor was a damned blackguard and liar, and that if Canada could only be kept on such terms as dealing with fellows like him, it was not worth keeping."[58]

In any event, the prince's itinerary continued. The next evening, the prince enjoyed dancing at the ball at Osgoode Hall. His first dance was with the wife of John Hillyard Cameron, a prominent leader of Toronto Orangemen, whose wife was honoured by the prince because Hillyard Cameron was the treasurer of the Law Society of Upper Canada, the host of the evening.

Sunday morning brought the second of the weekend's contretemps, one that very nearly ended in a riot. Everyone expected the prince to attend Sunday service at St James Cathedral, and it was anticipated that to get there he would pass under the Orange arch in front of it. A large crowd of Orangemen gathered near the arch to cheer the prince's progress. The coach carrying the prince took a detour, however, avoiding the arch entirely. The incensed Orangemen outside the cathedral were joined by brethren who had grabbed banners and flags from their nearby lodge rooms. While the service continued inside the cathedral, Orangemen decorated their arch so that the duke would see it in its full glory. At this point the street theatre grew colourful indeed. Various Orange leaders, some of them civic officials, intervened and tried to remove the decorations. As they climbed ladders to take down the banners, other Orangemen shook the ladders. Alderman W.W. Fox was shaken to the ground and his ladder smashed in the process.[59] The *New York Times* reported how the crowd "hooted and yelled, calling out all manner of insulting language." Inside the cathedral, the worshippers could hear the rising tumult outside.[60]

When the duke and the prince left the cathedral at the conclusion of the service, they could not help but see the brilliant banners of the Order hanging from the arch. Orangemen cried "Down with the Duke!" Newcastle's face signalled stern resolve. When the royal party got into their waiting carriage, some Orangemen tried to cut the horses' traces so that the carriage could be pulled under the arch, but a coachman applied the whip to the team and the cortege passed through the angry mob and drove off to Government House.

Later that day, the duke learned that Orangemen were saying that he was holed up, daring not to make an appearance for fear he would be assaulted. "This of course could not be submitted to," wrote the duke privately. To maintain his manly pride, Newcastle took a couple of members of the suite and walked over to the Orange arch and inspected it. A crowd, yelling and hissing, surrounded them as they returned to Government House. *Le Canadien* of Québec called it a "charivari," implying that the crowd was attempting to shame him.[61] Newcastle was not cowed, however. He reported privately that when returning to Government House, he had purposefully "walked slower and slower to shew them that I knew they dare not touch me, and when I reached the gate I stopped and there were nearly as many cheers as groans." In his own eyes, at least, by walking the duke had asserted his power and proven his courage.[62]

On another day of the prince's stay in Toronto, he and his suite made a day trip through the countryside north of the city, travelling via the lone track of the Northern Railway as far as Collingwood on Georgian Bay. The travellers sat perched atop a flatcar to view a fast-developing agricultural frontier. More Orange shenanigans ensued. At towns along the route, Orangemen had raised and decorated arches of welcome over the track, knowing that no detour by rail was possible. As the royal party passed beneath the decorated arches, the prince and others smiled, but the duke remained expressionless, purposefully ignoring the obvious. The London *Times* said that no one else aboard the train "could forbear a smile at the obstinate pertinacity displayed by the Orangemen, and the ingenious manner in which they had compelled His Royal Highness to pass under their party emblem, all bedizened as it was with the most obnoxious of their banners."[63]

On the morning of 12 September, the prince made a splendid departure from Toronto and continued on his way, visiting the southwestern part of the province and the Niagara Peninsula, where he encountered no Orange difficulties. Newcastle, patting himself on the back, wrote: "The flags which were prepared in many places to plant in our faces were all furled, not an emblem nor a motto were shown elsewhere, nor a cry heard." He believed that by his resolve he had subdued "a violent & overbearing minority."[64] In fact, after the prince's departure from the province, Newcastle's behaviour continued to be fiercely debated, and it surfaced as an issue during the provincial election of 1861, when Macdonald and the government were put on the defensive.[65]

The Orange difficulty gained enormous attention, not only in the Upper Canadian press but also in newspapers in the rest of British North America, the United Kingdom, and the United States. Both the Reform and the Conservative press of Toronto regretted the imbroglio. Canada was not fit to host the prince, declared the *Globe*, torn as it was by dissension "because Lower Canada ha[d] been ruling Upper Canada for years in defiance of the expressed wishes of her representatives." The Conservative *Mail* placed the blame on Newcastle, who had wrongly applied his experience in another place – "caste-ridden" England – to a situation in this "freer country" and thus shown "the fatuity of Imperial statesmen who have an undue love of interference and are unable to read history properly." The Québec newspaper *Le Courrier du Canada* boasted that "in Lower Canada, where the population is almost entirely

French and Catholic, everywhere the prince was welcomed with the most respectful loyalty," whereas in Upper Canada "he found only an excessive and brutal pride." The *Irish-American*, published in New York, gave readers a history lesson, recalling the tradition of Orangemen in Ireland who had built arches with Orange devices so as to humiliate Catholics by compelling them to give "involuntary homage" by passing "'under the yoke.'" The Orangemen of Canada West had revived the practice on the occasion of the royal visit as a way to "pay off old scores against the Catholics," while hoping to gain "*eclat* and official recognition from the presence of a scion of royalty." Fortunately, however, the attempt had backfired and brought the Orangeman scorn.[66]

Conclusion

During the prince's visit to Canada West, the Orange difficulty focused on the right of access to public space, official recognition of the Orange Order, and appropriate forms of public ritual. Badges and banners, emblems and music became flashpoints of difference. Triumphal arches of welcome, so proudly raised and richly praised throughout the tour, in this particular context became symbols of oppression and brakes on the freedom to participate. Marching in public processions, so widely taken up and lavishly extolled during the visit, proved to be a hotly contested matter when it was Orangemen doing the marching. Orange arches of welcome and participation in public processions provoked clashes in the streets that bordered on rioting. Public ceremonies intended to enhance imperial relations ended up exposing long-standing social tensions. Rituals meant to demonstrate loyalty and community became triggers of confrontation between rival factions. For many Torontonians, the bitterness that was caused by the dispute, and the political fallout from it, called into question the value of the prince's visit to Canada. For all its appeal to authorities and the public alike, the royal tour had come with serious risks.

Toronto's extensive arrangements for an elaborate welcome for the visiting prince paid off. "Words cannot describe that vast volume of sound, thrilling, soul-stirring, heart-heaving," boasted the *Globe* of the first evening of the Toronto visit. "The Prince has arrived and received a welcome which in spirit and enthusiasm has not been equalled in any place which His Royal Highness has hitherto visited."[67] It had to be admitted, however, that the Orange difficulty took some of the shine off the spectacle. John A. Macdonald said as much in a speech he made in October 1860, when he was touring the province trying to repair the political damage he had suffered because of his handling of the Orange issue. Thanks to the royal visit, he declared, Canada had been "called to the attention of the whole civilized world in a manner never before known." While it had been "a source of great pleasure to the people," it had nevertheless "been accompanied in some respects with disappointment, in some degree with heart burning, in some degree with mistakes."[68]

As we shall see, this occasion was by no means the end of divisive displays in Victorian Toronto. "Heart burning" characterized other public controversies, including on religious occasions when denominational differences became flashpoints of intense dispute.

4
Religious Processions and Disorder

In mid-Victorian Toronto, passions were sometimes aroused by public religious displays of difference. On two occasions – the 1864 Corpus Christi celebration and the Jubilee pilgrimages in 1875 – the clashes played out both physically, in skirmishes and rioting, and verbally, in meetings and in the press. These troubles erupted not in connection with Sunday services within church walls, but rather when differences in religious belief, practice, and dress were displayed in the open and on public streets. In both years, the tranquillity of the Victorian Toronto Sabbath was disturbed when angry Protestants violently attacked Roman Catholic processions. The dissonance carried over into weekday sniping in meetings and newspapers. "The lining of the streets through which the processionists march, the playing of music and singing, the sprinkling of holy water and other unusual performances," declared one Protestant organization, were "calculated to inflame the public mind and to lead to strife and disorder."[1] From this perspective, Catholic religious practices were bizarre and, when displayed in the open, a danger to public order in a city where at least three-quarters of the population was Protestant. Sectarian conflicts feature prominently in the historiography of Victorian Canada; this chapter tells the story of two such conflicts to deepen understandings of liberal discourse as it relates to public order.[2]

The intensity of the two disputes derived both from differences in religious belief and from established patterns of public behaviour. Protestant convictions, Orange associational solidarities, and the Order's marching tradition mixed to fuel Protestant objections to Catholic processions. For their part, Catholics stood their ground as a religious minority asserting its presence and rights, as believers doing what was willed by God and the Church, and often as members of an Irish Catholic ethnic group as well. From various perspectives, many observers insisted on the need to maintain public order and halt disturbances of the peace, especially on the Sabbath. Some sought peace by pleading for toleration of people holding beliefs that set them apart from the majority. Others recoiled from the calls for tolerance and from what they believed were ostentatious and threatening Catholic displays. The Catholic processionists, by taking religion into the open air and public streets, challenged a certain Protestant understanding of worship's proper place: in the sphere of home and chapel, where it would not endanger a unified Canada built around common public institutions. For Catholics, the expression of religious particularism formed part of a wider struggle in English Canada to maintain the faith, build separate Catholic institutions, and belong. In the city of Québec, the Catholic majority held Corpus Christi and other religious processions unchallenged by Protestants, but in Montreal, where the Protestant population was substantial, controversies arose.[3]

These clashes took place against a backdrop of long-standing religious disputes in which ethnic differences were entangled. Protestant/Catholic tensions, of course, stretched back to the Reformation and were kept alive by clergy who persistently reminded their congregations of doctrinal differences. In mid-Victorian Canada, deep-seated mutual suspicions between many Catholics and Protestants were revealed during various political struggles when Catholics asserted rights, notably on the question of public funding for confessional schools and at the time of Louis Riel's resistance movement in 1869–70.[4] Nineteenth-century immigrants, especially from Ireland, brought sectarian disputes with them, which were then nurtured and reshaped in particular settings throughout North America, including in Toronto, where the Irish made up roughly 40 per cent of the population and were divided between a Protestant majority and Catholic minority.[5] While the Catholics belonged to one church, the Protestants were divided among many. As historian Roberto Perin shows in his recent book, *The Many Rooms of This House*, the differences among Toronto Protestants derived from the different national traditions of immigrants and various schisms that had taken place over time.[6] Seldom would there be unanimity among the denominations, even though Protestants were often referred to as a group.

Victorian English Canada has been characterized as a place where liberal values came to prevail, a reasonable proposition when the focus is on private property and freedom of contract.[7] However, calls for liberal tolerance of religious diversity, though voiced in Victorian Toronto, were on these two occasions nearly drowned out by irate opponents of tolerance. The most persistent rights talk came from the city's illiberal ultramontane archbishop, John Joseph Lynch.[8] These incidents also highlight the ways in which collective violence, far removed from the ideals of rationality, self-restraint, and deliberative democracy, exposed challenges to constructing a liberal order and provoked heated public rhetoric that relied not on reason alone but also on appeals to faith.

The Confrontations

With more fanfare than usual, Bishop Lynch announced that on Sunday, 29 May 1864, Toronto's Roman Catholics would celebrate the feast of Corpus Christi with a procession that would proceed "around the gardens" of St Michael's Cathedral.[9] A group of Protestants approached their friend, Mayor Francis Henry Medcalf, to ask him to ensure that the procession remained on the cathedral grounds.[10] Medcalf wrote the bishop, inquiring where the procession would go and warning him, on the advice of the Protestant delegates, that if a "procession was attempted in the public streets, they had every reason to believe that it would occasion a very serious breach of the peace." The message was ambiguous: was the Orangeman and chief magistrate concerned for the public peace, or was he conveying an Orange threat of violence? Certainly a threat lurked behind the carefully crafted rhetoric of the Protestant delegation's expression of concern for civic order. Lynch responded publicly that while Catholics had every right to process through the streets, the procession would be confined to the grounds of the cathedral and bishop's palace, and he reminded Torontonians that the exercise of the Catholics' religion had been guaranteed by the Treaty of Paris (1763).[11] Meanwhile, at the cathedral in the centre of town, Catholic laity decorated the grounds with religious banners and evergreen arches surmounted with crosses, set up outdoor altars, and, as a sign of loyalty, raised the royal Standard of England.[12]

Just after five p.m. on the Sunday, the procession exited the cathedral and wended its way through the grounds. Bishop Lynch in his pontificals led the way, holding the Holy Host high beneath a canopy carried by four men and an honour guard, while clergy in their vestments solemnly chanted. Girls and young women in white joined the procession, underscoring the purity of the adoration and the religious procession's inclusiveness. As expected, the hundreds of Catholic men, women, and children within the grounds uncovered and knelt as the Host passed them. Just outside the fence stood a large crowd of Protestant men and boys, some curious to witness the anticipated trouble, others bent on ensuring that the Host was not carried into the street. The mayor too was there, surrounded by Orange brethren, as pointed out by the *Irish Canadian*, Toronto's Irish nationalist newspaper.[13]

Bishop John Joseph Lynch. His magnificent pontificals would have struck evangelical Protestants as ostentatious.
Source: Library and Archives Canada, MIKAN 2192000.

The skirmish began when some Protestants sitting atop the fence jeered at the processionists using foul language. Some of the Catholics responded by telling the Protestants to uncover and kneel as the Host was carried past them. Predictably, they refused, in the belief that to kneel before the Host was an act of idolatry. Scuffles then broke out as some of the Protestants pushed past the Catholic guards at the gates; others toppled sections of the fence and pressed into the Catholic gathering. The *Canadian Freeman*, the Toronto Catholic weekly supportive of Bishop Lynch, alleged that some men in the in-rushing mob brandished six-shooters.[14] The Protestant intruders, whatever their original intention, were now challenging the right of Catholics to hold their religious procession even on cathedral grounds. Amid the noise, cries of "Fire!" drove people from the cathedral and, according to one male reporter, Catholic girls in the procession "broke from the ranks with screams." The bell of a nearby fire station gave the signal to city firemen – and Orangemen – to rally. Women and children scrambled to the safety of the vaults, leaving combat to the men. For nearly two hours, unrestrained by any police, the warring parties shouted, shoved, and squabbled, until seven o'clock, when it was at last possible to say the benediction.[15]

Incensed by the attack on the seat of Catholicism in Toronto, Bishop Lynch complained to provincial authorities. In a letter to Premier Sir Étienne-Paschal Taché, a French Canadian Catholic, Lynch described "the flagrant outrage," "the brutal conduct of the mob," "their blasphemies most insulting," and "their revolvers, bludgeons, and other deadly weapons." Lynch also complained of "their successful efforts to create a panic amongst the children and women by their cries of fire, murder, etc." In keeping with the gender conventions of the day, Lynch positioned women and children as prone to panicking and therefore deserving of far more chivalrous treatment than meted out by the Protestants, whose manliness was thereby questioned. Lynch went on to explain that the mayor, an officer of the Orange Lodge, had failed to preserve the peace and provide police protection from Protestant rioters. The bishop warned that, if not protected, Catholics "will be prepared to defend themselves." Lynch received a sympathetic though not concretely helpful reply from the co-premier, John A. Macdonald, an English-speaking Protestant.[16] On the Sunday following Corpus Christi, Lynch tested the waters by holding a special procession. It came off peacefully. To the processionists that day, Lynch vowed he "would not surrender one iota of rights secured to Catholics by the constitution and laws of the country, even at the sacrifice of his life."[17]

Angered by the insult to Catholics during the Corpus Christi celebration, Hibernians made a stand later that year on Guy Fawkes Day. On that important date in their ritual calendar (5 November),[18] Orangemen marched in city streets in the afternoon according to the conventions of their fraternity, which regularly asserted claims to public space and recognition, and vowed to burn effigies that night of Guy Fawkes, Daniel O'Connell, and Pope Pius IX. Fortunately for the city's peace, they conducted their evening activities indoors, so when the Hibernians took to the streets that night in their own display of masculine strength, they had no one to confront.[19] Still, the Hibernians marched through town in well-drilled squads carrying pike poles and, in some cases, swords and revolvers. Momentarily, they must have felt empowered by this paramilitary show. Police charged one man with firing a pistol and took another to court after a search of his home revealed a cache of pikes.[20] Newspapers reacted in horror at the arms and at the threat of violence, which was heightened by the rise of Fenianism – Irish republicanism that in the case of some American adherents condoned violence. The *Freeman*, however, defended the Hibernians and railed at the severity with which the law was applied against Catholics when, it alleged, Mayor Medcalf had ordered the police away from the scene of the Corpus Christi riot. Lynch publicly deplored the display of weapons but defended the Hibernians as necessary when Orangemen marched in processions "calculated to excite the worst passions and to revive burning memories that should be permitted to be forgotten." Critics of the bishop and his "Lynch law" countered that Orangemen on parade were unarmed and loyal, whereas the Hibernians were neither. What began in May as a dispute over Catholic religious processions ended in November with another about the marching rights of Orangemen and Hibernians.[21]

Eleven years later, on Sunday, 26 September 1875, two Catholic processions took place in Toronto: the first of the Autumn Jubilee pilgrimages, and another to mark the opening of the first provincial council of the Roman Catholic Church in Ontario, during which visiting bishops and other clergy were to proceed through downtown streets with Catholic societies lining the route. A few days prior to the processions, a group of prominent Protestants presented Medcalf, once again mayor after a five-year absence, with a requisition asking him to put a stop to the bishops' procession, "an ostentatious display on the Lord's Day." It was described by the archbishop himself as being accompanied by "'Music,' 'Bands,' and 'Singing,' and by 'Bishops,' 'Children,' 'Students,' 'Thurifers,' 'Acolytes, 'Priests,' 'Deacons,' and other orders, dressed in 'Dalmatics,' 'Copes' and all the paraphernalia of 'Full Pontificals,' and 'Regalia.'"[22] The requisition warned that the procession would "likely lead to serious breaches of the public peace." Although phrased as a cautionary concern (like the warning given by the Protestant delegation in 1864), some people saw it as a threat.[23] The mayor wrote Lynch, now archbishop, relaying the message. Lynch replied that the bishops' procession would go ahead. It did. No trouble occurred.

That afternoon, however, some 8,000 pilgrims converged on St Michael's Cathedral for a Jubilee walk to St Patrick's Church, led by four acolytes carrying a crucifix and a banner representing the Immaculate Conception, followed by men, women, and children. Crowds gathered in streets near the cathedral, most in the mistaken belief that they were witnessing the bishops' procession and expecting some excitement. They were not disappointed. Large numbers of Orange Young Britons blocked the procession and, when the pilgrims altered the route, reappeared and pelted them with stones. Some of the male processionists sent the missiles back into the ranks of the attackers. Unsympathetic reporters claimed that some pilgrims fired revolvers into the crowds, which included women and children. Many suffered injuries, none serious. The mayor and police were on hand, but did little.[24]

Newspaper editors hoped that the last of the Jubilee processions scheduled for the following Sunday might be cancelled in the interest of peace, or that a strong police and military presence would be arranged to prevent violence. City councillors asked Mayor Medcalf to cancel the procession, but he said that the city solicitor had advised him he lacked such authority.[25] The police commissioners sent a letter to Lynch asking him to discourage processionists from carrying firearms. At its meeting, the district Orange Lodge defended its own right to hold processions but urged authorities to suppress Catholic religious processions because they led to disorder.[26] An Orange deputation asked the mayor to call a public meeting. When it convened on the Friday evening, the overflow crowd at St Lawrence Hall was determined to make clear its objections to public Catholic processions. Medcalf voiced his opposition to "popery" but begged the brethren to avoid violence and "to give the Roman Catholics the privilege of walking." He did not speak of their right to do so. Ogle Gowan, the veteran Orange leader, proposed a resolution urging Catholics to abandon the procession but committing Orangemen to non-confrontation if it went ahead. The meeting soundly defeated his motion, exposing both a split in Orange ranks and the militancy of the meeting's majority.[27]

Preparations for both the procession and possible trouble continued throughout the week. The archbishop sought the assurance of police commissioners (who included Medcalf) that a strong police presence would be on hand to protect the legal right of Catholics to walk through the city. Lynch agreed to reduce the procession's length so that police resources would not be spread too thinly, and he issued a statement that any pilgrim carrying weapons or engaging in stone-throwing would lose "every blessing and indulgence attached to the jubilee." In exchange, the commissioners informed Lynch that they had made "arrangements for the preservation of peace and order." According to the *Irish Canadian*, Oliver Mowat, Ontario's Reform premier, attorney general, and ally of Catholics, had written Medcalf to remind him of his duty to ensure the public peace.[28] Perhaps the reminder prompted the police commissioners to co-operate this time. Local authorities also requisitioned 100 cavalry and 500 other militiamen for the occasion. Meantime, it was rumoured that Hibernians from Toronto had visited Buffalo, Cleveland, and Montreal to recruit Fenians to join the procession and to ward off attackers with imported American firearms.[29] Even if unfounded, the news increased tensions in town and reflected Protestant suspicions that local Hibernians were really Fenians: revolutionaries in disguise. That Sunday morning, no girls or women were to be seen on the streets; only boys and men attended Protestant churches, so certain were people of trouble that day.[30]

About 2:30 in the afternoon on Sunday, 3 October, some 2,000 pilgrims assembled at St Michael's Cathedral for the walk to St Mary's

Church on Bathurst Street in the west end. After blessing the pilgrims, the archbishop told them to avoid retaliating if attacked and to rely on authorities for protection. This time, women pilgrims lined the sidewalks, keeping pace as the men walked in the street, led by a group of bishops and Ontario's newly appointed lieutenant governor, Donald Alexander Macdonald, a Roman Catholic Scot from eastern Ontario.[31] Greeting the processionists was a crowd of 5,000 to 10,000 onlookers and demonstrators, and behind them a substantial militia presence. Before long, the crowd began pelting the processionists with stones. The bishops and Macdonald led the procession along a different route, but the well-armed stone-throwers, who had stockpiled ammunition on the grounds of Metropolitan Methodist Church, regrouped and pelted the pilgrims anew.[32] Shots rang out in Queen Street. Some among the processionists fired back at the demonstrators with stones and, in a few cases, with pistols. At Simcoe Street, an all-out attack led by Protestant youths failed to break through the procession. Police protected the pilgrims, repeatedly charging into the demonstrators and wielding revolvers, which they normally did not carry in daytime. Though constables were frequently knocked down, they kept opening the way for the procession. When the pilgrims approached St Mary's Church, Catholic women and children retreated inside and the confrontation climaxed in the street. One of the demonstrators, William Patton, with a phalanx of supporters, drove a horse and wagon into the Catholic ranks. Police Sergeant Williams, with revolver drawn, threatened to shoot Patton's horse. Patton allegedly replied, "Damn it. It ain't you we want to get at, but the other party."[33]

After the St Mary's service, the demonstrators' fury subsided, but groups of Orangemen attacked delivery carts and other Catholic targets in downtown streets that evening, including Owen Cosgrove's tavern, a popular Hibernian watering hole. Many on both sides were injured that day, including constables and at least two clergymen, though apparently no women or children. The lack of injuries to women and children and the fact that no one was killed was partly a matter of luck, but also reflected self-imposed restraints typical of participants in the ritualized street clashes in Victorian Toronto.

This time around, the police's unusual behaviour surprised people. Catholics were delighted that the police had actually enforced the law and helped to protect pilgrims, drawing as they did on their recent training in crowd control. Lynch urged they be paid a bonus for their "noble conduct," and prominent Catholics established an honorarium.[34] By contrast, Protestants were disconcerted by the unanticipated police behaviour. When testifying on behalf of her son, the mother of

Jubilee riot near Metropolitan Methodist Church. With the church as an appropriate backdrop, the artist draws attention to the central figure of the police officer with his club confronting a rioter while endangered women cower in the foreground.
Source: *Canadian Illustrated News*, 12:16 October 1875. Credit: Early Canadiana Online.

Protestant rioter William Lougheed was perplexed, if not indignant, that he had been apprehended and charged. After all, she had even "told Sergeant Williams that [her son] was a good Orangeman and [the police] should be easy with him."[35]

Police charged twenty-nine men with rioting, fifteen of whom were tried at the winter assize court, where again the results surprised some Protestant Torontonians. The trials, which took place in the impressive York County Courthouse on Adelaide Street East, were of great public interest. Crowds thronged the courtroom each of the six days of the trials, and newspapers filled many columns with news of the court proceedings. Ten of the accused were Protestants and five were Catholics. Both the judge, Ontario Chief Justice Robert Alexander Harrison, and the Crown prosecutor, Kenneth Mackenzie, tried to keep the focus on lawbreaking and deflect attention from sectarian matters, but it wasn't possible to do so completely. All but one of the accused had a working-class job and little property.[36] The exception, Fallis Johnson, a prominent Orangeman, who owned a grocery store, a fine residence, and properties he rented to tenants, was given better treatment by the court and could afford two experienced defence lawyers. Nearly all the evidence against the accused was presented by police who had made the arrests. Johnson was acquitted, but so too were all the Catholics, which surprised Torontonians familiar with the frequent convictions of Catholics in the city. The judge sentenced the nine Protestants convicted by the jury to two or three months of jail time, not heavy sentences given the seriousness of the charges. Orange influence likely resulted in the court's leniency toward accused Protestants.[37]

Blame and Context

In analysing the confrontations of 1864 and 1875, Toronto newspapers revealed the contentious cultural politics of religious processions in mid-Victorian Toronto. The first response of nearly every commentator was to deplore the violence and insist on the need for public order and respect for the law. "We have no sympathy with law-breaking in any cause," declared the Conservative and Orange-leaning *Leader* in 1875. Its arch-rival, the *Globe*, insisted: "Mob rule must not be triumphant in the streets of Toronto." The *British American Presbyterian* responded with disgust, observing that "stone throwing and rioting are not the legitimate means for settling religious controversies."[38] No one defended disorder.

Commentators quickly turned to apportioning blame. In both 1864 and 1875 Toronto newspapers sympathetic to Catholics blamed Orangeism for the attacks. In 1864 the *Irish Canadian* asked rhetorically: "Who gave the Orangemen of this city the power to dictate the course that Catholics should pursue in regard to the festivals of their church?" And drawing on history it added: "Time and again have we been placed at the mercy of these remorseless Thugs, till our blood flowed and our property lay in ruins and in ashes." After the Jubilee riots the *Irish Canadian* blamed Orangemen and Young Britons, "the worst characters that could be possibly scraped together from the foulest sources"; and after the second riot it emphasized the high degree of premeditation by the Orange Young Britons. In 1875 the *Globe* never wavered from the position that the perpetrators were mostly irresponsible Orange Young Britons, "rowdy lads bent on mischief, or those who were worse than rowdy being either of the actually criminal class or of those who are trembling on its borders."[39]

Some commentators, however, pointed out that Catholic men had joined the mêlées, contributing to their escalation. The *Leader*, though admitting the Jubilee demonstrators were the first to throw stones, said the fighting "was almost entirely due to the processionists taking to throwing stones and firing off revolvers." Militant Irish nationalists among the Catholic processionists had been the real troublemakers. In reply to such criticisms, the *Irish Canadian* said Catholics were forced to stand up "in self-defence." The *Mail* purported to take the middle ground by blaming both factions. Newspapers outside Toronto chimed in, with the Belleville *Intelligencer*, for example, saying: "No matter who began it, the whole proceedings are of a most disgraceful character and will be reprobated by every well wisher of peace and order in Canada."[40]

Orange Young Britons objected strongly to the Jubilee pilgrimages but bristled at reports that their organization had authorized the use of physical force. Newspapers registered this objection, but for a public familiar with the frequent rowdyism of the Young Britons, it made sense to blame them for the rioting. After all, said the *Globe*, they were "void of anything like common-sense" and were "ignorant of the very first principles of what they assailed or what they wished to champion. We very much doubt if a great number of them know whether William of Orange lived in the days of St Patrick or of Julius Caesar, or if they could give a reasonable account why the objects of their dislike should be stoned."[41] Embedded in the put-down was a class dynamic: the *Globe* spoke for the mature, respectable, middle-class public, who condemned working-class irresponsibility and ignorance.

Yet this contemporary analysis highlighting the role of organized men in stoking the fires has real explanatory power. Historian Brian Clarke, in a perceptive analysis of rioting titled "Religious Riot as Pastime," explains that the Orange Young Britons emerged as an organization for the first time in Toronto during the 1860s and grew substantially over the following decade. As one of many fraternal organizations of the day, it offered conviviality in a partly structured setting to urban men in their late teens and twenties who wished to congregate during their leisure hours, now that industrialization had given them daytime jobs with free time in the evenings. Typically, male bonding occurred in lodge gatherings that involved evenings of heavy drinking, followed by spontaneous marches to fife and drum through city streets until long into the night. Such gatherings were also intended to teach young men the tenets of Orangeism. Religious rioting grew from the young men's Orange world view and their leisure pursuits. The presence of Hibernians or Young Irishmen in city streets only added to the likelihood of an outing of Young Britons becoming a brawl.[42]

Not everyone agreed that the demonstrators were all rowdy youths, however. In a letter to the editor of the *Globe*, L.S., a witness injured in the final Jubilee riot, said many mature men had participated. Moreover, in an unusually explicit comment on class, L.S. maintained that the demonstrators included members of the Young Men's Christian Association, "wearing the finest of silk hats and kid gloves, who would be more than surprised if you called them boys." The *Irish Canadian* reprinted the letter and accused the YMCA's smug, middle-class Protestants of hypocrisy because they preached Christian behaviour but "stone their fellow-creatures, men, women and children, for the sole crime of kneeling at a different altar!"[43]

Gender conventions proved useful to commentators who favoured the Catholics. Processionists who were Catholic women and children could be presented as victims of Protestant male aggression. "It must not be forgotten," declared the *Irish Canadian*, "that the pilgrims were composed of whole congregations – men, women and children, infancy and old age, the child in arms, the grey-haired of four score – and that these 'brave' Orangemen attacked them indiscriminately."[44] In secular parades of the period, only men and male youths marched, women being relegated to the sidelines as admiring spectators. Thus, attacks on those marching in parades were always instances of men attacking men. Catholic processions differed in their inclusivity; the faithful included women and children, as well as men. Attackers of the processions could be portrayed as unmanly because they were unchivalrous, showing a lack of respect for the weak. Galling as the charges must have been for the Protestant demonstrators, they chose to ignore them in public, signalling they had been rhetorically outmanoeuvred.

Some commentators insisted that Catholics were the true perpetrators of the disturbances. The Toronto weekly the *Nation*, speaking of the first of the Jubilee processions, said unequivocally: "It was a religious procession that caused the riot." "Loud, gaudy, and vulgar," they must be outlawed because they "might in time develop into grander processions in which the Host would be carried in the streets and in public."[45] Many of the processions' critics placed the blame for the troubles on Lynch, who pushed aggressively against the Protestant mainstream and identified closely with Irish nationalism. In 1864, Protestants were especially sensitive due to the growth of Fenianism. It had been reported that Michael Murphy, leader of Toronto's Hibernians, had attended a conference of Fenians in the United States and that, during St Patrick's Day festivities held shortly before the Corpus Christi celebration, Lynch had shared a platform with Murphy, who had spoken with revolutionary fervour.[46] Who knew what the bishop might attempt with the Holy Host? By 1875, Lynch's Catholic assertiveness had only increased. The *Leader* took exception to Lynch inviting Catholic societies to line the route of the bishops' procession on the grounds that it amounted to a claim on public space. Moreover, Lynch's invitation looked "suspiciously like as if [sic] a riot was what was desired." More delicately, the *Mail* questioned "the taste of the Archbishop in obtruding upon the community, largely Protestant." In reference to Lynch's role in authorizing the final pilgrimage, the *Leader* observed: "we must hold him responsible to some extent for the bloodshed and rioting which occurred."[47]

Lynch, of course, had not sought bloodshed, but he was defiant about the processions, a defiance based in his ultramontanism. In the nineteenth century the worldwide Catholic Church had undergone renewal, as the ultramontane movement reinforced the Church's hierarchical and centralized structure, and the empowered clergy undertook to reinvigorate the laity. In Toronto, the Catholicism of immigrant Irish gained a new vigour after 1850 as men and women formed an array of voluntary associations, some under clerical direction and others with Irish nationalist goals at a remove from the clergy.[48] The new piety, which included participation in Corpus Christi processions, saw many bishops in the Catholic world putting greater emphasis on such forms of devotion.[49] Moreover, Lynch's offer of indulgences to the jubilee pilgrims conformed to the wishes of Pope Pius IX, who promoted indulgenced devotion. Later archbishops of Toronto would have different views, but, for the faithful, the archbishop's blessing for the walk meant that it was willed by God.[50]

Lynch's determination to proceed with the processions was also in keeping with the role he had carved out for himself in the province. By the 1870s the archbishop had positioned himself as Ontario's chief Catholic defender and was dedicated to making the faith known widely.[51] Never shying from the limelight or controversy, Lynch took his role seriously, giving weekly Sunday evening public lectures to ticket-paying Catholics and Protestants, who filled the cathedral to hear his spirited defence of Catholic doctrine and his attacks on Luther and Protestantism. The Protestants in attendance were perhaps there to be outraged, but it is possible that their presence points to the open-mindedness of at least some Toronto Protestants, people whose outlook and behaviour contrasted starkly with those who attacked Catholic processions. Certainly Lynch's topics were red flags to the Protestant theologians, including as they did papal infallibility, transubstantiation, penance, purgatory, indulgences, and the mediation of saints. Synopses of the lectures appearing in Monday newspapers greatly widened his audience, as did frequent verbal assaults on those lectures from Protestant clergy, including those from an outspoken recent arrival from Ulster, the Rev. James Gardiner Robb of Cooke's Presbyterian Church.[52] Equally provocative was Lynch's pamphlet explaining Catholicism to Protestants, which sparked a spirited reply from a Presbyterian cleric in his own pamphlet. These public disputes had little to do with rational debate and deliberative democracy.[53] Denunciatory in tone, the rhetoric on both sides relied on revealed truths or faith-based assertions.

Lynch's determination to take Catholic religious processions into the community and defy the Protestant majority stands out amid the predominant pattern described by Ann Taves for the United States, where Catholics behaved cautiously when the public sphere was dominated by Protestants.[54] In Toronto, Lynch defiantly paraded Catholic differences in public. He persistently justified his position by pointing to the right of Catholics to practise their religion in Canada. In both 1864 and 1875, he reminded the public of the particular historical right of Catholics granted by the treaty between France and Britain at the time of the Conquest, when (French and Catholic) Canadians became British subjects.[55] Historian E.A. Heaman provides a context for the discourse of illiberal ultramontane Catholics like Lynch, who argued for rights in nineteenth-century Canada, when she distinguishes between the "rights talk" used by liberals as an assertion of individual rights, and that deployed by conservatives when advancing claims to group rights. In contrast to liberals, who defended their claims to individual rights by appealing to universal principles, conservatives grounded their claims to group rights in history. "Ultramontane leaders were openly hostile to the very concept of universal rights, seeing them as unwarrantable rationalism and independence of thought," she writes. "The ultramontanes were primarily concerned with the rights of collectivities ... rights that dated back to specific promises made at the time of the Conquest."[56] Lynch's resolve to proceed with the processions reflected his feistiness, an ultramontane challenge to the city's dominant Protestant norms, and a defence of such collective rights.

Lynch had some ground for hope in thinking that an appeal to collective rights might be effective in defending the Catholic religion in Toronto. In the 1840s and 1850s, separate schools in Canada West had been defended by appeals to the rights of collectivities. It was not only Catholics who had advocated separate schools; many Protestants had also done so in support of their own denominational schools and collective rights.[57] Indeed, supporters of separate schools had been powerful enough during the Confederation debates to have their rights embedded in the Dominion's new constitution. Of course, other people, nearly all Protestants, had persistently attacked state funding for separate schools, preferring a single, state-supported, so-called non-sectarian school system. Lynch, then, was making his case for the right of Catholics to practise their religion in a charged atmosphere in which he expected his statements would be strongly opposed but still find resonance.

In 1875, tensions in Toronto were reinforced by the Guibord affair in Montreal. At the time of the Jubilee riots, Montreal Catholics were rioting to prevent civil authorities from carrying out a court order to reinter the long-dead corpse of Joseph Guibord, a liberal, in a Catholic cemetery even though the ultramontane Bishop of Montreal had objected because he believed Guibord had died while excommunicated.[58] As Torontonians watched the affair, they divided sharply along sectarian lines. Archbishop Lynch publicly sided with the Montreal clergy, insisting that Guibord should not be buried in consecrated ground, the courts notwithstanding; he also maintained that at times, Church law superseded that of the state. The dispute between French Canadian liberals and the Church became, in Toronto, a debate about civil as opposed to Church authority. Many Toronto Protestants expressed horror at the Catholic Church's claim to supremacy over the state and deplored the Catholic vigilantes and rioters who physically blocked both Guibord's reburial and justice following its course. Even the *Globe*, which stood by Lynch and the Catholics during the Jubilee riots, strongly objected to Lynch's position on the Guibord affair.[59]

Commentators speculated that some of Toronto's anti-Catholic demonstrators were acting in retaliation against rioting by Montreal Catholics, which they believed both the Catholic clergy and the Montreal police condoned. The combination of the Guibord affair and the Jubilee pilgrimages led one newspaper editor to widen the lens: "Italy, Germany, France, Spain, England, Ireland, the States and Canada are all more or less engaged in contending against the encroachment of the papacy, whose arrogant thirst after supremacy in civil matters has fairly aroused the press and the Government of all these respective countries."[60]

For Tolerance and Against

Amid all this turmoil came a plea for tolerance. We cannot know whether tolerance made sense to the silent majority of Protestant Torontonians, who had not participated in the attacks on the processionists. Quite possibly it did. After all, not every Catholic procession resulted in public disorder. Clearly, however, calls for tolerance prompted outraged Protestant evangelicals to deplore toleration in this situation.

The *Globe* made the plea for tolerance. Although George Brown and his newspaper had expressed intolerance often in the past, especially regarding French Canadian Catholics, in 1875 his call for tolerance was heartfelt and sat comfortably alongside his mellowed view of Catholics now that they formed only a minority in the new province of Ontario. Couched in liberal language, the case he made for tolerating processions fit with his liberalism more generally. It was politically expedient, moreover, because the *Globe* and the provincial Reformers had an understanding with Lynch. The *Globe* argued that in a free society it was incumbent on people to exercise self-restraint. If other people had beliefs and practices that one did not share, it was best to be prudent and Christian by turning the other cheek. Attacks on those who are different occurred "because men had a very inadequate idea either of the rights or the duties of free citizens in a free state." The *Globe* had no doubt about those rights, declaring: "This is a free country, and our streets are therefore free to all who choose to use them in a decent and peaceable manner. Every colour and every class are free to settle among us, on one single condition – obedience to law."[61]

In his address to the jury hearing the cases of the men charged in connection with the Jubilee riots, Chief Justice Robert Alexander Harrison, an Anglican, a Conservative, and a son of Ulster immigrants, made a similar case for tolerance. Harrison observed that processions were of questionable value, but "in a country like this where we have so many conflicting interests, so many different Churches, and so many points of dissension, it is all important that each should give way a little in order that all enjoy peace and quiet." He added, "Toleration is a Christian feature, and without toleration there cannot be peace."[62] The claims of ultra-Protestants to public exclusiveness had to be rejected in a well-ordered, plural society.

Calls for tolerance provoked a fervent response from certain evangelical clerics and voices in the Protestant religious press. Both the Methodist *Christian Guardian* and the *British American Presbyterian* saw dangers in tolerating Catholic processions.[63] Their objections began at the practical level. Processions blocked public streets to the inconvenience of other citizens, and blockages on the Sabbath were especially objectionable because they hindered Protestant children from attending Sunday school, thus jeopardizing their Christian education.[64] More generally, evangelical commentators criticized the processions for provoking the Orange Young Britons and others who had disrupted the day of rest and made it "hideous ... with noise and riot." While rioting was no way to defend the peace of the Lord's Day, Protestants must insist on strict Sabbath observance. As the *British American Presbyterian* put it, "All kinds of 'pageantry feats and shows' are unseemly on the Sabbath, and should be discouraged by Protestants. That hallowed day belongs to the Lord."[65] Such a position fit into a long-standing campaign led by Ontario's evangelicals to impose their understanding of Christian observance on the public.[66] They petitioned officials for regulations to limit a range of Sunday activities, from train service to tobogganing – often with success in Toronto.

The strength of the Sabbatarianism among Toronto's Protestants reinforced their critique of Catholic processions on Sundays, but it had broader grounds still. The Protestant religious press condemned what it saw as Catholic bullying. "It is the most unbearable effrontery," declared the *Christian Guardian*, "that a Church, whose agents everywhere require unquestioning slavish submission to a narrow-minded Italian priest [the pope]," should expect Ontario Protestants to act toward them "as if the pretended dictates of their perverted consciences created rules by which Protestants were bound to govern themselves." It was not just a case of the minority dictating to the majority. Protestants who tolerated Catholic public practices were allowing idolatry to flourish, thus harming the spread of religious truth. "The fact that Roman Catholics believe that certain irrational and superstitious performances are acceptable to God," declared the *Christian Guardian*, "can be no reason for the [civic] authorities, or anyone else ... to act towards them as if they believed these superstitious falsehoods to be true."[67] At Cooke's Presbyterian Church, the most Irish of Toronto's Presbyterian churches, the Rev. James Gardiner Robb, a persistent public critic of Bishop Lynch, delivered a hard-hitting sermon the Sunday morning of the final Jubilee pilgrimage on the subject of processions. "There is a spurious liberality in the present day," he thundered, "which declared that because some men hold certain opinions other persons must fall in with them. Such was not the fact; ... they as Christians were bound to maintain what is true." George Brown sat in a pew listening to these words.[68] They might well have seemed directed at him, the voice of "spurious liberality," that to Robb sounded more like moral relativism than toleration.

Protestant commentators objected to Catholic processions as overly elaborate spectacles that desecrated the Sabbath. Evangelical Protestants contrasted their own modest forms of worship conducted within church walls with the ostentatious showiness of Catholic displays in the streets, which were not only vulgar but, they believed, in contravention of Jesus's teachings.[69] Items of dress as provocation had a long history. The British Relief Act of 1829 had conceded significant rights to Roman Catholics but contained a clause meant to prevent disturbances by banning public processions where Catholic ecclesiastical garments were displayed.[70] When Corpus Christi processions led to trouble in 1852, the British government issued a proclamation forbidding all public displays of Roman Catholic vestments or religious symbols. Where Catholics defied the ban, Protestants harassed them.[71] Archbishop Lynch informed Torontonians that he had found when visiting Ireland that the law required clergy riding in open carriages to hide their purple robes with cloaks. In Canada no such bans applied to ecclesiastical displays, but some Protestants clearly objected to them in the same way as their Old Country counterparts. At a more quotidian level, Protestants sometimes jeered and assaulted Catholics wearing ecclesiastical clothing when going about their everyday activities in the street.[72]

Beyond dress, many Protestants particularly objected to those processions where Catholics carried the Holy Host publicly, as during the Corpus Christi celebrations, which was evidence of theological error. Lynch explained the sectarian difference from the Catholic perspective: "Catholics profess to have the true body of Christ and a true sacrifice to God in the Blessed Eucharist; Protestants have only the symbol of it, mere bread and wine, and no sacrifice."[73] Many Protestants in Victorian Canada viewed transubstantiation (the transformation of the wafer into Jesus's body) as theologically unsound and the veneration of the consecrated wafer as idolatrous.[74] Uncovering and kneeling in respect for the Holy Host, therefore, had long been resisted by some Protestants. In the context of the Protestant Reformation, Lutherans at Augsburg in 1530 had opposed the doffing of caps for sacramental processions. In the early nineteenth century in frontier districts of the United States, Catholic priests tested the climate of tolerance for Catholicism by gauging the reaction of Protestants asked to uncover when the Host passed in a procession.[75] Toronto Catholics in 1864 who defiantly refused to uncover or kneel were acting, then, in a well-established tradition. In 1875, one evangelical commentator warned Ontario not to permit the practice of Quebec, where Catholics "insolently knock off the hat of any one ... who refuses to do reverence to their wafer god."[76]

If they failed to combat such Catholic processions, reasoned the evangelical press, Protestants would concede public space to Catholics. Canadian Catholics had benefited, claimed the *British American Presbyterian*, from a liberal approach that "allowed them to choose their sites, build their Cathedrals, and raise their lofty steeples wherever their hearts desired." The processions, however, marked a dangerous departure because they turned public space into religious space for idolatry and, thereby, made the city itself Catholic. "A Popish religious procession is an act of worship," said the editor, one that changes "the whole city through which that procession moves into one great church devoted to the worship of the wafer." He concluded by asking, "are we prepared by allowing religious procession to convert the whole city into one immense Popish Cathedral, every street into a Popish Chapel, and every street corner into a Popish altar for the adoration of their host?"[77]

Evangelical commentators maintained that tolerating such prominence in public space left unwitting Protestants vulnerable to Catholic proselytizing. "The arguments in favour of religious tolerance," declared the *Christian Guardian*, "deserve to be cautiously urged when a tolerance is capitalized for Jesuitical purposes under the guise of holy zeal." The *British American Presbyterian* maintained that processions were "a deep laid plot for gradually familiarizing our youth to the Romish worship ... and subverting in Ontario the Protestantism which is the only barrier against the complete subjugation of this great Dominion to the yoke of Rome."[78] Comments in the *Canadian Freeman* about certain Protestants' admiration for the piety shown in Corpus Christi celebrations would have only increased suspicions, as would Lynch's remark in his Jubilee pastoral letter that "in England especially those extraordinary conversions [from Anglicanism to Rome] are being renewed."[79]

Conclusion

The Corpus Christi skirmish and the Jubilee riots buttress the perception that mid-Victorian Toronto was a place where religion and denominational identities mattered. The incidents show how far differences could go: Catholic processionists and their Protestant opponents exchanged blows, and the rhetoric got downright nasty. Anti-Catholicism in these incidents could not be separated from the history of sectarian disputes in Ireland and the Orange/Green conflicts that began among the immigrant Irish in Canada and spread to others. The clashes reinforce the fact that collective violence and religious conflict played a fundamental role in shaping politics and public life of mid-nineteenth-century Canada. Moreover, these violent incidents are another aspect of the making of Victorian Canada's public sphere, one in tension with deliberative democracy and liberal ideals of rational debate. In 1864 and 1875, differences about public order were fought out with violence. The incidents also provoked extended debates during which opponents appealed both to reason and to faith-based assertions that relied on revealed truths, the antithesis of rationalism.

Religious differences sparked the troubles and provided the central analytical tool for commentators, but class and gender entered the picture too. When the *Globe* treated the troublemakers as irresponsible working-class youths, at least one voice objected, saying that some demonstrators were mature men dressed in fine clothing. Hibernian militants, like their Orange counterparts, were mostly working-class in Toronto, but both groups took support from whatever class it came, whether from newspaper offices, the bishop's palace, or City Hall, and their behaviour and rhetoric prioritized religious rather than class divisions.

In the patriarchal society that was mid-Victorian Toronto, men took the lead in public life, directing the faithful from the bishop's palace, forming delegations to take Protestant concerns to City Hall, administering civic authority, manning the attacks on Catholic processionists, defending Catholic rights in the streets, and taking positions from pulpits and in the press on all that transpired. Habits of fraternal bonding gave both Orangemen and Hibernians the incentive to take a militant stand, assuming a role in the eyes of supporters as manly defenders and in the eyes of opponents as hostile aggressors or foolish youths. Women and girls sometimes avoided the confrontations as best they could, with female Catholics seeking shelter in the cathedral vaults during the Corpus Christi clash, and Protestant women and girls vacating the streets on the day of the last of the Jubilee walks, even if it meant missing church services. Yet some women and girls placed themselves on the front lines as Catholic processionists, a departure from secular parades of the period where only men marched. The presence of females in the Catholic processions facilitated their defenders' representation of the Catholics as victims of unchivalrous and hence unmanly attacks. Orangemen and their friends, left in an awkward spot, ignored the charges and diverted attention to the provocations of Lynch and the ultramontane Church.

Buttressing the convictions of both the Protestant demonstrators and the Catholic processionists were religious beliefs that lent authority to their choices and behaviour – or so the press implied with its ample airing of the matters at stake. In fact, many who marched or protested would have struggled to explain the religious issues involved. Nevertheless, many Catholics, having embraced the devotional revolution, and in deference to clerical authority, took their piety into the open air. Protestant reactions were shaped by Orange convictions about the dangers that submitting to Rome presented for the freedom of British subjects and for the Protestantism that was the bulwark of that freedom. Evangelical clergymen added their authority to that perspective, indicating doctrinal errors expressed by Catholic processions and warning of the dire spiritual consequences of enabling Catholics to proselytize in the open.

While those involved in the clashes and debates expressed themselves strongly, the vast majority of Torontonians did not do so, choosing instead to avoid engagement in street violence or direct participation in newspaper debates. Yet as consumers, they chose to subscribe to newspapers that gave voice to particular positions, which must say something about the range of views among the public. The popularity of Brown's *Globe* may indicate that his liberalism and defence of religious tolerance had many supporters, however isolated his voice sounded amid the clamour of the intolerant. Indeed, the fact that Corpus Christi celebrations could continue without incident in subsequent years suggests that ultra-Protestants called a kind of truce. In the decades ahead, certainly, the commitment to tolerance and liberal modernity would come more into the open and grow in association with both the privatization of religion and the growth of secularism. In 1875, however, the most immediate response to calls for tolerance was a backlash from evangelicals, who were anything but liberal or indifferent. Later in the decade, Orange and Green remained as combative as ever, although less directly around religious issues than political ones involving, for instance, the visits to Toronto of revolutionary Irish republicans.[80]

Victorian Toronto was part of a Canada in which the liberal order was becoming entrenched, but the process was no straightforward matter, as the confrontations of 1864 and 1875 well illustrate. Civic authorities with their Orange convictions sometimes ducked their obligation to enforce the law without reference to religion. Much of the mainstream press took an illiberal stand by making demands to limit the freedom of Catholics to exercise their religion in public places. The show of intolerance was led by the city's largest voluntary organization, the Orange Order, and its youth branch, some of whose members spearheaded the city's biggest riot of the era. Just as hostile to liberalism in this instance, the evangelical press backed up the Orange challenge to Catholic rights, marshalling religious arguments that insisted tolerance was no virtue when it came to matters of Catholic belief and practice. George Brown's *Globe* did provide a prominent contrary voice, yet his rights talk was accompanied by frequent assertions made by Bishop Lynch. As the local head of the fiercely anti-liberal ultramontane Church, Lynch argued for collective rights when asserting a minority's claim to practise its religion freely and express its distinctiveness publicly.

Deeply felt differences did not characterize every public occasion in Victorian Toronto, however. The following chapter provides a contrasting scenario where, according to the press, the city stood united in support of the militiamen who went to the North-West to suppress the Métis resistance of 1885.

5
Colonialism Triumphant: Celebrating the Suppression of the North-West Resistance of 1885

"REBELLION: Louis Riel Again Heading an Insurrection," screamed the Toronto *Globe* headline on Monday, 23 March 1885. For a few days the press speculated that a force of militia Volunteers would be sent at once to the North-West to quell the uprising. The situation was finally clarified on the Friday evening, when Prime Minister Sir John A. Macdonald announced in the House of Commons that troops would be called out and sent via the not-quite-completed Canadian Pacific Railway (CPR) to what is now Saskatchewan to re-establish order. Toronto newspaper offices received Macdonald's announcement by telegraph, and the news "soon filtered into the streets and the word passed from mouth to mouth like flame."[1] Late Friday evening Lieutenant-Colonel William Otter, the commandant of "C Company" Infantry School in Toronto, provided details for reporters keen to learn about the city's contribution to the force going to the Prairies. From Toronto he would be taking 250 men of the Queen's Own Rifles (QOR), 250 men of the 10th Royal Grenadiers, and 80 men from the Infantry School. According to the *Mail*, when two dozen sergeants who had gathered that evening in their mess learned what Colonel Otter had said, "hats were thrown into the air and the cheering renewed again and again."[2]

Overnight, orderly sergeants from the companies of the QOR and the Royal Grenadiers in hired cabs rushed around town thumping on doors and rousing sleeping militiamen.[3] As early as midnight, said the reporter from the *Mail*, the streets resonated with the steps of men who already "marched with the tread of the military conqueror." Perhaps contradictorily, hotel barrooms were said to be suddenly packed with men who were soon "gloriously merry."[4] Well before sunrise on Saturday, scarlet-coated Grenadiers and soberly clad riflemen began congregating at the drill shed for the morning's muster and the officers' selection of local men for the North-West Force. "The men gathered with as much glee to any Queen's Birthday outing," reckoned the *Telegram* in an article headed "Eager to Smash Riel and the Rebels."[5] Ordinary citizens were also afoot early that morning as news spread thanks to the new-fangled telephones, and soon crowds plugged the streets near the drill shed. "War fever had taken hold," declared the *World*. "Everybody was talking about the squelching of Riel and his crowd of malcontents." A lieutenant boasted that the Volunteers were "as good soldiers as you can get the world over." When the interviewer pressed him about their lack of active service – probably a widespread concern – he replied in words possibly burnished by the reporter: "Well, have those infernal half-breeds ever seen active service? No, sir, never; and I tell you when they see about a thousand well-drilled men in front of them there will be a general skedaddle."[6]

This chapter examines the coverage that Toronto's daily newspapers and illustrated press gave to the mobilization of Canada's citizen soldiers for the North-West campaign of 1885. While the rebellion has been extensively studied, hometown support for the Volunteers who suppressed it has not.[7] In covering the mobilization of militiamen for the North-West campaign, Toronto's press rhetorically constructed and actually helped foster the massive show of public support for the campaign, most vividly displayed in the send-off of the local militia going to the North-West and the celebrations welcoming Volunteers as they returned home. The city's dailies presented a story of the vigorous suppression of rebels and re-establishment of law and order, the triumph of state power rooted in empire, and public admiration for the values of patriotism, order, discipline, and duty shown so admirably by Canada's soldiers. Simultaneously, journalists made it a story of the people's power that lay behind the state and the military, of the resolve of ordinary, local citizens who donned the uniforms of Volunteer militia regiments and risked their lives to keep their country safe. The press's handling of the 1885 mobilization provides a vivid illustration of Canada's militia myth in action: the people rallying behind the military because they had a popular faith in an active citizenry as the country's best defence in times of crisis. Equally vividly it shows how a moment of militarism could spark and flicker brilliantly for a few months in 1885, twenty years before the launching of much more concerted attempts to foster and sustain militarism in Canada.[8]

On various topics connected to the 1885 conflict Toronto newspapers differed sharply, but on the need for vigorous suppression of the resistance and on the patriotism of the Volunteers there was no dispute. Even the *News*, Toronto's most radical newspaper and one that attacked the military elite, fell in line with the others.[9] Papers were in perfect agreement that once violence erupted it had to be suppressed by the Canadian military, and all of the dailies heaped praise on the Volunteers.[10] In the early weeks of the uprising, Toronto newspapers devoted most of their editorial comment to assessing who was to blame for the uprising, a matter on which partisan differences were especially stark. Upon the outbreak of conflict in the North-West, Toronto's two party organs, the *Globe* and the *Mail*, began an extended and intense partisan battle, each naming the other political party as the catalyst for the violence. Other Toronto dailies took less overtly partisan positions, but they all agreed the Conservative government had helped bring on the rebellion.

None of the Toronto newspapers, including those that maintained the Métis and others in the North-West had legitimate grievances and deserved sympathy, saw the violence as acceptable, and all presented Louis Riel as an outlaw whose presence had sparked the violence. From the start, Toronto newspapers represented the resistance as "Riel's rebellion" and spoke of him as a notoriously familiar figure to Ontarians because of his previous leadership of a rebellion. From their perspective, back in 1869–70, Riel, a Roman Catholic, francophone "half-breed," had led an uprising in the Red River community that threatened Canada's expansion into the North-West. His illegal so-called provisional government had murdered Thomas Scott, a white, patriotic, Ontario-born Orangeman – one of the province's own. Now in 1885 Riel was at it again. Once more, the movement he led seriously threatened the prospects for Canadian development of the North-West, which had not been nearly as rapid as had been hoped over the previous fifteen years. Riel and his followers had twice threatened the steady westward march of settler colonialism.[11]

The certainties Toronto journalists shared about Riel being a traitor who was leading a rebellion against the Queen's authority have dissolved over time as historians have brought to light a more complex picture.[12] Many historians now see the uprising as a resistance movement rather than a "rebellion" because the Métis and Aboriginal insurgents saw the land as theirs and had no sense that they were breaking away from a state that had sovereignty over them.[13] Some have argued that First Nations never allied with the Métis during the resistance movement, although the press of the day saw a frontier "Indian war."[14]

When Toronto journalists unanimously praised the city's Volunteers and the military campaign of suppression, they were showing an awareness of their readership. Known as "the Queen's City," the Toronto of 1885 was nearly entirely English-speaking, 93 per cent British (including Irish) in origin, and nearly 85 per cent Protestant.[15] Historian

J.M.S. Careless aptly describes Toronto as a "very British city in the 1880s, flag-waving imperialist though no less adamantly Canadian in national hope."[16] The events of 1885 vividly reinforce that observation. Resentment of French Canadians ran deep in the city, nurtured in the mid-nineteenth century by Reform cries of "French domination" within the political sphere, by the popular Orange Order's anti-Catholicism, and by the arrival of English, Scottish, and Ulster immigrants whose Britishness was deeply rooted in a suspicion of Catholics and France.[17] After Confederation, political alliances at the federal level that crossed the Ontario/Quebec boundary were always fragile and susceptible to breakdown when flare-ups developed over issues of language, religion, and ethnicity. Because of this predominant viewpoint, sometimes Toronto newspapers depicted Riel in 1885 as one more instance of francophone Catholics asserting themselves inappropriately – in this case, violently and in a way that risked sparking a terrifying "Indian war." According to the Anglican *Dominion Churchman*, the uprising would not have broken out had its "leaders been utterly without support from the Romish Church and the mad effort been sternly discountenanced by the priests, for the rebel leaders were all bigoted Romanists."[18]

Along with Britishness came a firm conviction about the superiority of the British race, The late Victorians' perception was that humankind was composed of a hierarchy of races with white, Protestant Britons at the top; this fostered a deep suspicion of interracial sexual relations that produced hybrid and possibly degenerate offspring.[19] In 1885 the Toronto press sometimes racialized the enemy in the North-West, representing the Métis as "Half-breeds" and "Indians" whose racial inferiority to whites partly explained their turning to violence when starving or when frustrated by inaction on rights claims. Negative stereotypes were associated with this terminology. The *Globe*, for instance, referred to the "Half-breeds" as having "a character ... composed of that of the child and of the savage."[20] By this logic, such a depiction explained why the Métis were so easily misled into violence by the dastardly Riel, himself a half-breed. The hybridity of the Métis enabled the Toronto press alternatively to highlight their French rather than their Aboriginal aspect. "The French half-breeds were in the hands of the French Jesuits," opined the *Telegram*, "and could hardly therefore be expected to have much love for British law or British institutions."[21] If the newspapers are to be believed, then Torontonians' sense of the racial superiority of the white Volunteers on the one hand, and their confidence about the racial inferiority of the non-white rebels on the other, can only have reinforced the sense of mission that fired support for the troops and their campaign in the North-West.

When Toronto's Volunteers responded to the call in 1885, they joined other Volunteers from across the country to reassert law and order in the North-West. In legal terms, the force was acting as an aid to the civil power in response to a request from Edgar Dewdney, lieutenant governor of the North-West Territories. It would be the first real test of the Canadian militia as a battle force acting on its own. Originally designed to assist the professional soldiers of the British army garrisoned in Canada, the militia became Canada's main defensive force in 1871 when a cost-cutting imperial government withdrew the last of its garrisons from the Dominion. Canada's tiny professional army could only provide training for the militiamen and some permanent officers. Canadians expressed pride and faith in their militia force even as taxpayers showed a marked reluctance to spend much money on training or equipping it. In 1885 Ottawa relied on local initiatives to cobble together a force, which it placed under the command of Major-General Frederick Dobson Middleton of the British army.[22]

Organization and funding for the militia fell largely to locally prominent individuals, who provided leadership and assumed substantial financial burdens in exchange for prestige. That system worked best in the cities. Militia companies had a club-like aura, recruiting through personal contacts among those who had money for a uniform and the time for weekly drilling and parade, target-shooting, athletic events, occasional manoeuvres, and attending frequent social functions and public events.[23] Only some workingmen enjoyed such contacts, savings, leisure time, and either self-employment or the approval of employers for time off work. It appears that the militiamen were mostly young businessmen, professionals, and clerks in shops and offices. Such men were sometimes urged to join militia units on the grounds that their masculinity needed toughening because of the sedentary work they did.[24] General Middleton described them privately as being mostly "well-to-do tradesmen's sons or in business." Certainly the Canadian militia's composition set it apart from the British army, whose foot soldiers had long been recruited from the bottom rungs of society. In a private telegram to the Minister of Militia, General Middleton midway through the 1885 campaign praised the Canadian militiamen's gentlemanly conduct, referring to their "superior class and education compared with other armies."[25]

The North-West Field Force was recruited mainly from Toronto and rural Ontario east of the city, Halifax, Quebec City, and Montreal, as well as from Winnipeg and new settlements in the North-West, where units were created on the fly. Macdonald's Conservative government took pains to ensure that the force for this popular campaign was a national one drawn from across the country and that the unity of Canada was thus on display. For reasons of politics, French Canadians had to be included, especially as Riel and many of the rebels were French-speaking; hence the Hon. Adolphe Caron, the federal militia minister and Quebec County MP, called up his province's only two francophone city battalions, the 9th Voltigeurs from Québec and the 65th Carabiniers Mont-Royal from Montreal. In the end a force of 6,000 men from across Canada was assembled, only 363 of them regulars from the Dominion's professional army.

Reinforcing the militia myth, the press in 1885 insisted that the Volunteers called to serve in the North-West were acting solely out of a deep sense of civic and national duty. The *Mail* quoted one Torontonian, a clergyman who declared to his congregation: "It was not from mere love of adventure; it was not from a desire to display muscular courage; it was not from a cowardly fear of reproach should they have remained at home, that our citizen soldiers hastened ... to the defence of their country." Rather, "these gallant men were moved by a patriotic feeling and by a noble desire to perform their duty for their country's good."[26] Readers of the *Mail* in 1885 might well have wondered whether adventure, a wish to show bravery, or fear of criticism did not play some considerable part in the Volunteers' behaviour. Private sources hint at the naivety of the Volunteers, unfamiliar as they were with battle and caught up in the general excitement. Midway through the campaign, General Middleton wrote to a friend expressing his dismay at the losses to his troops and stating bluntly that the Volunteers had "thought they were going on a picnic." Dick Cassels, a young Toronto Volunteer who kept a diary, expressed a similar view when he wrote on the day of his departure from the city: "I am very lucky to have a chance to go," adding that for him active service promised adventure and an opportunity to see the North-West for the first time.[27]

The Toronto newspapers' quick dismissal of concerns about the Volunteers' preparedness for military engagement thinly papered over legitimate worries that were probably widely shared throughout the city, especially by relatives concerned with the welfare of their serving family members. The journalists' bravado fit with the positive spin they gave to the militiamen's patriotic campaign in general. Perhaps, too, it was an attempt to reassure worried parents and others close to the soldiers. And Torontonians hoped – even expected – that the sheer size of the Volunteer force would quickly overpower the small force of Métis combatants, a view eventually borne out by events. From the start there were warnings that the Métis had an advantage because they were fine horsemen and sharpshooters familiar with the country where the fighting would take place.[28] Nevertheless, such uneasy thoughts were overshadowed by robust expressions of confidence in the power of numbers and the advantage of disciplined troops.

Mobilization and Send-off

Daily newspapers judged the turnout for the call-up of Toronto Volunteers on the morning of Saturday, 29 March, to be larger than expected given the short notice, and officers soon selected 500 men for active service. It was widely reported that 800 could easily have been found – possibly even 2,000 – so keen were the city's Volunteers to see action. Only a few militiamen were rejected for duty because their health was poor, and only a few more objected to going because they would probably lose their jobs. Victorian understandings of manly duty were much in evidence in the press's depiction of the young men's eagerness for active service. Because this generation of militiamen had never before had an opportunity to fight in a war, they were keen to be off – to get on with what could well be the chance of a lifetime. After discovering that the men's clothing and equipment were woefully lacking, however, Colonel Otter delayed the battalions' departure for a couple of days to enable women, city and military officials, and others to collect underclothes, boots, mufflers, and equipment suitable for the mission.[29]

The delay gave the city's reporters an opportunity during the weekend to roam the streets amid the swarms of residents who were out and about showing their community's interest in the Volunteers. On Saturday evening they described the streets near the armoury next to Osgoode Hall as thronged with people eager to admire the soldiers on parade, and on Sunday the interest only escalated. "There was nothing else talked of yesterday," observed the *World*, "either in the home circle, at church, or on the streets. War, war, war was the cry, and war it will be till Mr. Riel and his followers bite the dust." The crowds in the vicinity of the drill shed grew enormous when the officers obliged the public with a Sunday afternoon parade of the Volunteers.[30] Parades of local militia regiments had a strong popular appeal in ordinary times, but the Riel crisis magnified the public interest.[31] The military parade was such a familiar form of street celebration that an impromptu one could be easily arranged that weekend. Military officers did not need to negotiate with the city to gain approval to march; their authority went without question, and, of course, the risk of the parade sparking any trouble was minimal. Well-drilled militiamen knew what to wear and how to march, and their well-practised bands provided stirring music that set the tempo and appealed to the crowd.[32]

The Tenth Royals and Queen's Own Rifles Marching Out of the Drill Shed. With the austere drill shed in the background, the image depicts the well-ordered troops watched by lively crowds featuring women admirers on 28 March 1885.
Source: *Illustrated War News*, 4 April 1885.

The climax of the mobilization came with the send-off of the city's force from Union Station. "Toronto never before witnessed such a sight," the *World* exclaimed. "The departure of Volunteers to repel the Fenian invasion nineteen years ago was not a patch to it."[33] Neither was there any resemblance whatsoever to the quiet departures from Toronto of the force of several hundred Ontario militiamen who, with Colonel Garnet Wolseley's British regulars, went west in 1870 to the Red River settlement five months after the outbreak of Louis Riel's resistance there. On that occasion some of the militiamen had complained that even the regimental band failed to appear at the railway station.[34] Throughout both resistance movements, the Toronto newspapers were equally fired up about the dangers the troublemakers posed to

Canada's development of the North-West, the unconscionable behaviour of Riel, and the need for a military force to proceed to the region. Still, the send-offs could not have been more strikingly different. The circumstances surrounding the troops differed in 1869–70 and 1885. In 1885, Torontonians, fearing that the violence would escalate, believed that troops should be dispatched immediately to nip the uprising in the bud; the CPR and spring conditions made doing so a practical if challenging proposition. The troops therefore departed within a few days of the outbreak of hostilities in the North-West, when public excitement, according to the newspapers, was at a fever pitch. In 1869–70, the resistance erupted at the beginning of winter, and by springtime, when it became feasible to send a force up the Great Lakes and overland from Minnesota (without a railway) to the Red River settlement, Torontonians knew that the violence had already subsided in the North-West. Judging by the May newspapers, they were more interested in news of the negotiations over the provisions of the Manitoba Act. Moreover, the composition of the military forces differed significantly in the two instances. In 1870, Wolseley's expedition was chiefly composed of British regulars, with Canadian militiamen in only a supporting role. In 1885, apart from a few officers, the force was entirely Canadian and composed of Volunteers, characteristics that heightened Torontonians' sense of investment in the force's expedition and what has been called "Canada's First War."[35]

When covering the 1885 send-off, Toronto's daily newspapers featured the enormous crowds, the general jubilation, and touching departures. The program for the day – Monday, 30 March – included a rendezvous at the drill shed, a parade through downtown streets, and final farewells at the station. According to the press, the public leapt at the opportunities for involvement. "All was orderly commotion," reported the *Telegram* in reference to the drill shed where officers had ordered the men to muster that morning. "Officers shouting orders in hoarse voice and the clank of bayonet and the thump of rifle butts on the pavement merged with the tramp of rushing orderlies." Once the men had been called to attention, Colonel Otter told them they had been summoned to the North-West "to crush the rebellion," and he declared that they had but one motive and that was "to do their duty to their Queen and country." In addition, he took the opportunity to play father to his troops, saying that he knew some of the men had liquor in their water bottles. "I urge you to abstain from intoxicants and empty out any liquor you may have, for you are going on a mission that requires the possession of all your faculties."[36] The reports did not mention any immediate draining of water bottles.

The real story was not the colonel's address but the throngs of people who stood in the galleries of the drill shed, clogged nearby streets, and lined the flag-draped route of the parade. "At every window in every building a group of people were gathered, and every housetop was covered, and every verandah crowded," declared the *Mail*.[37] Those people who could afford it paid high prices for perches above the streets, from which well-dressed women showered the Volunteers with flowers. As the force marched down Yonge Street, the Grenadier Band played "Auld Lang Syne" and the Queen's Own Band "trilled out 'The Girl I Left Behind Me.'" "Wild with excitement," onlookers "shouted themselves hoarse."[38]

According to some press accounts, the sight of the two regiments marching evoked a Canadian patriotism rooted in British traditions and a wide, imperial world. The *News* said that the Grenadiers in their red uniforms reminded older Torontonians of the British redcoats no longer seen in the city. "Straight, stalwart and resolute," the *News* reported, "the Grenadiers marched along as steady as a clock, and apparently undisturbed by the tumult around them." These were "gallant young men" whose "moral courage and stamina showed that the military spirit which has characterized the progress of the English-speaking race the world over ... can manifest itself in no uncertain way when occasion demands."[39] The voice of Toronto's Irish Catholic minority, the weekly *Irish Canadian*, gave equally firm support for the Volunteers' mission, observing that the government's call to arms had been "responded to with an enthusiasm that reflects honor on the patriotism of our Volunteers" and adding that "in this free land there is no standing room for rebels." Rebellion might be a legitimate response to oppression in Ireland, but the *Irish Canadian* saw no such justification for it in the North-West or anywhere in Canada.[40]

Featured prominently in the daily newspaper coverage of the time were sentimental accounts of personal departures that closely followed gender codes. At many doorways, a mother, wife, sister, or sweetheart sobbed as a departing soldier tore himself away and "strode manfully along with a lump in his throat and a wild desire to rush back to get one more loving embrace."[41] Visible tears belonged to women, not men. At the drill shed a Queen's Own sergeant clasped hands with his "aged father," who "made brave effort to hide his emotion."[42] Late in the day, the *World* reported, "sobbing females were frequently met, and in some cases, men found handkerchiefs useful to hide red eyes or remedy a blurred sight." According to the *Globe*, at the station police had to carry off women who had fainted because their "nerves had become unstrung at the thought of their husbands, fathers, and brothers leaving home for the frontier."[43]

The climax of the day's events came at Union Station when the Volunteers boarded two trains bound for the North-West. "Fully 10,000 people were gathered, probably the largest number ever assembled in one spot in Toronto," reported the *Mail*, while the *World* declared the numbers were in "the tens of thousands" and the *News* put the crowd at 50,000. Even the station's roof was "black with spectators," and the whole place was "aflame with patriotic enthusiasm." Before the Volunteers arrived, University of Toronto students amused the crowd by singing Civil War songs in "doggerel parody": "'Tramp, Tramp, Tramp' and 'We'll hang Louis Riel on a sour apple tree.'" (The *Globe* reporter sniffed that it was scarcely the time for the "clumsy antics of a lot of very callow youths trying hard to be funny." In response, the university's student newspaper, The *Varsity*, accused the *Globe* of "studento-phobia.")[44] Once the troops appeared at the station, everyone surged forward and cheered. The lieutenant governor made a public appearance, adding viceregal dignity and authority to the occasion. A two-page spread in the *Illustrated War News* featured the enormous crowd near the CPR train, while close-ups showed the bustle of activity, final farewells, women drying their tears, and "the last glimpse."[45] As the first train pulled away, the two regimental bands joined together in playing "God Save the Queen." The *Varsity* said that, as the students of "K" Company "silently uncovered to our cheer, we felt a thrill of fellowship such as we had never known before." Soon the last train had disappeared and only smoke remained. Thousands of people scurried away amid driving sleet. The *Globe* remarked: "In little over 48 hours from the first summons, Toronto's young men, deserting office and workshop, started on their three-thousand-mile journey."[46]

Journalists thus interpreted the public's occupation of city streets as the community's solid endorsement of the campaign to suppress the resistance. Perhaps many who gathered to send off the Volunteers were simply curious or did not want to miss the excitement, but the dailies did not allow such a possibility. Still, community support for the event had to have been considerable. Organizing the departure had been rushed, and there was no opportunity for the top brass or other prominent figures to choreograph an elaborate send-off. It could reasonably be seen as a spontaneous effusion of ordinary people and thus all the more impressive a display of patriotism.[47] Jubilation carried the day, according to the press, and nothing marred the scene in the slightest. On display in city streets, the military was equally on display in the press. Military might and imperial state power were much admired, but the admiration was undergirded by awareness that local boys, citizen-soldiers, "our brave Volunteers," were the ones who embodied authority and militarism.

"Take your discharge? – Certainly not." The artist depicts the ideal Volunteer, whose wife supports his determination to serve despite the dangers of the frontier.
Source: *Illustrated War News*, 4 April 1885.

Backing Up the Boys

During the nearly four months between the Toronto send-off and the men's return, the city's dailies featured news items and opinion pieces that kept the Volunteers in the public eye. Front and centre were reports of military engagements, especially involving Toronto's two regiments: the QOR at the battle of Cut Knife Hill and the Grenadiers at the battles of Fish Creek and Batoche. The press strongly played up the men's fighting abilities and reported victories where military historians have seen other results.[48] As historian Sarah Carter has shown, Canada's reading public was also made fully aware and then some of how the uprising endangered white womanhood in the North-West.[49]

The dailies sent reporters "embedded" with the troops on the trains bound for the North-West. Typical of the coverage was a report in the *Mail* from "our special correspondent," who wrote within a couple of hours of the men's departure from Toronto. "The utmost enthusiasm prevails amongst all ranks," he declared, "and the men are anxious for the field." Those aboard the train were enjoying the tobacco the Canadian government had provided for them, filling every nook and corner with smoke. "I pity the non smokers from the bottom of my heart," he added parenthetically. All of the men enjoyed singing Civil War songs – "John Brown's Body" and "Tenting on the Old Camp Ground" – and, more patriotically, they also sang "Rule Britannia" in "every imaginable key."[50] Such reports were uniformly upbeat, evidently meant to lift the spirits of all who read them, Volunteers and civilians alike. Reporters even gave a cheerful spin to the gruelling and hazardous marches in the gaps along the rail line north of Lake Superior, when many men suffered from severe frostbite and snow blindness. Reports focused on the soldiers' pluck and stamina.[51]

Eagerness to see action in the North-West pervaded the ranks of militiamen still at home. This enthusiasm had to do in part with press reports that focused on the bravery of the men selected for active duty. Such reports cast everyone left at home in the same light: as spectators and supporters of the masculine virtues of the chosen. In a sense even militiamen eager to serve but not called up played this feminine role, their masculinity thus threatened. A hint of the consequences comes from a telegram sent to the militia minister by a private in the QOR not chosen for service. He expressed his deep regret that his whole regiment had not been called up because "if the Regiment had gone we should have [all] had ... a chance to prove our courage."[52]

Also in the news were stories about home-front activities in support of the troops. The Orange Order offered supportive words, expressing admiration for the brave, loyal, and patriotic Volunteers.[53] Torontonians debated how best to support the hard-pressed families of some of the married Volunteers. In the end, military officers provided the names of soldiers with dependents in need, and, after a City Hall committee investigated their situations, it gave support to wives judged deserving.[54]

Women appeared in many newspaper stories, cast in the role of dependents; they also appeared as highly active volunteers who prepared bandages, comforts, and such for the soldiers. Newspapers urged readers to respond generously to requests from the Ladies Volunteer Supply Committee. "The citizens of Toronto," observed the *Mail*, "cannot better signify their appreciation of the fortitude with which [the Volunteers] are bearing up than by doing what they can to ensure their comfort in the performance of their duty."[55] The dailies closely covered the work of these public-spirited local women, reporting for instance on a meeting in early May when the Ladies Volunteer Supply Committee resolved to send flannel smocks for all the Toronto men on active service and 100 nightshirts for the sick.[56] The *Illustrated War News* featured their work in a three-scene engraving titled "Toronto Ladies Receiving and Packing Contributions for Volunteers at the Front."[57] In this image a few men are depicted doing the heavier tasks such as handling frightened horses, hammering shut the packing cases, and moving them on the warehouse floor. The more numerous women in fine dresses and elaborate hats sort items, fill the crates, and chat with one another, presumably about the task at hand. In its context the image stands out amid the many others featuring males, especially soldiers. Coverage of this sort deliberately underscored the inclusiveness of the public that had mobilized behind the North-West campaign, a message the press was keen to convey.

City streets recently crammed for the spirited send-offs were soon packed with mourners for the two local casualties of the campaign. The bodies of Lieutenant William Charles Fitch, twenty-six years, and Private Thomas Moor, eighteen years, both Grenadiers "who fell before the rifle-pits at Batoche," were shipped home just four days apart for burial services at Mount Pleasant Cemetery.[58] Reporting on the 1 June funeral procession for Private Moor, the *Globe* doubted "if ever before in Canada so many people assembled on such a mission," adding that "it was apparent that the heart of the city was moved."[59] Although the sombre tone of the newspaper coverage of the funerals stood out amid all the jubilation elsewhere in the press, its focus on the Volunteers' patriotism and the popular participation fit neatly with the rest.

Planning the Reception

By late May the North-West Force had quashed the resistance and Riel, having surrendered, was awaiting trial for treason. Discussions began about welcoming the heroes home to Toronto. Planning the Volunteers' reception consumed the energies of a considerable number of citizens, whose debates and activities the press detailed. Public commentators and the newspapers underscored that the welcome would be from the people, arranged by grateful residents eager to honour the country's citizen-soldiers, especially the local boys.

The *News* took the lead in urging civic officials to plan a grand reception, publishing five editorials calling for action.[60] Mayor Alexander Manning eventually called a public meeting at City Hall that established the Toronto Volunteers Reception Committee, a large body composed of citizens and aldermen, the people being thus represented in two ways. Sub-committees were also put in place: the barricade and route committee, the arch committee, the music and decorations committee, the luncheon committee, and the monument committee.[61] Advice on the program for the reception flowed through the pages of the press, with disputes inevitably developing as to how best to proceed, and readers were thus made to feel part of the process. Organizers quickly rejected the idea that there should be a banquet for all the Toronto men or any elaborate formalities and "tedious" ceremonials. The main objective was succinctly put in a *News* editorial: "that as many people as possible be able to see and cheer the returning heroes and that the latter should be able to return to their families and friends as soon as possible." Organizers focused on arranging refreshments for the Volunteers while en route to the city and, once they arrived, on processions through brilliantly decorated city streets, music, and an illumination and fireworks display in the evening.[62]

Finalizing the arrangements presented some modest challenges. The processional route, which was debated at several meetings of the reception committee, needed to be long enough for plenty of spectators to see the heroes, but not so long that it exhausted troops who deserved their rest. Would detraining at Parkdale Station in the west end mean a too tiring (three-and-a-half-hour) march into town? Was North Toronto Station a better choice for the procession's commencement? Opinions varied, not least because each neighbourhood wanted to be at the centre of things. Because the CPR authorities preferred the North Toronto (Summerhill) Station, which they fully controlled, it became the focus of activities.[63] The thorny question of precedence also cropped up. The reception committee placed the stay-at-home members of QOR and Grenadiers at the end of the procession route, that is, in front of City Hall, where the brief formalities were to occur. Though the committee intended it as a compliment to the regiments, the stay-at-homes did not see it that way. They insisted they appear at the railway station so as to be among the first to welcome their fellow-Volunteers when they stepped down from the trains. As the procession moved off, the home boys said they would fall in at the rear.[64] In the end the barricade committee agreed to this plan. Also assigned places in the procession were militiamen from units not sent to the North-West, including Captain Carter's Colored Corps and band.[65] When showing appreciation for the heroes, everyone wanted to appear generous, but city officials, worried about budgets and criticism from ratepayers, pared down requests from the various committees.[66] At first the reception committee opted not to build an arch of welcome for the Volunteers, but, after it was pointed out that arches were always built for British troops returning from battle, the decision was reversed. In the end the city spent at least $2,250 of public funds on the reception, a modest sum when compared to Toronto's budget of $12,000 for welcoming the Prince of Wales in 1860.[113]

Decorating the town involved both the corporation and its citizenry. According to the *Mail*, city workers made "strenuous efforts ... to make the old City hall building look as well as possible, but it was a big job." The reception committee asked residents to decorate their homes and streets and owners of vacant lots on the procession route to build viewing platforms on them. A day or two before the arrival of the Toronto regiments, the *Mail* was reporting a brisk demand for evergreen boughs.[67] Indeed, "all classes of citizens" were "entering into the spirit of the thing with the same zeal and heartiness." A reporter poked fun at some of the results, however. A welcome banner raised on top of the usual signage on a storefront ended up reading "Welcome – Fresh Fish"![68]

Toronto welcomed three battalions of Volunteers before the city's own boys returned: the Midland battalion (men drawn from counties east of Toronto) and the 9th Voltigeurs (from Quebec City), both arriving on Sunday, 19 July, and the Halifax provisional battalion, received two days later. The series of receptions gave citizens a chance to practise for the main event, the arrival of Toronto's own, and they built excitement in anticipation of the local lads' arrival. Toronto's reputation for hospitality was at stake: the local press reported that newspaper readers across the country were watching to see how the city would welcome the visiting Volunteers. This sort of reflexivity within the national press community fed urban rivalries.

When the Boys Come Home

"Never since Creation has there been such a home coming," hyperbolized the *News* about 23 July 1885, the day the Toronto Volunteers returned. "Toronto fairly rocked with joy. ... It was a most glorious, resplendent, brilliant, effulgent ending to a gallant national movement." The *Telegram* declared: "Such a day never was seen in Toronto before. Possibly such a day will never be seen in Toronto again." The *World* judged it equally: "Over one hundred thousand people yesterday joined in the warmest welcome that was ever given in this fair dominion to citizen soldiers who had served their country in suppressing armed rebellion. The oldest and youngest inhabitants agreed for once that it was the greatest day Toronto ever witnessed."[69] In their detailed reports of the day, journalists stretched their descriptive powers to bring to life the patriotic display and the emotional reunions.

On the eve of the boys' arrival the streets were clogged with residents and visitors "viewing and criticizing the decorations." The *Irish Canadian* thought the city's "gay appearance" resembled "the gala days" of Toronto's 1884 semi-centennial "only the enthusiasm, if any thing, is greater."[70] One of the several images in the *Illustrated War News* featuring the decorations shows residents admiring the elaborately and patriotically festooned offices of the *Globe* – both a reminder of the press's importance to the campaign and an opportunity to publicize the *Globe*'s message: "WELL DONE BOYS."[71] Along the parade route had sprung up six temporary arches, festive structures appropriate for the city's Volunteers, who would pass through triumphal arches in the same way that victorious Roman legions had in classical times.[72]

There was much more. Fire halls appeared elaborately adorned to resemble castles, demonstrating once again, said the *Mail*, the firemen's "genius for decorating." Main streets were thickly draped with streamers, shields, and banners, with mottoes of welcome.[73] Some decorations were elaborate. At his Yonge Street home, a citizen had erected a gallows-tree with a noose from which hanged an effigy of Louis Riel. The reporter for the *Mail* observed that it was "evidently popular" but that he found it "rather a ghastly spectacle."[74] (French Canadian commentators would have bitter words for this kind of display.)[75] In front of Randall's news depot were red-and-white banners reading: "Long Marches, Hard Tack, Rough Camping, Lead to Victory and Triumph."

A. McGregor, a painter, had created a scene on his window that "represented a Grenadier with fixed bayonet charging at a redskin in warpaint, who was doing his best to make himself scarce." The caption read: "This is the way Our Boys did it at Batoche." Butchers working in St Lawrence Market placed a banner at the building's south entrance: "The knights of the cleaver salute the Cut Knife heroes, the Frog Lake butchers' avengers, and the sharp steel chargers of Batoche."[76] Aligning themselves with the popular patriotic campaign could have done nothing to hurt the commercial prospects of the businesses doing the advertising, and indeed several businesses placed display advertisements in the press associating their products and services with the popular campaign.[77]

Not only were the main streets much adorned, but side streets too were "flamboyant with flags and streamers, and redolent of the delicious resinous odour of the cedar [boughs]."[78] The *Globe* waxed sentimentally about "the outpouring of individual sympathy for the gallant fellows" shown in the modest decorations displayed outside unpretentious dwellings, such as a "little arch of evergreens over a small gateway."[79] Popular participation was made evident in reports of a large group of women, amply supplied with flowers from the gardens of many residents, who made up 1,000 bouquets, each one mounted on a stick so that it could be stuck into the barrel of a soldier's rifle.[80]

On the afternoon of the men's arrival, the city was bursting both with residents enjoying the holiday declared by the mayor and with visitors who had streamed into town for the celebrations. The *Christian Guardian* said the crowd numbered 100,000 and formed "one dense mass of men and women excited to the highest pitch of enthusiasm."[81] People gathered all along the parade route and especially near the North Toronto Railway Station. Admittance to the station was by ticket; members of the reception committees thus ensured that they and other local worthies would have privileged access to the heroes.[82] Just before five o'clock the first of the trains chugged into view, carrying the QOR, and "in a moment all was confusion." While the soldiers had to await orders to detrain, impatient civilians rushed up hugging and kissing their loved ones, who reached out from the carriage windows. Meanwhile, the ladies of the Volunteer Supply Committee boarded the trains and presented each man with a nosegay consisting of "a shield covered with white flowers with the initials of the regiment in the centre and the words 'Cut Knife Creek' above and below."[83] Once off the train, the men posed for a photograph and listened to Mayor Manning welcoming them back: "You have proved yourselves no mere holiday soldiers,

Queen's Own Rifles pose at the North Toronto Station, 23 July 1885. The photograph shows the returned men in tidy lines still displaying military discipline.
Source: Toronto Public Library.

and we feel with just pride that our Volunteers in discipline, endurance, and steady bravery can favorably compare with any regular troops."[84] Shortly afterwards the scene was repeated with the arrival of the Grenadiers and the mayor again invoking the militia myth.

When the bands struck up "When Johnnie Comes Marching Home," the two battalions began their march down festooned Yonge Street past the cheering onlookers. It was a military display with civilian marchers limited to the civic officials who played host. No other groups, such as trade unions or fraternal orders, marched that day. The great mass of the population participated as spectators, cast in the role of admirers of the militiamen. The newspapers reported the exact order of marchers, which organizers had carefully worked out ahead of time. City officials led the way, followed by the various regiments of mounted and marching soldiers. The wounded rode in carriages. A clear distinction was made between the returning men and the militiamen who had stayed home, with the former taking precedence. Included prominently in the procession was Captain Howard, a soldier in the US army who had gone west to man the Gatling gun, a new and terrifying, though still often inaccurate, rapid-fire weapon.[85] At the head of the military procession rode Colonel George T. Denison, whose reminiscences confirm newspaper reports of the day. "What struck me was the extraordinary enthusiasm of the people," he observed. "If we had been returning from a second Waterloo, concluding a long and anxious war, we could not have been received with greater warmth. I repeatedly saw both men and women cheering wildly, with the tears running down their cheeks with excitement. It was a most interesting study."[86]

As the procession continued down Yonge Street, the crowds cheered endlessly. "Old men shouted themselves out of breath," said the *Globe*; "young ladies cheer[ed] as they pelted bouquets of flowers at the veterans; mothers wept with joy, and the babes in their arms cooed and waved their stubby little hands as if by instinct."[87] At City Hall the girls' choir "broke forth in patriotic and welcoming songs," which the men acknowledged with "regulation campaign cheers." The lads were in a jolly mood, not only because they were home but also because they had been supplied with well-iced kegs of beer donated by O'Keefe's brewery and loaded onto the trains at Orangeville.[88]

The crowd was said to be moved by the appearance of the Volunteers, who, declared the *Globe*, "looked like soldiers every inch, albeit much patched-up, sunbrowned, and dusty warriors." Some who had been overweight on departure had trimmed down considerably. And their discipline was admirable. When called to attention, the entire battalion "stood erect, immovable, like bronzed statues."[89] In its editorial, the *Mail* said that the troops had shown "all the soldierly qualities we expected of them" and "sustained the warlike traditions of their race." Moreover, on that glorious day of the reception, they had "received the warm welcome which British subjects always give to British soldiers when they return from those services of danger which we have learned to consider invariably the occasion of victory."[90] In parallel, the Catholic *Irish Canadian* gave a special welcome home to Captain James Mason of the Grenadiers, who had sustained a bullet wound: "He has nobly upheld the valor of our race and enabled us to say that in the North-West fight the Irish were in the van."[91]

People in the crowd that day were transported by the exhilaration of it all, or so it was said. The *Mail* reported that in a sermon the Rev. E.A. Stafford of Metropolitan Methodist Church spoke at length about a rare

Colonialism Triumphant 127

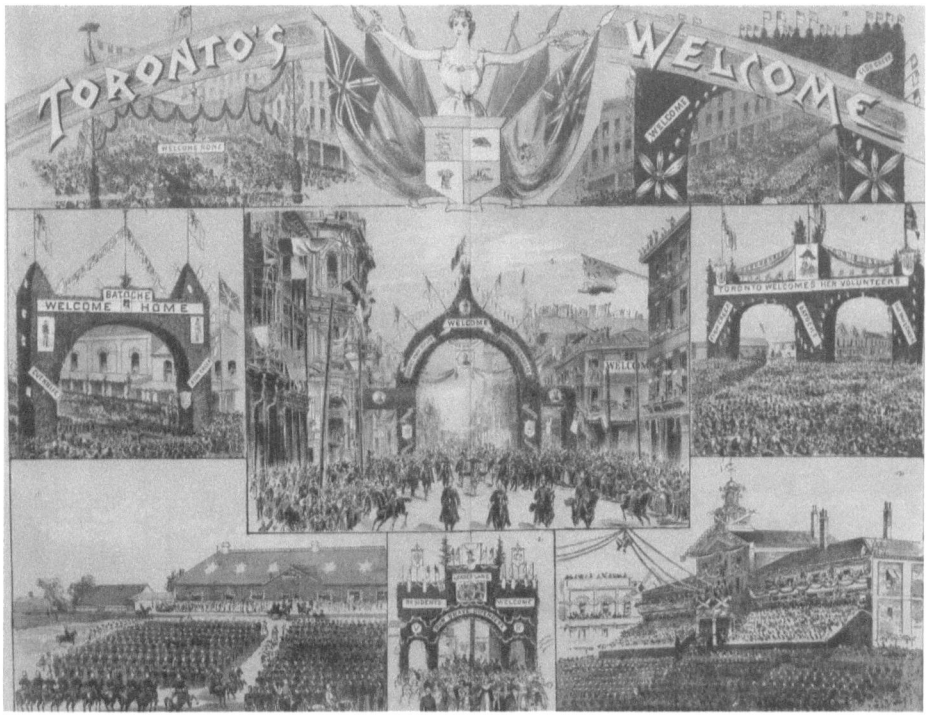

Toronto reception, 23 July 1885. A montage highlighting the arches and welcoming crowds along with the then familiar figure of "Miss Canada" showing them off.
Source: *Illustrated War News*, 25 July 1885.

and valuable sense of oneness that the crowds experienced during the reception. "The whole people had their minds bent on one thought," he mused, adding, "such enthusiasm lifts us out of the common-place and into the poetical – out of the little into the great." Moreover, this feeling had prompted "an increased growth of national feeling." Another publication described the "atmosphere of naturalness" that pervaded the city, when "differences in rank and position were for the moment forgotten." The crowd's "truth and spontaneity were so fully apparent, that the coldest temperament melted into geniality and good feeling." Another editorial remarked: "Everybody was glad, everybody cheered and did various other things that in a colder blooded mood they would never have thought of doing."[92] Such remarks confirm historian H.V. Nelles's generalization about popular parades: "Colour, spectacle, a

The returned men of K (University) Company, Queen's Own Rifles.
While carefully posed in front of University College, the young men
assume relaxed positions, signifying their job is done.
Source: University of Toronto Archives.

massing of bodies, ordered formations, and an impelling tempo, by inspiring awe and adulation, dissolve distinctions."[93]

On the day of the men's return, one of them, Dick Cassels, wrote in his private diary using language that echoed the public rhetoric of the press: "At the roar of welcome that greets us, our labours, our trials, our dangers, our hardships, are all forgotten and gratitude and enthusiasm alone remain." For its part, the University of Toronto showed gratitude by excusing the returning student militiamen from sitting their exams, giving each of them automatic credit for the academic year.[94] To commemorate their experience, the "K" Company veterans posed in uniform on the steps of the front entrance to University College, the officers standing with hands resting on their upended rifles, and the students sitting in a relaxed manner, signifying that for the present their duties had concluded.

On the Monday following the reception, local newspapers printed summaries of Sunday sermons that focused on the citizen-soldiers who had done their country proud. The *Mail* provided accounts of seven church services and one at "the synagogue" (Holy Blossom) where the cantor, the Rev. Herman Phillips, welcomed the men of the congregation home from the North-West and "eulogized the troops for their prompt service at the call of duty, for the hardships undergone and blood shed in the cause of law and order." For those attending service at Grace Anglican Church, the minister underscored how recent events had proven that "the people of Canada were united, not merely by an Act of Parliament, but by patriotic feelings, by pride for their wide domain, and by faith in the future."[95]

The city's permanent recognition of the Volunteers' campaign in the North-West saw the eventual unveiling of a monument in a prestigious location at Queen's Park commemorating those who had died suppressing the resistance. Well before the Volunteers returned home, Mayor Manning and others had formed a civic committee to undertake public collections for the construction of a monument that was estimated to cost $15,000 to $20,000. "It is to be emphatically a citizens' monument," reported the *Telegram*, "erected by the citizens without distinction of class, politics, colour, creed or nationality." The *News* called it "a memorial of patriotic heroism ... intended to be worthy alike of those who fell, and of the city which honors itself by erecting it." It proved difficult to find adequate support, however, once the moment of militarism had passed, which happened noticeably soon. Eventually, however, the funds were found, and Walter Allward, a talented young Toronto sculptor (and the designer much later of the Vimy Monument), won the commission to design and execute it. Reflecting a distance from the militarism of 1885, the sculpture unveiled in 1895 consists of a single female figure, Peace, standing on a tall, white marble base, and holding up an olive branch and with a sword sheathed at her side. The base of the Northwest Rebellion Monument better reflects the spirit of 1885. On it are inscribed the names of the battles and a bronze plaque at the front reads: "Erected in memory of the officers and men who fell on the battlefields in the North-West in 1885. Dulce et decorum est pro patria mori."[96] Today the monument site has been appropriated by the organized Métis community, which, with an acute sense of irony, uses it as the gathering place for annual Riel Day ceremonies on 16 November, the date of Riel's state execution in 1885.[97]

North-West Rebellion Monument, Queen's Park, Toronto. The monument features the uplifting female figure "Peace."
Source: Author's photograph.

Conclusion

In 1885 Toronto journalists certainly outdid themselves in their lively, extensive, and sometimes over-the-top coverage of the Volunteers' campaign to suppress the Métis resistance fighters in the North-West. From the first news of the resistance's outbreak until the boys had been welcomed home with grand receptions, the city's dailies lavished attention on the people's support for the undertaking. Newspapers constructed a public composed of active citizens intensely involved in the events of the day and completely committed to the idea of the citizen-soldier as the country's best defence. According to journalists, popular convictions gave weight to the manly virtues said to be at the heart of the Volunteers' mobilization: patriotism, duty, and discipline. Military and civilian authorities called for the vigorous suppression of resistance, and Toronto newspapers reinforced the call at every turn. The press assisted the process of settler domination in the North-West, marking 1885 as a triumph of colonialism in Canada.

Historians are accustomed to discovering evidence of contention in public celebrations, such as the "civic wars" Mary P. Ryan locates at the heart of democratic public expression in American cities in the nineteenth century.[98] Disputes about Toronto's 1885 send-offs and receptions, however, are noticeably lacking in the pages of Toronto's dailies. Scenes of playful mockery that challenged hegemonic displays of welcome during Canada's first royal visit or occasionally in Labour Day parades are similarly absent in the press's depiction of Toronto and its soldiers during the summer of 1885.[99] Newspapers depicted the crowds as ceaselessly jubilant (except during the funeral processions for the fallen Volunteers), but never playful. The labour reform weekly newspaper from Hamilton, the *Palladium of Labor*, provides the only Ontario press evidence I have found of a critical perspective on the receptions. It condemned the campaign of the government and the Volunteers and in passing objected to the receptions on class lines, dismissing them as "plenty of cheap and showy displays of gratitude" got up for the common soldiers, who were given no compensation "of a solid, substantial character."[100]

Generally speaking, the position taken by Toronto's dailies echoed across Canada as local journalists gave a vigorously positive spin to their communities' patriotic celebrations in support of the Volunteers.[101] In Montreal, French and English newspapers alike fawned over the local men called to service and praised the huge public participation of both French and English Canadians in the celebrations surrounding the mission.[102] That city's homecoming was spectacular. In Montreal, unlike in Toronto, however, newspapers acknowledged local dissent in connection with the troops. It was reported, for instance, that a few members of the 65th Voltigeurs had deserted before departure for the North-West.[103] Moreover, newspapers closely covered the large, open-air meetings called by Montreal's Le Club National, where French Canadian nationalists voiced support for the French-speaking Métis, denounced the government's campaign of suppression, and railed at the remarks hostile to French Canadians published in the Toronto *News* and elsewhere.[104] Journalists in Montreal said the city's opposition voice was that of only a small minority, but they abandoned that stance once French Canadian dissent ballooned during Riel's treason trial and especially after his hanging. Until then, the scene in Montreal mostly resembled that of Toronto in its keen support for local militiamen going to the North-West.

This chapter has focused on newspaper representations of Toronto's support for the Volunteers of 1885. In this regard, a legitimate concern is the accuracy of the press depictions. When the great bulk of historical evidence is in the form of newspaper accounts, assessing their accuracy is difficult, especially given the consensus among them in praising the military campaign and public support for it. Internal press evidence points to some inconsistencies. For instance, where one paper said the crowd at the train pull-out numbered 10,000, another said 50,000. It could not have been both, but what seems apparent is that the crowds at the send-off and the later receptions were very large. We may legitimately doubt whether the public was really so uniform in its support for the troops. It is reasonable to assume that quite a few people in the crowds appeared in city streets merely out of curiosity or for a diversion, rather than to show patriotic support for the Volunteers, the preferred official and press interpretation of what was happening. It's obvious there was exaggeration and hyperbole in many accounts. When mothers watching the returning heroes of Batoche "wept with joy," it is unlikely that literally "the babes in their arms cooed and waved their stubby little hands as if by instinct"![105] Such exaggerations would have been apparent to readers, and the touch of humour helped make plain the crowd's approval.

At all times, Toronto journalists put the best spin possible on the troops, seeing skill and victories where limitations and disappointments are more apparent in retrospect. Upon the return of the troops, the *Mail* commented on the difference between the complete public approval of them and the situation at the outset of the campaign: "It can hardly be offensive now to say that the general public did not hold volunteering as a very useful pastime. Men of business grudged the time it occupied for some of their young men ... Cynics sneered sometimes at the parade that was made of volunteer uniforms."[106] Such an admission was in sharp contrast to the various newspapers' earlier depictions of the admiration Torontonians had for the militia. The press bent the truth to fit the needs of the hour, all the while telling a story of worthy Volunteers patriotically answering the nation's needs.

In 1885, newspapers played a key role in both representing patriotism and encouraging displays of it. Military officers, the mayor, clergymen, and others made remarks that journalists then used to build a picture of determined support for the Volunteers' campaign to suppress resistance. No gap can be discerned between the message authorities wanted to convey and what city dailies said at every turn. The daily press reinforced the voices of power. This was essential to making hegemony work.

That hegemony was also apparent when Toronto newspaper editors and other members of the local elite turned their attention to other topics, such as youthful perpetrators of disorder in city streets.

6
Boys, Young Men, and Disorder

Boys and young men figured significantly both in the disorder that occurred in mid-nineteenth-century urban British North America and in the concomitant search for social order, as this case study of Toronto shows. From the 1840s through the 1870s, the considerable rowdiness in Toronto was mainly fuelled by lads hanging about the streets eager for action and by their fierce ethno-religious and partisan differences. The city's largest riots usually pitted Orange (militant Protestants) against Green (Roman Catholic Irish), but even minor clashes of young men in the streets often derived from ethno-religious tensions, or at least that is how they were represented by newspapers.

Toronto's lively press, essential in this work as a historical source, reported and commented on street violence and attempts to prevent it. Newspapers, especially the mighty *Globe*, which could afford to hire roving reporters, covered all manner of social conflict in the streets and in the courts. The press's intense gaze on crime and violence points to the voyeuristic fascination of many newspaper readers, who derived reassurance about their own respectability and social distance from street violence.[1] In addition, the press publicized the authorities' attempts to combat crime and disorder, as well as middle-class activists' campaigns to reform troublesome boys.

This chapter deals both with boys and with young men because of the similarities in experience, behaviour, and treatment of them when they were in city streets, where they were most likely to engage in conflict or come within the purview of the law. Boys learned about masculinity by watching males older than themselves. As Craig Heron argues about a later period, for young men, being "one of the boys" was about performing masculinity in ways learned first on the streets as young boys and then in ongoing ways that extended that childhood experience.[2] In the mid-Victorian city, too, the continuity from childhood through adolescence and into a bachelor life (if not beyond) also gave substance and meaning to the imprecise but frequently invoked expressions, "the lads" and "the boys." Playful behaviour in the streets sometimes led to trouble. Boys liked to throw stones, and sometimes those stones broke windows or hit people, behaviour that older fellows took up during riots. Boys sorted out differences by fighting, just as young men used their fists to establish their place in the pecking order or to challenge men from rival fraternal orders. Indeed, much of the violence of the mid-Victorian city grew out of the recreational life of boys and young men, and critics of rowdiness and crime struggled to find ways to curb both. At a time when calls for "peace, order and good government" were gaining increasing traction on the national scene, urban reformers sought to achieve the same rather elusive goal.[3]

Women and girls in mid-Victorian Toronto behaved, and were represented, differently from men and boys. Girls and women were virtually missing from accounts of collective street violence, and girls figured much less frequently than boys in the city's crime statistics. Reformers, however, did target wayward girls, whose morals were subjects of intense concern. For reformers, "girls embodied delinquency in a way boys could not," observes historian Tamara Myers. "Their maturing sexuality and promise of maternity were read as harbingers of society's destiny."[4]

Youthful Violence during Riots

Newspapers reported that young men and boys participated in the frequent riots that erupted in mid-nineteenth-century Toronto and that they sometimes instigated them. There is, of course, a long history of youthful violence. To cite but one example, Natalie Zemon Davis in her study of violence in early modern France observes: "Adolescent males and even boys aged ten to twelve played a strikingly important role in both Catholic and Protestant crowds."[5] In 1849, the Toronto press characterized the perpetrators of serious social violence as reckless youths. As we saw in chapter 1, in March of that year the Reform government allowed William Lyon Mackenzie, the rebel leader of 1837, to return to Toronto for the first time since the rebellion. Some Conservatives held a demonstration and burned effigies to protest his reappearance, activities overlooked by municipal authorities and a police force with Orange and Tory sympathies. The Reform press disparaged the demonstrators, underscoring their youth. "Young lads, half grown," reported the *Globe*, "were observed in small groups of two and three, generally carrying sticks, moving about in the neighbourhood. They were joined by some men and the procession moved off." The *Examiner* described the "the squalid and vicious looking cortege" as being composed of "unshaven, dirty looking, half-intoxicated men, and aged boys." Instead of the 2,000 demonstrators promised by the Tories, the *Globe* maintained that "they numbered from 100 to 120, many of them lads, and mostly raggamuffians [sic]." They had been mustered, the *Globe* charged, by Tory aldermen who "have a few rowdies whom they can move or restrain at pleasure." Their numbers included "a few college boys, or the off-scourings of Orangeism." The point of the rhetoric was to defend the moderation and respectability of the city and to dismiss the significance of opposition to Mackenzie and the Reform government by representing the protesters as few in number, young, and lacking independence, respectability, and good judgment.[6]

In 1855, the "circus riot," one of mid-nineteenth-century Toronto's largest riots, involved youthful violence fuelled by nativism and Orangeism. The trouble began on the evening of 12 July, the "Glorious Twelfth," the Orangemen's most important annual celebration, when social tensions always ran high in Victorian Toronto.[7] This time trouble erupted in a bawdy house on King Street when a local man knocked the hat off a circus worker – dubbed a "clown" – from an American circus visiting town. A brawl ensued in which the circus visitors sent the local fellows running "like nine pins."[8] Revenge would be swift. The next evening, young locals set the circus's ticket wagon on fire and rolled it down to the bay. The fire bells were sounded, a signal that called out not only the volunteer firemen, who were Orangemen, but all their brethren too, including those dressed in the costume of the Orange Young Britons, the order's youth wing. A crowd of perhaps 2,000 people gathered on the fairground, where young local men tried to confront the circus personnel. When the circus men refused to venture out of the big tent, the crowd hurled stones at it, set it on fire, and attempted to axe its guy ropes. Local men roared that "they would have out the livers of the Circus men" and shouted "murder the d – n Yankee son of a b – s." The volunteer firemen refused to douse the circus's property, both because the firemen sympathized with the incendiaries and because an Orangemen, Joe Bird, had been badly injured by a circus worker. The constabulary similarly did little, even when the mayor, George William Allan, implored them to restore the peace. When news circulated that Bird was nearly dead, the local lads demanded the police arrest the circus men, adding, "Why should our fellow citizens be murdered by a parcel of Yankees?" The confrontation lasted for a few hours before burning out.[9]

Witnesses to the violence underscored the leading role young men played in the riot. A city councillor noted that – particularly in its early stages – "the crowd consisted chiefly of boys, and did not seem to be very serious." The mayor declared, "One thing that struck him that night was the vast number of vagabond boys between 16 and 20 years of age who were present," adding that "those ruffian boys ... were the pest and curse of Toronto."[10] The violence of the circus riot was thus exacerbated by young men eager for excitement, high on Orange festivities, and fired by nativism directed at the "Yankee" circus men visiting the city.

Processions of Irish Catholics on St Patrick's Day (17 March) and by Orangemen on the Glorious Twelfth (12 July) could be well-ordered and impressive in their size, but, as often noted, some years saw serious clashes between Orange and Green.[11] Tragedy struck during rioting on St Patrick's Day in 1858 when Matthew Sheedy, a twenty-two-year-old Catholic stableman, was fatally stabbed. According to the police magistrate's findings, the trouble began when a boy driving a butcher's wagon tried unsuccessfully to pass through the St Patrick's Day procession. Orangemen rushed to the scene and the riot began.[12] Apparently, then, a boy triggered rioting, and it led to the death of a young man mourned as a martyr by the Irish Catholic community after the acquittal of the Orangemen charged with the murder. Yet most remarkable is the fact that, notwithstanding intense Orange–Green hostility, Sheedy's death was the only one to arise from years of rioting, suggesting some self-restraint on the part of demonstrators most of the time.

As we saw in chapter 4, the biggest riots in Victorian Toronto were the Jubilee riots, when, in 1875, militant Protestants attacked Roman Catholic pilgrims as they processed through city streets.[13] Images from the *Canadian Illustrated News* featuring the Jubilee riots convey both the youthfulness of the participants at the heart of the combat and the event's proximity to play. Figure 6.1 shows young men throwing and dodging stones in what looks like a game. All is not fun, however. The boy in the foreground on the right has fallen or been knocked down and nurses a head wound. In an attempt to restore order, outnumbered policemen dash onto the scene. Indeed, the bloody riots resulted in injuries to many participants, police, and onlookers. Yet it was also an exciting confrontation that drew demonstrators and spectators – thrill-seeking youths – into the streets however troubled, or not, they were by the issues at stake.[14] The exhilarating occasion offered respite from a Victorian Toronto Sunday, normally pinched into dullness and inactivity by evangelical sabbatarianism.

Two of Toronto's newspapers blamed the violence of the Jubilee riots on the Orange Young Britons, an organization of young men in their teens and early twenties that was loosely associated with the Orange

Young men and boys throwing stones during the Jubilee riots.
The artist captures the action but makes it appear like sport, except
for the stunned, fallen fellow in the foreground.
Source: *Canadian Illustrated News*, 12:16, 16 October 1875.

Order but lacked its discipline and growing respectability. According to the *Globe*, these fools were a "thoughtless class of lads" who purported to stand up for Orange principles about which they knew nothing. As for "their affected zeal for God's truth or God's law, or the sanctity of the Lord's Day," that was "one of the most transparent frauds that ever was attempted to be palmed off upon a long-suffering and highly charitable community."[15] The *Irish Canadian*, the city's voice of Irish nationalism, also blamed the Orange Young Britons for the attacks on the Jubilee processionists, who included many women and children, and it objected when authorities looked the other way. "The Young Britons," surmised the *Irish Canadian*, "had made up their minds to break up the procession and slaughter the weak and defenceless – if that could be done with impunity." They were emboldened in the knowledge that their unlawful conduct was permitted by the civic authorities.[16] This analysis connected the events to ongoing political struggles as the Irish Catholic minority resisted Orange dominance at City Hall.

Sectarian conflict persisted in part because of city authorities' toleration of Orange violence. The Orangemen consistently positioned themselves as staunch loyalists in a British colonial setting where loyalism carried weight.[17] Yet they professed their loyalty even as they challenged constituted authority. The colonial state, similar to the imperial state, both deplored Orange violence and tolerated it when it served state and political purposes.[18] As fierce defenders of the Protestant Crown, which had long privileged the Protestant minority in Ireland, Toronto's Orangemen promoted grassroots activism in the name of loyalty, campaigning successfully in municipal elections so as to dominate at City Hall and gain access to jobs, including on the police force. In the 1840s and 1850s, the Orange Lodge created and defended not a liberal order but an Orangemen's order. Equality before the law and "peace, order and good government" were not its goals; instead, Orange bullying ran free, and the mayor's office, police court, and the most of the constabulary acted with a blunt and undisguised bias in favour of its brethren and Protestants more generally.

Sectarianism did not underlie every large confrontation in nineteenth-century Toronto, however. College students were sometimes criticized in the press for the rambunctiousness in the streets, especially at Halloween, when, as historian Keith Walden has shown, they gained the attention of the press annually from 1884. The ritualized behaviour conformed to a pattern: male students would gather on Halloween evening on college grounds, march to a theatre where they would disrupt the performance in various ways, then parade through city streets, singing and shouting, damaging property, and sometimes clashing with police. It is significant that on these ritual occasions the property damage was of a minor nature, such as overturning fruit stands and outhouses or smashing wooden fences. Walden argues that this behaviour was not only an expression of youthful exuberance but also part of the young men's "adjustment to an emerging modern urban situation." He dubs the men "respectable hooligans," underscoring that college men stood steps up the social ladder from the lads who usually caught the attention of police.[19]

Sectarian differences were similarly not prominent during the two 1886 strikes by streetcar operators, examined in chapter 7, but boys acted as catalysts to some of the violence. The first to hurl handfuls of mud and snowballs at scab-run streetcars and their operators, boys triggered men in the crowd to do the same. Young lads had good fun taking potshots at their targets, enjoyment that resembled the mischievous activity many of them undoubtedly engaged in daily in the streets.[20] In this situation, the sympathetic crowds offered some protection from the usual police reprisals, and in any case, police initially tolerated the public-supported unruliness. On the first day of the March strike, police apprehended only two individuals, one aged thirteen and the other twelve. During that strike, boys gained attention when they assisted older males in hounding operators to abandon their streetcars. Once they were successful, youngsters would jump aboard the vacated streetcars to the cheers of the throng celebrating the victory. At certain points, however, the boys' behaviour became violent. During the second strike, they threw not just mud but stones at scab-operated streetcars, provoking men to do the same. A spokesman for the strikers' executive committee, who regretted the violence, maintained that "the trouble commenced by the boys throwing rocks at the cars. A few of the rowdy element, taking advantage of the large crowd and enthusiasm displayed, took a hand in and finished the work the boys had commenced."[21] His observation neatly characterizes the manner in which boys participated in riots.

Quotidian Violence

In addition to riots involving large numbers of people, mid-Victorian Toronto saw countless incidents of violence that involved fewer people and appeared spontaneous. Young men were accused of "rowdyism" when, for recreation, they congregated in groups and preyed upon respectable residents in the streets. "Gangs of rowdies collect about the corners," the *Globe* reported in October 1853, "and they make a fiendish delight in insulting and maltreating all whom they think unable to defend themselves." On Yonge Street, a man and "an aged lady" were not only hassled but knocked down, "apparently from no other motive but a diabolical delight in working mischief."[22] On another occasion, around midnight a witness watched some "very rough-looking characters," armed with sticks and stones, attack and knock down passers-by indiscriminately.[23] In the newspapers, groups of rowdies were casually referred to as "gangs," but it appears they lacked the coherence of organized gangs.

Mid-century Toronto's most notorious gang, "the Brook's Bush Gang," was composed equally of men and women in their late teens and twenties. About a dozen men and an equal number of women in summer lived rough in Brook's Bush, a wooded area east of the Don River bridge on Queen Street East, and in winter they took shelter in nearby abandoned buildings. Gang members, who often harassed pedestrians crossing the Don Bridge, appeared before the police court many times in the 1850s and 1860s, usually on drunk and disorderly or streetwalking charges.[24] Members were involved in two murder cases. In 1856, Michael Barry, twenty-five, was convicted of manslaughter for killing a young Black man, Isaiah Sewell, who lived out on the Kingston Road and had stopped to talk to one of the women gang members on the edge of Brook's Bush. Barry had been drinking heavily and impulsively used a bottle he had in hand to clobber Sewell from behind. As he attacked, he shouted "You black b – g – r, go away!"[25] Thus, whiskey and racism combined with tragic results. In December 1859, John Sheridan Hogan, an assemblyman, stood talking to a woman gang member on the Don River bridge, which provided the opportunity for the gang to rob him, bind him up, and toss him into the river. His disappearance was a mystery until the body literally surfaced sixteen months later, and the story came out during a sensational inquest, hearings, and trials.[26] Eventually one gang member, James Brown, was executed for the murder.[27]

A rare case of murder where the victim, Samuel Reid, was a young man (he was eighteen) illustrates how things could escalate into violence and tragedy. It occurred in the working-class St John's Ward on the night of the municipal election in 1855. Election nights were routinely a time for carousing and disputes, and this was no exception. Although Reid was too young to vote, he was active in the election because as a carter he needed a city licence and thus had an interest in seeing his Orange brethren maintain their grip on power and patronage. James Spence, his uncle and a candidate in the election, while walking down Elizabeth Street with a friend shortly after the polls closed, encountered two swaggering men from the rival political camp who said "Clear the planks," demanding control of the sidewalk. The uncle and his friend refused, and in the ensuing fight Spence was knifed and cut badly. Young Reid and a companion watched his parents clean up the wound, and they volunteered to go to the druggist for a sticking plaster. On their way back, they encountered two men they mistakenly believed had perpetrated the dispute and set upon them. One of the men pulled out a bowie knife and stabbed Reid in the thigh, severing an artery. "Boys, I'm done," cried Reid, "They've stuck me." And, indeed, he bled to death. Eight men were arrested as suspects in the killing and testified at the week-long inquest, but eventually another man, John Irving, was charged after his initials were discerned faintly etched on the murder weapon. He confessed to the stabbing. Recoiling from the damage done in a street fight, the coroner's jury urged a law prohibiting the importation and sale of bowie knives. The jury observed that they were too readily available, being found for sale "not only in hardware stores but in nearly all clothing stores, to the great demoralization of our youth."[28]

Newspapers and the police sometimes pointed to violence involving young boys. Much of it was petty and connected to play, but authorities and middle-class commentators took it seriously, worried that as boys grew up their violence would become more threatening. One day in

March 1855, for instance, three cases involving youngsters came before the Toronto police court. First, three "little boys" appeared on a complaint from a resident who alleged that they had broken a window in his house. The police chief took the trouble to appear and speak against them, saying that the lads "were part of a gang of incorrigible boys who frequent the corner of Church and Richmond Streets for the purpose of indulging in obscene language, committing petty larcenies, and insulting passers-by." In response, the boys defended their behaviour by saying they were "only fooling." They were sentenced to forty-eight hours in solitary confinement. Also appearing that day was Michael Hardy, "a lad of not more than fifteen years of age" whom Police Constable Jones maintained had been "pummeling two urchins to the infinite amusement of a crowd of boys." Because it was Hardy's first offence, he was discharged with a warning. And lastly, Patrick Donovan, also not more than fifteen, was charged that day "with conducting himself in a very improper manner on Sunday evening." A policeman observed Donovan entertaining a crowd of "ragged urchins" by "flourishing a stick over his head in Donnybrook style." When the constable approached, the young showman whistled and everyone fled, but he tumbled into a snow bank and the officer nabbed him.[29] All these incidents appear to have closely connected to "fooling around."

Given that the Orange/Green celebrations and conflicts were so prevalent in Victorian Toronto, it's not surprising that young boys were involved in them. In 1858, on the evening of the Glorious Twelfth, a Catholic boy about thirteen triggered a riot by plucking an Orange lily from the chest of one Charles Manson, who was walking in a poor Catholic neighbourhood. As Manson testified in court, he turned around "to punish the boy" and was attacked by a dozen men, who struck him and kicked him in the head. Manson's friend and fellow Orangeman came to his rescue, firing a shot at one of the assailants and wounding him in the cheek. A crowd of some 150 gathered, and various scuffles occurred. Eventually Manson's friend was convicted of shooting the assailant.[30] Almost a year later, on another Orange commemorative occasion, a boy playing Protestant tunes on a fife in Cuthbert's Saloon, Adelaide Street, provoked a gang of working-class Catholics to smash the tavern's windows. Retaliation followed, when "a number of lads" marching through the streets playing militant Protestant music entered Stanley Street and broke many windows of Catholics' homes.[31] Thus, small acts by young boys could lead to serious trouble in the highly charged sectarian atmosphere of mid-century Toronto.

Mid-Victorian statistical reports on Toronto crime reinforce the point that boys and young men were accused of crimes and often convicted, but boys' crimes were overwhelmingly non-violent.[32] Boys and men under thirty-one made up about two-fifths of the police court appearances by males and about one-third of total appearances. The trend was toward more appearances before the court over time, including increased numbers of boys and young men, a development explained both by population growth and by a more active constabulary. Within the population under thirty-one, criminal appearances increased with age. Male appearances greatly outnumbered female ones in the lower age groups.

The reports mention boys in the case of only two types of crime: drunk and disorderly, and larceny and suspicion of larceny. It was reported in 1861, for example, that thirty-two boys appeared for being drunk and disorderly, and fifty-three boys for larceny or suspicion of larceny. At the time, individuals licensed to sell liquor were prohibited from selling intoxicating drink to any child or apprentice without the consent of a parent, master, or legal protector.[33] Determined lads, of course, found ways to gain access to alcohol.[34] Sometimes the police court exposed evidence of organized, premeditated larceny by youngsters. In February 1854, one newspaper alleged that about fifteen lads had formed a gang to steal from stores and the market. "Some of the secrets of the gang have come to light recently," reported the *Globe*, "which show that the members have a regular system on which they work, such as changing coats whilst committing a robbery – passing the article stolen from hand to hand, etc."[35]

Authorities deplored the extent of youth crime. Judge James Hagarty, in his address to the grand jury at the winter assizes held in Toronto in December 1865, reviewed the provincial and city statistics on crime and declared that "the darkest item in this black catalogue is that relating to young prisoners." Noting that, in 1864, there were 130 children under sixteen held in the demoralizing Toronto jail, he called it "a most melancholy fact." When the number of prisoners ranging in age from sixteen to twenty was added, the total came to 300. "We have hardly to ask," Hagarty said, "what may be the probably [sic] after-life of those who begin the world under such degrading conditions."[36] The *Globe* took up the judge's concerns, calling the 130 children serving time "a disgrace."[37]

One lad's plight tugged at Victorian heartstrings. In October 1860, Louis Palmer, about nine years old, appeared before the Police Court charged with vagrancy. The boy, "who presented a very emaciated appearance," had been afraid to return to the home of his guardian, a watchman, because he had not sold enough newspapers that day and expected a beating as a result. A constable found Palmer in a place on

Yonge Street, where he had been sleeping and hiding from his "protector." Disgusted, the police magistrate dismissed the charge and called in the guardian, whom he reprimanded for his bad treatment of the lad.[38]

In the 1870s the local conflicts most troubling to authorities involved groups of young men, both Orange and Green, whose recreational activities sometimes included street fighting. As commerce and industrialization increased in Toronto, more young men had fixed workdays and thus clearly defined leisure time in the evenings. Many of them joined either the Orange Young Britons or, on the Catholic side, the Young Irishmen's Benevolent Association, fraternal organizations where youthful, masculine conviviality could be enjoyed with likeminded fellows.[39] Newspapers reported favourably on the picnics and other outings the organizations arranged, and reporters admired the young men's appearance in colourful uniforms during processions. On the other hand, commentators disapproved of gatherings that involved heavy drinking, late-night carousing, and violence.

The *Globe* denounced street violence, whether initiated by the Young Britons or the Young Irishmen. In August 1877 the Young Irishmen held a dance at a hall, after which several men visited nearby Sholes' Saloon. "Whiskey being indulged in large quantities," observed the *Globe* report, "the young men's wits got out, and the result was a free fight, and the smashing of the windows of the place." When a constable entered the tavern and used his revolver to stop the fight, "six or seven roughs" attacked him, disarmed him, and beat his face to a pulp.[40] In August 1876 the Young Britons' excursion to St Catharines aboard the crowded steamer *Picton* turned violent: fighting erupted on-board and continued in St Catharines, resulting in more than "a few broken heads and disfigured countenances."[41] Reports such as these shaped the public's negative view of the young men and besmirched their organizations.

Those negative impressions deepened when members of the two organizations clashed. Sometimes the confrontations were unplanned. In July 1871, two Young Britons wearing orange neckerchiefs and "some other youngsters of the opposite persuasion" got into a scuffle aboard the ferry *Princess of Wales*. According to one report, "imprecations, mingled with the screams of the females on board, filled the air."[42] Sometimes these clashes were more concerted. One incident was said to have grown out of regular fights between Young Britons and Young Irishmen, who all frequented Bailey's Tavern on Front Street. After being bested too many times, eighty members of the Young Britons marched on the tavern one evening, but on their way they encountered a band of 200 Young Irishmen "and a regular fight ensued." After police dispersed the men and cleared out Bailey's, the Young Britons – marching four deep and playing party tunes – stoned a rival's house, shattering its shutters, and then proceeded to Dummer Street to fight Catholic youths.[43] Such activity occurred repeatedly during the first half of the 1870s.

Historian William Jenkins has explored the connection the daily press made between Toronto's Catholic Irish and poverty, indolence, and crime, particularly when it came to depicting, or rather caricaturing, residents of Stanley Street and Dummer Street.[44] Young militant Protestants were frequent targets of complaint and ridicule too, but significantly, similar caricaturing was not applied. For instance, in 1870 the *Globe* simply observed that "the name of 'Young Briton' has come to be very nearly synonymous with 'rowdy.'"[45]

Young Britons came in for opprobrium when, in June 1869, some of them smashed windows and the lamp over the door of Police Station No. 2 because police had detained raucous members and seized a drum used in nightly marches. The *Globe* observed that even if the police handled the Young Britons unwisely, the youths should not have attacked police and a public building, which they would have realized "if they were not foolish beyond all hope of remedy." The *Irish Canadian*, the newspaper speaking for the city's Irish Catholics, objected when the men were released, charging that it showed the police were "pandering to the tastes and wishes of these young sprigs of Orangeism."[46] Even Protestant members of the public denounced Orange raucousness. Protestant residents of the middle-class suburb of Yorkville complained in court about the band practices of Young Britons: their music was "loud, shrill, discordant, tremendous, and annoying," set the neighbourhood dogs barking, and prevented sleep.[47] Magistrates sometimes fined Young Britons heavily, indeed to the point where the district master advised cheering Young Britons that, if they were attacked, "never to mind taking their assailant to the Police Court, where, perhaps, he would get but scanty justice, but just to have satisfaction there and then." The *Globe* fumed at the remarks, saying it was "a deliberate inculcation of mob rule and violence, and an attempt to bring law and justice into contempt." The worry was that the district master's advice would be followed by "the reckless lads" and "peppery young simpletons."[48]

When the courts or newspapers criticized the Young Britons and the Young Irishmen for rowdiness, officials of the organizations sometimes responded by maintaining that their benevolent associations did not condone violence and by insisting that every sectarian scuffle did not involve the organizations. It is true that neither organization formally condoned violence; however, their clashing world views and encouragement of recreational drinking and public strutting clearly fostered conflict.

The Search for Order

In mid-Victorian Toronto, reformers and commentators troubled by the violence of boys and young men proposed various means to discourage it and bring order to the city. In the 1840s, reformers in the Legislative Assembly introduced measures intended to suppress Orange violence. The 1842 Freedom of Elections Act, one of many mid-century alterations in election procedures, aimed at making intimidation and violence at the polls less likely. The 1843 Act to Restrain Party Processions in Certain Cases banned processions, the target being Orange processions in particular.[49] Seething with a sense of injustice at being singled out, Orangemen defied the ban by walking in procession on many occasions. Because the law proved unenforceable, a Reform government repealed it in 1851. Thereafter, when violence related to processions occurred, voices demanded a ban, but opponents ensured that no legislative action succeeded by pointing to the failure of the 1843 act.

A changing culture within the Orange Order proved to be more effective in reducing Orange unruliness. Orange leaders, often higher up the class ladder than the majority of the brethren, worked to make Ontario Orangeism more respectable and self-disciplined. Lodges increasingly used their disciplinary powers to prohibit drunkenness and unruliness at lodge meetings, in effect joining in the popular mid-century temperance campaign. To enhance the Orange Order's public face, lodges introduced dress codes and standards of behaviour for Orangemen taking part in public processions. Members also touted the order's philanthropic activities. Orange leaders denounced violence, and when the Young Britons persisted, the Orange Order in 1881 brought the Young Britons firmly within the order and its discipline.[50] Squabbles in the streets became increasingly rare. Many young men of Orange propensities got an opportunity in 1885 to engage in violence – this time state-sanctioned – when, as young militiamen, they ventured to the North-West as part of the Canadian military's bid to suppress the Riel resistance. The lads could imagine themselves to be avenging the "murder" of Thomas Scott, the Ontario Orangeman executed by Riel's provisional government in 1870. In their 1885 military action, in contrast to their previous street violence, they had the complete support of the Toronto public (see chapter 5).[51]

Another strategy for diffusing violence was to channel rivalries into organized sports. Both Protestant and Catholic groups formed clubs to engage in popular sports, such as lacrosse, football, and rowing, sometimes with teams competing across the ethno-religious divide. Increasingly regulated, the games never completely suppressed violence, but at least it was less threatening when it was represented as rugged, manly athleticism. In August 1859 a team of twelve Irish Catholics challenged players from the English Protestant St George's Society to a game of football, to the delight of 3,500 spectators. In May 1873, 8,000 spectators watched the Montreal Shamrocks, the visiting Irish Catholic lacrosse team, beat the Orange-dominated Toronto Lacrosse Club, a victory hailed by Shamrock supporters as "a great day for Ireland." The Irish Catholic Union's tug-of-war squad competed with the Orange-dominated regimental and police teams. Sports historians Dennis Ryan and Kevin Wamsley argue that, for Toronto's Irish Catholics, "competitive sport provided legitimate venues for the celebration of physical forms of masculinity, demonstrations of strength through victory, and masculine honour because the contests were rule bound and sanctioned by the Protestant majority."[52]

Police reform offered another means to discourage violence in Toronto. Incidents such as the circus riot had exposed the ineffectiveness and Orange bias of the force.[53] In 1858 a new Board of Police Commissioners gained control from corrupt municipal politicians. The following year, it fired the entire Toronto police force, including the chief, and created a new force that re-employed fewer than half of the former constables and fewer Orangemen. Using Boston's system of police patrols as a model, the constables were put on regular patrols to deter lawbreaking and to model public behaviour.[54] The constables were to be more detached from the local community so that they could fairly apply the law. It is likely that the newly structured force did deter some street crime, given formal reports that such crimes declined in the 1860s. Certainly the new chief constable boasted that, thanks to improved policing, "street rows and wanton assaults, committed on respectable persons, by disorderly and turbulent people, commonly called rowdies, and which were formerly of frequent occurrence in Toronto, are now very rare."[55] Like all the city's municipal institutions, the police force continued to be overwhelmingly composed of Protestants, and charges of ethno-religious bias continued. The reforms marked a step toward a liberal order, but the Orangemen's definition of order had not vanished. The reformed force nevertheless was said to have been an effective deterrent to disorder on several occasions, including during some parades.[56]

In contrast to attempts to rein in young men as part of a strategy aimed at all adult males, reformers saw unruly boys as a distinct social category that required specialized responses. A few well-educated social reformers mounted a campaign to address "the boy problem," by which they meant the presence in the streets of destitute lads whose pathetic appearance and lack of Christian virtue both drew at the heartstrings of sentimental Victorians and demanded stern measures of social control. Reformers urged that orphaned, neglected, and vagrant boys be provided with a substitute for the home life and supervision they lacked. Confident that the lads were young enough to be malleable, reformers believed the children could be taught good habits and a Christian outlook, thus saving them from a life of sin and hardship and an afterlife of torment, as well as saving society from crime and its many costs.[57] The projects pursued by the reformers drew upon ideas circulating among reforming elites in the North Atlantic world, a public sphere that promoted liberal modernity.

In Toronto, reformers adopted several institution-building strategies to address the boy problem, three of which focused on schooling. First, they supported free common schools for all, justifying them on numerous grounds, including the belief that everyone would benefit from a schooling regime that would reverse the descent of vagrant and neglected children into crime and unruliness.[58] Experience soon showed, however, that few such children attended the common schools, and in any event, the parents and teachers of children who did attend regarded the urchins as an unpleasant and disruptive element that should be excluded. Second, reformers proposed building separate institutions, "ragged schools," specifically for the urchins, where philanthropists or churches would provide clothing and lodging. When a bill was drafted in 1862 to establish them, however, the public objected to this diversion of funds from the common schools, and this provided the momentum to kill the measure.[59] Third, reformers advocated that the state open industrial schools so that authorities could compel the attendance of incorrigibles who would be schooled and taught practical trades. Such schools would provide a viable alternative for magistrates who maintained that sentencing boys to the jail and the reformatory only increased the likelihood of recidivism. Ontario's 1874 Industrial School Act enabled school boards to found such institutions, but parsimonious boards were slow to do so.[60]

Reformers also campaigned to create home-like institutions to substitute for the proper families that the urchins lacked. In the 1830s, Toronto's House of Industry began its decades-long assistance to orphaned boys and girls, mainly by apprenticing them on farms, where it was hoped they would be useful, learn skills, and benefit from the family setting.[61] In the 1850s, reformers proposed building a provincial reformatory but were divided over whether it should house only juveniles convicted of crimes or if authorities should compel neglected children – "incipient criminals" – to be incarcerated as well. When the state established a reformatory for Canada West at Penetanguishene in 1858, it housed a heterogeneous population: convicts and others, and small lads and young men up to twenty-one years of age.[62] It was not the specialized facility envisaged by reformers. The Toronto police magistrate hesitated to sentence boys to the reformatory because he "never knew of a boy being sent there without becoming worse."[63]

Finally, reformers also promoted and established "children's homes," philanthropically supported institutions intended to replicate an ideal middle-class family situation, where street children could be cared for, disciplined, and instructed in Christianity, morality, and the habits of industry. Part of a transnational response to neglected children, the so-called family plan had been developed in France and Britain and transferred to Massachusetts and Ohio shortly before it arrived in Ontario.[64] The metaphor of the family was both inclusive, giving troublesome children a proper place within the community, and hierarchical, justifying and reinforcing the authority supervisors had over them. In Toronto, a group of Protestant men and women, inspired by a similar institution in London, England, opened the non-denominational (but Protestant) Toronto Boys' Home in 1859. It soon became one of more than a dozen children's homes in the province.[65] Its purpose was to house destitute boys who had not been convicted of crime but who lacked families to care properly for them, and in this way to aid in "the prevention of juvenile crime."[66] G.W. Allan, heir to a local fortune, headed a board of prominent men, but its driving force was "lady volunteers," women from establishment families.[67] The venture was financed from donations and a small grant from the city council, which endorsed the home but hesitated to be generous in an era when public funding for welfare was viewed with extreme scepticism.[68] At the home, a male superintendent and a matron assumed the role of stand-in parents for the boys, but how many boys embraced that viewpoint is unclear. The plan was to train boys and send them to paying jobs – preferably in family settings – and a large portion of the boys were sent out to work.[69] Many other boys stayed in the home for a while and then were released to a parent or relative, often to the distress of the home managers, who feared the lads were returning to exploitative or risky family settings.[70] After a long campaign, reformers in 1872 succeeded in securing the right of the home's managers to assume legal guardianship of neglected children, thus preventing "unworthy" parents from taking control.[71] Charlotte Neff persuasively argues that for all their shortcomings, this home and similar ones provided destitute and desperate parents with appreciated services, gave the first official recognition to child neglect, and laid a foundation for child welfare work taken up later by the foster parent movement.[72]

A decade after the 1859 founding of the Boy's Home, Toronto had two examples (one Catholic, the other Protestant) of a more specialized type of home for boys who worked principally as newsboys but also as bootblacks and at other trades. The condition, habits, and reputation of these boys drew the attention of reformers. The opening of a home for newsboys in New York was widely publicized and provided inspiration for other cities, including Toronto.[73] In 1868 the Roman Catholic Church, as part of a vigorous period of institution building, opened St Nicholas Home.[74] Newsboys and bootblacks were expected to work at their jobs in the daytime and return in the evening.[75] Boys in the street trades were by no means all Irish Catholics; an 1868 count found more than half of 200 such boys reported being Protestants. In 1869, a discussion in the Toronto diocesan synod of the Anglican Church and the activism of Professor Daniel Wilson of University College led to the opening of the News-boys' Lodging Home with accommodations for fifty boys.[76] Hailed as an improvement over miserable lodging houses where the boys "squander their petty gains in gambling and dissipation," this home encouraged boys to avoid pauperization by paying twelve cents a day for food and lodging from their earnings. In 1873 the News-boys' Home reported that it had sheltered 628 boys since its opening and had sent 246 of them to jobs in the countryside.[77] Even so, the home's record disappointed its advocates. Its strict regime led many of its targets to opt for the freedom and pleasures of the penny boarding house or to remain with their exploitative or lax parents.

None of the specialized institutions intended to address the boy problem fulfilled advocates' expectations. Inadequate philanthropy and state support left the institutions struggling to reach their goals. Moreover, their approach failed to address the underlying structural problems of poverty, unemployment, and inadequate incomes that contributed to the hardships these boys faced, nor could they counteract the appeal of independence and transgression so central to the subculture the street boys had created for themselves.[78] Moreover, the unruliness of boys extended well beyond the underclass that preoccupied these reformers; it was part of a much broader boy culture, if not bred in the bone.

Conclusion

This chapter has demonstrated that in mid-nineteenth-century Toronto, boys and young men played a significant role in social disorder, which in turn spurred the search for order. When riots erupted, young men and boys were usually there. The press often highlighted their role as a means to dismiss the seriousness of the disorder and defend the city's respectability. Boys and young men also engaged in minor confrontations that grew from many causes, including lads hanging about the streets looking for a diversion, playful but destructive stone-tossing, performances of masculinity that determined the pecking order on the street, and Orange/Green and other partisan tensions that led to fisticuffs. Such incidents meant that boys and young men also encountered authorities when police and the courts attempted to suppress lawbreaking and disorder. Evidence strongly suggests that the behaviour and encounters of Toronto boys and young men were not unusual. This chapter is an invitation to scholars researching disorder in other localities or regions to look for the presence of boys and young men.

Boys and young men, moreover, were prominent in mid-Victorian Toronto's search for order. Middle-class commentators and authorities scolded and shamed young men in ways more likely to antagonize than to quell young hotheads. Top-down attempts to contain young men's disorderly practices were subsumed within broader suppressive strategies aimed at males of all ages: the provincial state's discouragement of intimidation at the polls and its ill-fated ban on Orange processions, and the municipality's police reforms. Disorder was also brought under attack, and partly under control, by the Orangemen's campaign of self-discipline, which took special aim at the rowdiness of the Young Britons. Organized sport steered rivalries toward less threatening pursuits. By contrast, authorities and reformers devised institutional responses tailored for youth reforms focused on the waifs and strays whose predicament, it was feared, made them criminals and "incipient criminals" and thus a threat to property and persons alike. Reforms aimed at disciplining youths reflected the growing power of bourgeois interests in an industrializing city. Through common, ragged, and industrial schools, the provincial reformatory, and boys' homes, reformers hoped to provide the specialized institutions that would convert disorderly youths into industrious and moral contributors to the expanding, industrializing city. In their approaches to constructing and resolving "the boy problem," Toronto reformers explicitly drew upon and acted in concert with campaigns launched by reformers in many cities, especially London and New York.

A little later, when labour disputes enveloped industrializing Toronto in the 1880s, youths once again played a prominent role in the street theatre that characterized major strikes, which in turn prompted calls to reassert public order.

7
Strikers and Their Supporters

Amid jeers of "Scabs!" and "Rats!" a crowd of thousands of working-class Toronto men and boys surged toward the horse-drawn streetcar operated by strike-breakers. Coal heavers had used their wagons to block its passage through the downtown street, and now it was an easy target. Youths grabbed handfuls of mud from the slushy streets, hurling them jubilantly at the car and at both the driver and the conductor, who stood exposed on the front and rear platforms. In frustration, the operators gave up the contest, abandoned the streetcar, and slinked away through the jostling masses. A ringleader from the crowd boarded the car to tell the women passengers they had better get out, which they quickly did. In triumph, a gang of men hefted the car from the tracks and, turning it at right angles to them, set it down ignominiously. Cheers rang again and again from the throng in celebration of their little victory.

It was 11 March 1886, the second day of a labour dispute triggered by unionists in the employ of the privately owned Toronto Street Railway Company (TSR), which had a monopoly on streetcar services in the fast-growing city. Commentators divided over how serious these public disturbances were. Judge McDougall, chairman of the Board of Police Commissioners, was concerned about maintaining public order and insisted it was imperative "to demonstrate the fact that a mob cannot do with this town as it pleases."[1] Yet William Howland, Toronto's urban reform mayor, appeared less perturbed by the crowd actions when he publicly chastised the TSR for provoking the dispute with its anti-union policy. Journalists writing for the daily press were struck by the good-humoured mood of the vast crowds and maintained that even the police, hard-pressed as they were to maintain order, seemed to enter into the fun at least in the dispute's early stages. The air of tolerance extended even to commuters, who, though deprived of their ride to work, seemed pleased to see the TSR getting its comeuppance.

This incident and similar ones arose during the first of two disputes in the spring of 1886, when about 300 male conductors and drivers employed by the TSR defended their right to belong to a union. The employees were being organized by the Knights of Labor during its heyday in Canada and the United States. The two linked disputes of March and May 1886 exemplify the struggle prevalent in the late nineteenth century between fledgling unions and determined employers who, unhampered by the law, would employ only workers who had signed an ironclad agreement not to join a union. Because the TSR held a municipal charter giving it a monopoly on the provision of streetcar service in the city, the large streetcar-dependent public was adversely affected by the disruptions, yet the vast majority of residents supported the strikers by avoiding the skeleton service the TSR managed to provide with strike-breakers. Meanwhile, thousands of working-class men and boys took to the streets to express opposition to the company and its strike-breakers and to participate in the excitement. Large, boisterous, and sometimes violent demonstrations caught the attention of the press, as well as city authorities responsible for maintaining law and order. Journalists shaped their accounts of events, presenting them as spectacles.[2]

Historians have studied this pair of strikes when documenting the rise of the Knights of Labor during Toronto's industrial revolution, when narrating the story of Howland's colourful two-year term as mayor, and when analysing the legal issues raised by the strikes.[3] This chapter uses the detailed coverage of the disputes in daily newspapers to re-create the dramatic street demonstrations and to argue that even these highly contentious disputes had their playful side. In contrast to the self-disciplined behaviour of manly unionists, large numbers of boys and men in the crowds displayed their aggressive masculinity in transgressive and, for them, pleasurable ways that entertained the public – for a while at least – and at the same time defied the TSR and worried police authorities and union leaders.

The crowd actions during the streetcar strikes are good examples of what Charles Tilly has called "contentious performances," where people gather to act out their objections to developments in ways that communicate their demands and challenge authority, drawing from a limited repertoire of actions that usually change only incrementally.[4] The eighteenth-century English bread riots, with their strong appeals to custom and community standards of fairness, are classic examples of spontaneous but purposeful crowd actions, and Tilly has called them contentious performances.[5] The crowd actions surrounding the 1886 Toronto street railway strikes were part of this tradition. Name-calling as a shaming exercise, mud-slinging, and the massing of unruly people were components of a repertoire long used by crowds to object to and prevent actions they deemed adverse to the community interest. During the 1886 disputes, the overwhelmingly male crowds targeted the strike-breakers, and in back of these handy targets lay the street railway monopoly and the municipal authority, which had granted the charter. Yet these strikes occurred on the cusp of the modern industrial age, for which street railways provided a symbol of industry and modernity.[6] TSR employees' responses – forming a union and striking – were equally indicative of the new industrial order, and the self-disciplined behaviour of the male picketers was a modern contentious performance that occurred alongside but differed from the more spontaneous and unruly crowd actions. At times, an atmosphere of jubilation prevailed on the streets that did not escape the notice of journalists and that they perhaps encouraged by the tone of their reporting. The newspaper reports of the colourful street clashes probably encouraged yet more people to come out to witness the fun and join in the action. My analysis expands on scholars' understanding of contentious performances by underscoring that crowds could be both purposeful and playful.

The daily press provides the best source for reconstructing these street performances during the streetcar disputes; indeed, aside from the dailies we have little evidence at all about the crowd behaviour.[7] In 1886, interest in public events was such that five daily newspapers met the demand of Toronto's reading public: the *Globe*, the *Mail*, the *Telegram*, the *News*, and the *World*.[8] A newspaper's political slant shaped its reporting on the strikes; for instance, the *Mail* was hostile to the strikers while the radical-leaning *News* sympathized with them throughout.[9] Nevertheless, there were similarities in the style of reporting across all the dailies. Each newspaper had a reporter or reporters (articles had no by-line) observing the events closely and telling stories about them in as lively a manner as the writer could muster.[10] In these reports, to the frustration of the historian, journalists did not conduct "man in the street" interviews, as would be done in later decades, so the voices of those engaged in the street encounters are muffled – except when they yelled "rats" and the like.

Following Jürgen Habermas, historians have pointed to the crucial role played by newspapers in forming a public and promoting deliberative democracy in nineteenth-century Ontario.[11] During the 1886 disputes, the press represented a divided public and highlighted actions or divergent modes of behaviour more than competing discourses. Some members of the public chose to ride the streetcars operated by strike-breakers. Picketers made use of the public streets strategically

Two-horse streetcar with driver and conductor, Toronto, ca 1892.
When strike-breakers ran such cars, the open platforms exposed
them to projectiles and verbal assaults.
Source: City of Toronto Archives (William James Family Fonds), Item 1356.

against those streetcars to persuade the company to back down on its opposition to unionism. A larger portion of the public formed crowds that physically and verbally inhibited strike-breaking operations and turned the streets into sites of both fun and danger. Much less visible in the press was another large portion of the public that stood aloof from the action. Ultimately, the divisions within the public had an impact on how the disputes ended.

The potential of street railway strikes to provoke crowd actions and violence has long been acknowledged. In the course of the disputes, the *Telegram* editorialized about recent street railway disputes in Chicago, St Louis, and New York, where "public sympathy for the strikers was expressed by obstructions on the rails and in several cases by assaults on the substitutes who manned the cars."[12] Labour historians have examined street railway strikes involving crowd actions in Canadian cities such as London, Hamilton, Saint John, and Winnipeg, as well as in American cities. As is evident from these studies, street railway disputes in Toronto were part of a wider pattern of public indignation and protest about streetcar service and company labour policies.[13] The Toronto disputes of 1886 are part of this well-documented pattern of violent confrontation; however, those conflicts included playful performances that have not been sufficiently appreciated in earlier histories of them, or of other street railway disputes, for that matter. The stories told by newspaper journalists about the Toronto disputes were intended not just to inform but also to entertain. Labour historians have consistently pointed to the serious issues and risks for working people that strikes inevitably involve, but it may be worth paying more attention to crowd dynamics, the appeal of joining large crowd actions, contrasting collective expressions of masculinity, and shifts in the mood of confrontations over the course of a dispute.

Setting the Stage

By 1886, the TSR's charter from the City of Toronto was a quarter century old and the company had developed an extensive network of routes throughout the metropolitan area, whose population stood at 160,000.[14] More than 300 employees drove the horse-drawn streetcars, worked as conductors collecting fares aboard them, or toiled in the company's large barns at George and Front Streets near the city's commercial centre. The drivers and conductors were not regarded as skilled workers at the time. In an era when it was widely known how to handle horses, drivers and stable hands could be quickly trained and easily replaced. Conductors were routinely taught the job in about a week. In 1886 the TSR paid most of its employees only $9 per seventy-two-hour week (six days of twelve hours). The possibility of steady work, however, made it relatively attractive employment at a time when most common labourers expected frequent breaks in employment, including long winter layoffs. The main threat facing street railwaymen was sudden dismissal, often without explanation. Reports in Toronto's daily press occasionally detailed the hardships of TSR employees. On a rainy day in April 1885 a conductor told a *Globe* reporter that his pay was only nine dollars per six-day week and that he actually worked fifteen hours a day, so that by the day's end he was exhausted. That day he was drenched to the skin because he had been standing outside on a car platform for his entire shift. He also pointed out that it was up to conductors to come up with the eighteen dollars required each day for tickets and making change.[15] Streetcar workers thus had good reasons to organize for protection and improvement of their jobs, but until the coming to Toronto of the Knights of Labor in the 1880s, unionization appeared impossible because existing unions were composed of craftsmen, who relied on their scarce skills to build effective organizations.

Toronto's 1886 street railway disputes marked a local high point in the continent-wide surge in labour militancy and class conflict during the 1880s. As historians have shown, amid industrialization, unions proliferated, none more so than the Knights of Labor, which arrived in Toronto from the United States in 1882.[16] The Knights organized craftsmen into "local assemblies" that closely resembled craft-union locals; more innovatively, it also organized other workers into "mixed assemblies" of wage-earners from various workplaces or with varying levels of skill. Unusual too for the time, the Knights reached out to previously excluded workers, including women and Blacks, though not Chinese workers. Their approach was well-suited for workers in the many new factories opening in cities such as Toronto during the period of rapid industrialization that had begun in the 1870s, and it worked for the street railway employees, too. Throughout Ontario, and especially in Toronto, membership in Knights' assemblies and strike activity surged from October 1885 to March 1886, a moment dubbed by contemporaries "the great awakening." During that eight-month period, Toronto workers established no fewer than thirty-five local assemblies before the Knights' key Toronto leader, the Irish Canadian printer Daniel J. O'Donoghue, called for a breather. The Toronto assemblies challenged their employers, often over issues of workers' control, and sometimes struck, notwithstanding the preference of the Knights, as an organization, for methods of settling disputes other than by strikes, which were seen as a risky last resort.[17]

The Toronto disputes arose amid ongoing tensions between the public and its sole provider of streetcar services. While the TSR's monopoly agreement with the city made sense, given that competing street railway systems would have been impossibly unwieldy, it meant that few residents had any other option than to travel on the TSR system, which carried more than 8.5 million passengers in 1886.[18] Many riders viewed the TSR as complacent, unchecked by competitors, and insufficiently responsive to public complaints about the quality of service. Moreover, fuzzy language in the charter had left the city unable to compel the company to keep the tracks level with the roadways. The TSR's failure to maintain the streets in good condition and its success in ducking its obligation to do so in a much-publicized legal case added to public grumbling about the TSR.[19] And there was a litany of additional complaints. Suburbanites groused that they lacked adequate, well-connected services. Sabbath observers decried the TSR's bid to operate Sunday streetcar service. Women declared the cars uncomfortable.[20] In wintertime, residents objected to the company practice of clearing the tracks of snow by piling it to the sides, thus blocking the roads to the inconvenience of all other vehicles. At one point Yonge Street residents hired boys to shovel the snow back onto the tracks.[21]

The TSR and its president, Senator Frank Smith, had many critics but also some admirers. A prominent Torontonian, Smith was Conservative leader in the Senate, a cabinet colleague of Sir John A. Macdonald, and a wealthy businessman with diverse interests, including liquor wholesaling.[22] Still, it must have been easy for street railway employees and other workers to imagine that Smith derived his riches and power from the too generous terms of the TSR charter and the company's cost-cutting, which had resulted in a mean-spirited labour policy. Toronto's many Orangemen were no admirers of wealthy Irish Roman Catholic power brokers like Smith, and charged that he gave preference in hiring to Catholics and was using his connections to bring in French Canadian Catholics as strike-breakers.[23] Toronto's Irish Catholics probably had a different view of a dispenser of federal Tory patronage to local Catholics, an employer who at least did not discriminate against them, and a Horatio Alger whose rags-to-riches life showed what Catholics could achieve locally, though many Catholic workers objected fiercely to Smith's anti-union policies.

The surge in the Knights of Labor in the mid-1880s alarmed the president of the TSR, who in 1885 ordered his employees to sign an ironclad agreement, whereby each man vowed on the pain of discharge never to join the Knights or any other labour organization. Smith wanted nothing to do with unions; he must have seen them as a threat to his profits in a business where wages made up a substantial part of operating costs. At the time, the "ironclad" was a familiar employer's weapon, and it had recently been given local prominence when the *Mail* imposed it on its printing staff.[24] Smith's imposition of the ironclad prompted some TSR employees to form a Knights of Labor assembly in early November, but Smith succeeded in halting the union drive. Four months later, in early March 1886, pro-union street railwaymen revived their organizing attempt, enlisting a few dozen men in the Knights of Labor.[25] It became clear almost immediately that Smith and his superintendent knew about the renewed activity, for the company hired several men who began a week's training to be drivers and conductors, apparently in readiness to replace the unionists once they had been weeded out. In response to this provocation, late in the evening of Tuesday, 9 March, unionists held an emergency meeting at the Knights' offices in the fashionable Arcade Building on Yonge Street. Smith's timekeepers stood at the door, noting down the names of employees entering the hall. The blatant intimidation did not stop the meeting – a sign of the determination of at least a core of the company's employees.[26]

The March Dispute

Armed with up-to-date information on the activists, the company made its move on the morning after the union meeting. When employees arrived at the streetcar barns early on Wednesday, 10 March, the union men were barred from entering. Nearly all the other employees there at the time – 150 to 200 men – opted to act in solidarity by not starting work. The TSR was able to send out only a few streetcars early that morning.

Toronto newspapers immediately cast blame for the dispute. In its report headed "Trouble in Toronto," the unsympathetic *Mail* blamed the disruption of an essential service on employees who had "readily assented" to signing the ironclad but had now broken their contracts by organizing a Knights of Labor assembly.[27] By contrast, the pro-union *News* presented the dispute as a lockout and "another illustration of the arbitrary and inconsiderate policy actuating the management of the monopoly."[28] During the early hours of the dispute, confusion prevailed. The union had not known when the dismissals would come exactly, nor the extent of support from drivers and conductors not in the union. Understandably, men clustered in knots in the streets outside the TSR barns conferring about the turn of events and what to do next. Also on the scene from the start were at least sixty police constables, who pressed the groups of men to disperse.[29]

Into the scene stepped locked-out unionized driver Matthew Maloney, who shouted to the men, saying there would be a meeting in the union hall and inviting all to attend. By taking charge of the situation, he aimed to rally the unorganized men to the Knights and to get the street railwaymen off the streets so that they would not be tempted to disturb the peace and thus antagonize the public or trigger arrests. Under the criminal law, the activities of picketers were tightly bound and authorities had discretion in making arrests for "watching and besetting" and "obstructing," vaguely defined offences that gave much latitude to law enforcers.[30] On orders from the chief constable, Francis Collier Draper, an officer charged Maloney with disorderly conduct. None of the reporters described anything at all disorderly about Maloney's behaviour, but certainly it was conduct not in the interest of the TSR. In any event, the locked-out men were soon off the scene, discussing their situation in a meeting closed to the press. The *Telegram* nevertheless reported that at the meeting 100 new members joined the union.[31]

Most Torontonians got wind of the dispute when no streetcar arrived to take them to work. Residents walked to their jobs that morning, an unfamiliar but not impossible prospect for most residents in a city with still-limited sprawl. Large numbers of people who were not at work took to the streets in the vicinity of the barns. "The streets and sidewalks presented a surging mass of humanity," reported the *Mail*. "Men and boys stood ankle-deep in mud and slush, eagerly discussing the different phases of the rights between capital and labour."[32] The crowds soon showed sympathy with the locked-out men and hostility to the TSR. When the company used its remaining skeleton staff of mostly older employees to send out some streetcars, the crowds grew excited, hurling insults at the drivers and conductors who stayed on the job. Men shouted "Scabs!," "Rats!," and "Get off the car!" Men and boys slung mud at the streetcars, which were easy targets. It was good fun for those doing the throwing, no doubt, but the behaviour had meaning for the public. When the mud splattered the cars, it violated but did not actually damage company property. Such conduct indicates the ritualistic character of the demonstrations, as well as the self-imposed limits to the hostility, which reduced the likelihood of criminal charges but still conveyed a firm message. Furthermore, when the cars emerged from the city core into streets less crowded with spectators, the mud on the cars reminded any would-be patrons that it was not business as usual. The design of the streetcars ensured that drivers standing on the open front platforms and conductors standing on open rear ones received their share of muddy missiles.

After the unionists and the employees who supported them ended their meeting at the Arcade, according to the sympathetic *News*, they marched "in orderly manner" down to the barns and "formed themselves on either side of the street, laughing at the few men who came along on the cars."[33] Probably they jeered rather than laughed at the strike-breakers, but it certainly appears that as picketers they avoided behaviour that might have led to arrests. Journalists were agreed that, unlike so many in the excited crowds, the unionists and supportive employees showed self-control and behaved peacefully.

Around noon, the crowd near the barns grew much larger as men and boys released from their workplaces for mealtime joined in the action. The reporter from the *Telegram* observed that anyone expressing support for the company "was at once singled out as a target for a mud fusillade."[34] At that time about eighteen cars were still attempting to operate, but one by one the operators gave up. When operators signified their decision to stop working, "long and loud cheers rent the air, renewed again and again."[35] Forced to abandon his car and passengers by the crowd that had taken control of the streetcar, one older driver "made tracks as speedily as possible from the scene of his defeat."[36] These were indeed contests where militant demonstrators challenged the operators amid the roar of an audience.

Adding to the crowd's delight, a comedy routine played out in the street. Each time a constable arrived with a team of horses to remove an abandoned car, the officer would attach one horse and then, while he set about attaching the other, a lad would unhitch the first one. As quickly as the policeman could circle round and rehitch the other horse, the lad would undo the opposite one. The charade could go on for some time amid howls from the appreciative audience.[37]

In the afternoon the crowd actions escalated, while wagon-drivers intervened to disrupt streetcar service. Shortly after two p.m., coal carts, express wagons, and other vehicles blocked the passage of two North Toronto cars coming down Yonge Street. The coal carters, whose sympathy for the Knights was strong, showed special determination in using their wagons in a show of solidarity with the locked-out men. A scene deserving of vaudeville then ensued. Police urged the driver of the lead vehicle blocking the North Toronto streetcars to move along, and it moved a little ahead, but none of the others budged an inch. The constable was forced to proceed down the line urging each vehicle along. But of course, by the time the constables reached farther down the line, the lead vehicles had halted. Back the police had to go to the beginning of the line to try once again. The futile exercise amused the growing crowd of mocking observers.[38]

Within a few minutes many more vehicles had arrived on the scene, and the two streetcars, as well as a northbound one that had arrived in the interim, were at the centre of a huge jam. The *Mail* reporter called this situation "very dangerous," with so many horse-drawn vehicles being crushed together.[39] Men unhitched the horses from one of the streetcars, putting them in the charge of "a small boy" to take them to the barns. "As the boy mounted the horses," said the *News*, "cheer after cheer broke from the victorious crowd." The men then picked up the traces and pulled one of the cars along the tracks. When they rested, a crowd lifted the car and placed it crosswise on the rails, another marker of victory loudly celebrated by the throng. Eventually, after boys had plastered the entire car with mud, it was lifted back onto the tracks, boys boarded it for a free ride, and men exuberantly pushed it to the barns.[40]

Throughout the afternoon people continued to disrupt service and persuade the few remaining operators to abandon their duties When women passengers were travelling in a streetcar, the demonstrators showed their chivalry: "A ringleader would come late into the car and say: 'Now ladies, you'd better come out; they're going to turn her over.'"[41] They never did turn over a car, but instead turned cars crossways on the tracks.

So things continued until the end of the afternoon, when the company abandoned all attempts to provide service for fear of escalating trouble from protesters emboldened by the growing darkness. To ensure peace, 150 police were ordered out for duty that night, but they encountered no unrest. Reflecting on the first day of the strike, the press commended the police for tolerating some teasing and for desisting from forceful interventions. The *News* complemented the officers on their "excellent judgement" in exercising crowd control and averting "a riot of considerable dimensions." The *Mail* similarly praised the police for their levelheadedness but noted too that the crowd's good humour had prevented ugly confrontations. Whether the constables were under orders to go gently was not made clear, but it is likely that their approach was affected by the mayor's sympathy for the opponents of the TSR, widespread community indignation about its provocative labour policy, and the continuing good mood on the streets. The press might have represented the day's spirited crowd actions as violence bordering on riot, but according even to the unsympathetic *Mail*, "the whole performance appeared more like a practical joke than anything else, as the utmost good humour prevailed, injury being done to neither person nor property."[42]

Predictably there were also critics of the rowdiness and the police tolerance of it. The *Monetary Times*, Toronto's business journal, registered its concern that youths at the start of the dispute had gotten away with lawbreaking at a moment when law enforcement had been lax: "The street gamins got a lesson in violence which, for the rest of their lives, will give them false notions of the impunity with which the laws may be violated and property and life endangered."[43]

The crowds that flowed into Toronto streets on this occasion were some of the largest seen in the city during strikes in the nineteenth century. Similarly large crowds appeared in other cities during streetcar disputes. Historians have accounted for these exceptional numbers by observing that residents could not ignore the disputes because they were so inconvenienced when deprived of their essential means of transportation. Moreover, the disputes gave them an opportunity to express their many complaints about the monopolies that ran the systems, and not least about the injustices companies did to their employees, who came most directly into the line of fire of ruthless, cost-cutting monopolists. In the case of the Toronto dispute, a "moral economy" argument has been advanced. Sympathetic working-class residents perceived the lockout as a breach of public trust in that the TSR had deprived the public of an essential service, denied workingmen the fundamental right to form a union, and employed despised strike-breakers in a bid to defeat the workers and their union.[44] This argument is persuasive. In addition, however, the crowds were probably swollen by people drawn by the thrill of participating in a lively public event where the rules of behaviour had been temporarily suspended, where boys and men could let loose, and where the excitement was all the more intense because the outcomes of the conflicts were uncertain.[45]

Who were the people who formed crowds in the streets? The *News* referred to them as "working men" with, occasionally, the presence of a "boy." The less sympathetic *Globe* described some of the most active in the crowds disparagingly as "street arabs and message boys." It noted as well the presence on the sidelines of factory employees, who appeared at the windows and doorways of their workplaces to jeer the streetcar employees on duty. The *Mail* referred to "the idle element" and to "thousands of sympathizing artizans" who supported the locked-out workers, and it noted specifically the vigour of various "youngsters of the newsboy persuasion" and "stalwart boys." The reporter from the *World* preferred to speak of "crowds" or the "mob," though he noted there were "full-grown men" as well as "gamins."[46] What seems clear is that the demonstrators were overwhelmingly male, but of varying ages from young boys on up, and that they were working-class. Some of the demonstrators were employed men who found ways of participating during their noon meal break, but most appear to have been available to spend long hours on the streets, probably because they were unemployed.

Also unexamined and barely mentioned in the press was any presence of women either as demonstrators or bystanders. No doubt some women would have encountered the confrontations as they travelled through city streets doing their marketing and other errands. Other women would have come out to witness the excitement or to register their own objections to the company, as women did in the 1906 Hamilton streetcar strike, where such behaviour was documented.[47] Yet I have found only three brief asides that allude to women being in the crowds or on the sidelines in 1886. The women who do get mentioned frequently were "ladies" – middle-class women – who chose to ride the TSR streetcars operated by strike-breakers. The press emphasized again and again that the crowds were composed of men and boys.

The bolder boys and men in the crowds, the ones not content to be bystanders, expressed an aggressive and sometimes transgressive masculinity honed in boyhoods spent on the streets.[48] Patterns of behaviour learned in boyhood were practised by large numbers of working-class men when circumstances were right, as in the street railway disputes. Spontaneously and without thinking, they drew on a deep well of masculine experience. Theirs was a tough manliness that could transgress community standards and risk breaking the law. T. Phillips Thompson, the labour journalist and intellectual advocate of the Knights of Labor, saw the kind of violence engaged in by the Toronto crowd as reprehensible but understandable. "Whenever human rights are defied and trampled upon," he wrote in the *Palladium of Labor*, "there will be aroused a spirit of resistance which may overpass its bonds and find vent in actions which no reasonable or humane man can approve."[49]

All the newspapers stressed that, unlike the crowds, the union men avoided violence. "To the strikers' credit," said the *World*, "they took little or no part in the street disturbances."[50] Keeping their cool, the unionists expressed their masculinity in ways that had more to do with the proud family provider and model citizen or subject. When challenged by reporters about having broken the ironclad, one man asked rhetorically: "If my family was starving, do you not think I would do anything to get them bread?"[51] He positioned the workers as male breadwinners forced by the company to compromise principles in order to provide for their families, but now in a position to assert their rights as men and British subjects. Moreover, the self-control displayed by the street railway unionists in a hot situation, at a time when men around them were displaying physicality and impatience with the law, positioned the unionists as responsible men who were determined to win their cause by acting within the law. The opposite of the spontaneous and seemingly instinctual behaviour of boys and men in the surrounding crowds, the picketers' consciously controlled behaviour was meant to advance their collective goal of winning the right to unionize. Bonds of solidarity among the picketers helped regulate the behaviour so as to benefit their cause. No doubt the admonishments of the Knights leaders, who remained acutely aware of the need to avoid antagonizing the police and the community, curbed aggression and encouraged picketers to leave the unruliness to others with less at stake. That the Knights' leadership sought to keep the unionists out of trouble was underscored by their insistence at the close of the first day of the strike that the men "not ... loaf around" and instead go straight home and "abstain from intoxicating liquors."[52]

Senator Smith, the Unionists, and Mayor Howland

The first morning of the lockout, TSR President Frank Smith met the various city daily reporters in his office to publicize his view of the situation, framing it in a way intended to win him public support. Smith charged that the disruption was entirely the fault of the union, which sought to interfere in the company's good relationship with its employees. He was outraged that "outside agitators" (non-employees) were riding the streetcars trying to organize the men, and that the union wanted to judge whether the company's reasons for dismissing any employee were acceptable. The TSR needed full authority to dismiss men who broke the regulations by being drunk on duty (a threat to public safety) or failing to collect fares. "The union wants us to employ these thieves and scoundrels that we won't have," the *News* quoted him as saying. According to the *Mail*, Smith said, "it is a monstrous thing that a company cannot control its own affairs without being dictated to by men who are making capital out of agitation."[53]

Smith contended that the company could operate a full service, but the union was preventing willing men from working. He also attacked the city, which he held responsible for the company's lost revenues because its police protection for operators had been inadequate. "I will make the city pay every dollar I lose by the cars not running," he vowed. In reference to the stablemen, he declared, "I know where I stand in the law, and if they go out and leave the horses standing there to starve I will have them arrested for cruelty to animals."[54] According to the *Mail*, he said, "I will run the road independent of the Knights of Labour or will perish in the attempt."[55] Strong words but in line with the views of a great many employers in the late nineteenth century, who insisted on their right to command their businesses and employees untrammelled by unions.

In an attempt at full coverage, the press also gave space for the other side to air its views, though the speakers were left unidentified, probably to protect them. "As far as the men are concerned," reported the *Mail*, "the fight was a fair and square one on a question of principle." One employee explained that the company's ironclad was "an interference with the liberty of the subject when he is prevented from exercising his own free will," a liberal position that might well have resonated favourably even with residents who had little sympathy with unions. To the charge that employees had broken their contracts, unionists said they had only signed the contracts "under protest and owing to circumstances." Once they were better prepared to insist on their right to associate, they did so.[56]

Mayor Howland, who owed his election victory partly to organized labour's endorsement, sympathized with the unionists' fight for the right to associate and took exception to some of Senator Smith's public remarks.[57] The mayor denied that the city was responsible for lost TSR revenues and held Smith accountable for any costs because he had locked out the men. Moreover, Howland said that the TSR had violated the terms of its municipal charter by failing to provide regular service. Expressing his sympathy with the locked-out men, he said they were "simply ... exercising a legal liberty in joining a lawful body of society."[58] Howland's stance must have encouraged the strikers to stand up for their rights as the mayor intended, but inadvertently it probably also encouraged the rowdiness of crowds composed of men and boys whom Howland later called "scalawags and loafers."[59]

Late on Wednesday a delegation of the locked-out men met with Chief Constable Draper to object both to Maloney's arrest and to the assignment of additional officers to protect TSR property. Union leaders accused local officialdom of showing a class bias by acting against the workers, even though it was Smith and the company that had caused the service disruption. They also complained about police harassment of unionists. In response, Chief Draper simply promised to act as fairly as possible.[60] When the unionists approached the mayor, making the same points to him, apparently hoping he would intervene as he had in an earlier strike, he did not comply.[61]

By five in the morning on the second day of the strike, people were congregating near the TSR barns, as the *World* reporter put it, "to see the sport." However, it was not until 7:30 that the company sent out a streetcar. Coal carts obstructed it almost immediately, but once it had left the vicinity of the barns its progress was unimpeded. Another car made its way past the jeering throng, sustaining no damage "other than to the driver's and conductor's feelings."[62] On its return, however, a crowd stopped it and unhitched the horses. Police inspectors Seymour and Archibald were aboard the car, one at each end. Inspector Archibald "removed the dirty fingers of the little boys as they grabbed the rear platform."[63] Soon, said the *News* reporter, the inspectors "wisely saw that there was no use in keeping the car standing on the street, and so they told the boys to shove ahead." Amid cheers, the captured car and inspectors were pushed rapidly down the street.[64] Farther on, another crowd blocked the car, picked it up, and placed it crossways on the tracks to loud cheering. At this point several attempts were made to turn the car over, but according to the *News*, police intervened to prevent damage. The *Globe* reporter observed that the police "apparently ... enjoyed the situation as much as any of the spectators." And it credited the crowd of 1,000 engaged in the "lively scrimmages" with being "generally very good-natured."[65]

Eventually, after half an hour, a squad of police arrived, set the car back on the tracks, and hitched a team of horses for the car's return to the barns. At that point, one after another, wagons blocked its progress. Finally, the way was cleared and the car was run down to the barns. Along the way, it was pelted with frozen mud by boys, two of whom were arrested, John Landers, age thirteen, and James Ryan, age twelve. All the morning supporters of the locked-out workers taunted the men working inside the TSR barns by running inside and crying "rats" and "come out." Drivers of vehicles arrived every few minutes to watch the scene. The reporter from the *Mail* thought that they "seemed to have nothing to do but talk of the 'fun,' as some called it."[66]

After these morning incidents, the strike-breakers declared their unwillingness to operate streetcars without better police protection. Senator Smith supported them, calling off operations for the day. That afternoon further discussions took place about crowd control and policing. At a meeting of the police commissioners the TSR's lawyer made the case for a more aggressive police presence. But the force was already stretched. Consideration was given to swearing in special police to beef up the force if needed. In the end, the commissioners simply ordered the chief to dispatch such force as might be necessary for company operations to resume.[67]

On the Friday, the third day of the strike, 130 policemen assembled in the vicinity of the streetcar barns with orders to use their batons freely. Each car sent out had several police aboard to act as guards, and mounted police were detailed to clear the way in front of cars. The TSR superintendent stated that "determined and fearless" operators had been hired who could be relied upon to get the cars out and back "or perish in the attempt."[68]

Notwithstanding the preparations, Friday got off to a poor start for the police and the TSR. Constables lined the first few blocks of King Street, fully ready to prevent any interference with the King car, the first car scheduled to go out. The enormous crowd, estimated at 7,000, included "some women," as well as many men who had marched over from their workplaces to jeer operators and hinder the progress of any car sent out.[69] Inexplicably, after the King car left the barn it turned along Front Street rather than King Street. Demonstrators quickly surrounded it, which left the police scrambling to circle in behind the crowd. With difficulty the constables cleared a space around the car. But when the streetcar tried to proceed, a driver blocked its way with his lorry, managing to escape the swipes of baton-wielding police by standing in his lorry perched on a tall stack of boxes.[70] Demonstrators rushed to overturn the streetcar, but police stopped them with their nightsticks. Constables arrested two men and were able to get them to the police station only because a posse of twelve mounted police surrounded them and, "charging the crowd, ran over any who did not get out of their way."[71] The increased police presence no doubt explains the less playful and more violent confrontation on this, the third day of the dispute.

Police authorities then declared what today we would call a "zero tolerance" policy for anyone disturbing the peace. When the first man to step out of line, Edward Moran, was apprehended, people rushed to free him. A battle ensued, but mounted and baton-wielding police drove the crowd down to the lake and brought Moran to the police station. According to the *Telegram*, this was a turning point. The police, managing to stay relatively calm, brought order to the scene.[72]

The test came when another car was put into service. To block its way there appeared an enormous crowd of males of all ages and, according to the *News*, "even women." "Do you think you can get us through?," asked one of the operators. "I can take you to the devil," replied a defiant Chief Draper. An aggressive posse of mounted police rushed at the crowd, scattering people into doorways, alleyways, and anywhere they could escape. Police guards walked with the car, and fifty constables formed a moving cordon to keep back the surging crowd. Amid a fuselage of mud and deafening jeers, the policemen and streetcar made their way along its route. When another throng appeared, the mounted police again cleared the way. Soon the beaten crowd made no further attempts to block the car's progress, although people still "howled and hissed" and called out "'rats,' 'scabs,' 'suckers,' and 'skunks.'"[73]

Battles occurred throughout the day, including one shortly after noon, when a wagon blocked a streetcar on Yonge Street near Adelaide Street. When the crowd began stoning the car carrying police guards, a posse of constables, assisted by mounted police, rushed the crowd. One of the policemen was struck on the head with a stone, which, according to the *News*, "seemed to infuriate the rest, and batons were used with energy though indiscriminately." At one point, according to the *Telegram*, a drunken man came out of a saloon and egged on young demonstrators by shouting, "Why don't you kill the rats!"[74] The lads began throwing not just mud but stones at operators and constables riding the streetcars; two constables were hurt. Police arrested one mud-slinging demonstrator, identified as furrier Frederick Charles Klopp. Altogether that day police arrested one striker and at least fourteen other men, laying charges for offences such as disorderly conduct, obstruction, and assault. The Knights of Labor formally complained to civic authorities about the police's excessive use of force that day.[75]

The men arrested in the disturbances appeared before the Toronto Police Court magistrate, Col. George Taylor Denison, who dealt harshly with them. A familiar figure to readers of the reports on police court proceedings in the city dailies, Denison was known for his impatience with the rules of evidence, idiosyncratic rulings in rapidly heard cases, and fierce insistence on public order.[76] The *Mail* quoted the magistrate as saying of the street railway dispute, "The peace of the city must be preserved at any cost." He found most of the men brought before him guilty and fined them heavily.[77] T. Phillips Thompson in the *Palladium of Labor* attributed the harshness to the Toronto courts' "bias in favour of wealth and social position."[78]

That same Friday afternoon, the police commissioners met to consider swearing in 100 specials to augment the police presence, as well as calling out the militia in defence of the civil order. However, on the advice of Chief Draper, both measures were rejected, at least for the time being.[79] Mayor Howland took the opportunity to issue a proclamation forbidding assembling in the streets and threatening prosecution of "persons interfering with the free passage of street cars."[80]

Meantime, on the Friday afternoon, a deputation of aldermen approached Senator Smith in an attempt to end the dispute. After a long discussion, Smith agreed that the aldermen should tell the men that he was willing "to receive them back on exactly the same conditions as before the unfortunate difference arose." When informed the men could all go back to work "unconditionally," Knights leader Alfred Jury, thinking of the union men, asked "All the men?" The aldermen assured him that Smith would take all the men back, "no questions asked." At a general meeting of the union membership, the executive advised ending the dispute because it had taken "an unanticipated turn," a reference to the public violence and powerful police presence. The men accepted Smith's offer "amid enthusiastic cheering" and returned to work the next morning.[81]

There was no discussion in the press about whether the crowd actions had helped the TSR employees' cause. In retrospect, it is evident that the playful performances drew yet more people into the streets and that the escalating crowd actions were fed by increasing police aggression. Toronto had become a divided city: at least a substantial part of the working class had taken to the streets in support of the strikers, while many other residents opted to avoid doing so. As clear evidence of hostility to the strikers' cause, some residents had chosen to ride whatever streetcars remained in service. The growing conflict in the streets and the deep division of the city increased the public pressure on both the TSR and the union to settle. Both sides sought a quick end to the dispute. The negotiated settlement was not a lasting one, however.

The May Strike

In the weeks after the March dispute, the company systematically fired union men, picking off one at a time. The Knights held several meetings to discuss the dismissals and drew up a list of grievances, but Smith refused to address them. He insisted that in March he had agreed to take the men back on the same terms as when the dispute began; the ironclad had been in place then, as now, so he was justified in firing unionists. His critics pointed out that the men had returned to work jubilantly only because they had been led to believe that the ironclad had been lifted. Smith had let them think so at the time, pleased to get his business up and running at a moment when public censure of him was at a peak. He left the cleaning out of unionists for later.[82] Finally, on Friday, 8 May, the men voted to strike in protest of the dismissals and Smith's betrayal on the issue of the ironclad, and for an increase in pay to at least ten dollars per week for all employees. As the executive committee of the strikers put it, employees and the public needed to stand up to a company that "tyrannically deprives their unfortunate employees of their undoubted right to join or belong to any legal organization they may deem advisable."[83]

When the May strike got under way on Saturday, 9 May, people wondered whether there would be violence – a possibility now more worrying because the shocking events at Chicago's Haymarket had occurred in the interim since the March dispute. A *News* editorial observed that the Toronto strike leaders had taken the men out knowing that because of "the atrocities committed by anarchists in Chicago," shows of public sympathy would be "less prompt than on the occasion of the former strike."[84] Taking heed, the union's executive committee declared that "they do not contemplate, nor will they countenance any violence or any disturbance of the public peace."[85] At the outset of the strike Mayor Howland also took a firm stand against violence, emphasizing to the public that assembling or loitering in the streets was "unlawful, and especially under the present circumstances." On the eve of the May strike, civic officials announced that the police would protect TSR property and employees operating the cars during the strike. Special provisions included having the entire force at the ready, directing constables to carry revolvers during daytime duty, deploying constables on the streetcars, and ordering the mounted police detachment to do crowd duty.

On the first morning of the strike, the union posted picketers at the railway station to advise men coming into the city to refuse job offers from the TSR because a strike was under way.[86] It was quiet at the streetcar barns at 6:15 a.m., when an old employee named Cosgrove took out the first car. Police were on the scene. Only about 100 people had gathered there, including a dozen printers who, following their shift on the morning papers, had "dropped by to see the fun." No attempt was made to block the car. Indeed, peace prevailed not just at the outset but throughout the first day of the strike.[87]

By Monday, the strikers were better organized and succeeded in nearly stopping streetcar service altogether. They managed to do so without physical confrontations and while observing the moratorium on name-calling. According to the *News*, the only person who heckled a strike-breaker was "a young woman, who called 'scab' and 'rat' from a window of a house on Front Street."[88] It appears that her gender and location inside the house protected her from police action. As of the early afternoon, while thousands were walking the streets in the vicinity of the barns and the entire police force of 170 patrolled the scene, order continued to prevail. Occasionally police broke up gatherings on the street corners, but there were no disturbances.

Indeed, much less violence occurred throughout the far longer May strike, a development praised by many commentators, who commended the unionists and other Torontonians for their peaceful behaviour. "We could not have wished for a quieter day," declared a police official at the conclusion of the first day of the strike.[89] Ten days into the dispute, Mayor Howland congratulated the community for the orderly behaviour.[90]

It appears that the crowd performances of March were not repeated in May because of a combination of factors: the tougher stance of the mayor and police officials, the union leaders' acute awareness of the damage the Haymarket riot had done to the union's reputation, and Torontonians' collective memory of how nasty the March confrontation had eventually become. Since March, various judges had had an opportunity to expound on the illegality of intimidation and the serious consequences for perpetrators.[91] Moreover, by May, the spring season's increased demand for casual labour meant that far fewer men and boys had free daytime hours to spend on the streets.

During the May strike, the unionists and their supporters widened the repertoire of contentious performances by calling a large public meeting at the city's commodious St Lawrence Hall. Unionists planned to take charge of the occasion and to use the techniques of the meeting hall and a display of well-ordered opposition to the TSR to gain a measure of public endorsement for their cause. Following a convention familiar to Toronto residents, the meeting was called by Mayor Howland in response to a requisition signed by a large number of ratepayers.[92] Some 2,000 people, virtually all workingmen supportive of the strikers, packed the hall, and more were turned away at the door. Howland presided and praised the peacefulness of the strikers and the orderly conduct of those at the meeting. The Knights' leaders moved all three of the meeting's motions: one condemning Smith for depriving his employees of the right to belong to a lawful organization, a second expressing the meeting's support for the strike, and a third that condemned the TSR's refusal to comply with the terms of its charter and that endorsed an alternative bus service. These were enthusiastically supported.[93] Keeping to the orderly agenda, the evening closed with a conventional show of loyalty: three cheers for the Queen. The meeting got mixed reviews. The *Telegram* doubted its value where attention-seekers pushed to the front – a reference to the role played by the Knights' leadership. The *News* praised the initiative and the fine conduct of those in attendance but regretted that it produced no indication that a settlement was any nearer.[94]

At their own meetings the strikers also debated matters civilly and passed formal resolutions intended to pressure Senator Smith to end the strike. The strikers' executive, for instance, resolved to ask supporters to withdraw their deposits from the Home Savings and Loan Company, where Smith was president. A large meeting of the Knights of Labor opted to send a delegation to Ottawa to meet with Prime Minister Macdonald and urge him to remove Smith from the cabinet because of his opposition to organized labour.[95]

What violence occurred in the course of the May strike was generally the action of an individual rather than a crowd, and the perpetrators, if caught, were dealt with harshly. Charles Grassett, arrested on the first day of the May strike for simply calling strike-breaking drivers "rats," got a five-dollar fine or thirty days, whereas in March such calls were tolerated.[96] The following day, two carters, named Bryant and Doherty, were charged for obstructing the cars, and police arrested a dray man, named Bernard McGuffin, for having thrown a stone at a passing streetcar.[97] One boy nabbed by police for placing a foghorn on the street railway tracks, was fined ten dollars by Col. Denison, who threatened fifty-dollar fines in future.[98] Another boy named John Gowans was charged by police for stealing a cushion and switch pins from a streetcar. He pleaded guilty, and his mother asked the police court magistrate to send him to a reformatory because he had by "his outrageous conduct nearly broken her heart." Happy to comply, Col. Denison sent young John to the reformatory at Penetanguishene for three years. The most bizarre performance saw one Michael Durham shaking a dead rat "menacingly" at the streetcar men operating on Yonge Street. He apparently had a string attached to its tail, and when asked what he was doing, replied "I want the scabs to smell it." Later, in court, he had a different story, claiming implausibly that he simply had been removing the poor, dead creature for interment in some secluded spot. It appears that Col. Denison was amused by the tall tale, for he discharged the man.[99] Generally, though, Denison was so tough that the Toronto Trades and Labour Council resolved to request an interview with Ontario's attorney general to draw "the attention of the Government of the undisguised animus of the Police magistrate in cases the most remotely connected with organized labour."[100]

Rather than confronting the strike-breakers in the streets, the union opted for less direct tactics. Picketers pressured keepers of boarding houses and restaurateurs to refuse services to strike-breakers, apparently with some success.[101] Much more significantly, it sought to undercut the TSR's business by offering Torontonians an alternative means of public transport: a system of free buses operated as a cooperative by strikers. The Knights of Labor leadership very much approved of cooperatives, which had been attempted during various strikes in Ontario and during a recent street railway strike in New York, where a bus service was organized.[102] In Toronto, many riders were sufficiently ticked off by the TSR – for whatever reason – that they made extensive use of the buses and were even willing to make a donation to the cooperative each time they rode. Less comfortable than the streetcars, the buses, it was said, were not the preferred option of many "ladies." (No mention was made of complaints from working-class women.) The strikers' cooperative asked its bus riders to avoid smoking in an attempt to win over some of the middle-class women, but that tactic only partly succeeded.[103] Still, the Knights' service was sufficiently patronized that the strikers' main challenge was finding enough buses to meet public demand.

The largest street demonstration during the May dispute grew out of a union-organized parade intended to build morale by celebrating the arrival from Kingston on 25 May of seven buses and a contingent of supporters. Upon reaching the Don River on their way into town from the east, the visitors were met by a procession of twenty Toronto buses and hundreds of strikers and supporters, headed by the Irish Catholic Benevolent Union brass band. After an exchange of fraternal greetings, the procession of visitors and hosts passed through the city's principal streets as the band played "lively airs." Crowds along the route cheered the procession, then they and more vehicles fell in behind it.[104]

Without warning, the celebratory mood shifted. At the centre of town, some youngsters in the crowd attacked an eastbound streetcar, smashing its windows and injuring a woman passenger, whose cheek was badly cut. Farther west near Bathurst Street, the crowd pelted and damaged some passing streetcars. "The drivers and conductors appeared almost frightened out of their wits," said the *Mail* reporter, who thought that the fear of the employees "emboldened the mob which followed the K of L buses in their destructive course, as no car passing east or west escaped their violence."[105]

By this point some seventy vehicles had joined the procession and the crowd had grown to "alarming proportions." Pleas from the strikers' executive committee begging people to avoid damaging TSR property for fear of reprisals had little effect, "and the wildest excitement prevailed." To calm things down, strike leaders decided to break up the procession, but the brass band's attempt to lead the crowd away from the scene of the trouble brought only mixed results. A second rampage resulted in several streetcars having their windows smashed. At last, the crowd dispersed around St Lawrence Hall. Altogether some thirty to forty streetcars were damaged, most of them suffering broken windows. Passengers nearly all escaped unharmed. The only arrest was of a boy, Joseph McGilligan, age twelve, caught attempting to derail a streetcar by placing stones on the track.[106]

What success the cooperative bus company enjoyed resulted from the considerable public support for an alternative to the much-resented TSR service. The cooperative overcame obstacles, including its hasty formation, meagre capital resources, Smith's attempt to declare its service in contravention of the TSR charter, and hostile aldermen who tried to quadruple the city's licence charge per bus. However, the bus cooperative's temporary success was partly the undoing of the strike. Toronto riders were well-served by the two systems, so much so that the strike as a withdrawal of services lost effectiveness. Moreover, the committee behind the bus cooperative chose to plough earnings back into the cooperative rather than using them to assist needy strikers. Some suffering, unaided strikers drifted back to their jobs or to other work. Cynicism about political squabbles within the Knights' leadership between Conservatives and Reformers may also have played a role in some strikers' growing disillusionment.[107] Inevitably, the bus cooperative gradually lost riders as the novelty wore off. A disastrous fire at the bus barns on 30 June was the last straw.[108]

Senator Smith won the May contest, but organized labour and many supporters vowed that he would be punished when his municipal charter came up for renewal in 1891. Indeed, he was squeezed out, though he managed to do well financially.[109] Workers on the Toronto streetcar system struck successfully in 1902, gaining union recognition, a grievance procedure, and a wage increase as part of an organizing campaign by the Amalgamated Association of Street Railway Employees, first chartered in 1892 by the American Federation of Labor.[110]

Conclusion

The richly detailed press stories of these linked street railway disputes of March and May 1886 reveal two categories of contentious performances. First, there were the actions of the male union members and strikers, who expressed their masculinity in self-disciplined behaviour aimed at preventing the TSR from operating, thus minimizing public censure and police repression and earning support from residents. By presenting themselves as law-abiding but determined opponents of the company, the strikers succeeded in winning considerable support from the working class for their campaign to gain union rights. The Knights of Labor leaders choreographed the performances as best they could, urging self-control to avoid antagonizing citizens, and they publicly differentiated their own members' manly level-headedness from the erratic behaviour of the public demonstrators. Apart from street activities, the unionists' repertoire extended to an orderly public meeting, where Knights' leaders presented prepared motions and the lively participation never got out of hand, as well as to the organization of the bus cooperative, a peaceful strategy intended to reduce public use of streetcars run by strike-breakers. Near the end of the May strike, the *News*, the newspaper closest to the union leadership, summed up the unionists' performance style when it observed: "This self-respect and self-restraint has done more to restore public confidence to show that the men are determined to carry on their fight peaceably, orderly, and in a law-abiding spirit."[111]

In the second category of contentious performances were the many crowd actions characteristic especially of the March dispute. A portion of the wider working-class public took to the streets both to join in the excitement and to register their disapproval of the TSR in general and its anti-labour policy in particular. The exuberant, sometimes aggressive and transgressive behaviour could teeter on the brink of riot, yet contests between the crowd and strike-breakers and the police sometimes had an air of vaudeville about them, certainly as depicted by a daily press that aimed to entertain as much as to inform. Playful boys had an important role in the streets as eager risk-takers, the first to sling handfuls of mud at operators and streetcars alike. Their mischievous initiatives provoked men in the crowds, themselves not far removed from boyhood transgressions, who took the confrontations to new levels. On the first two days of the March dispute the crowd scenes had a joyous quality to them, reports of which probably drew yet more people eager to join in the fun and perhaps not strictly motivated by the issues.

Yet the mood of the crowd could shift. On the third day of the March dispute, at the insistence of Senator Smith of the TSR, the police took a much more forceful part in facilitating the resumption of streetcar service. Now the confrontations appeared less jovial, more threatening, and potentially dangerous. During the May dispute, a shift in mood was notable, too. While the procession welcoming the buses and supporters from Kingston began jubilantly, things turned nasty as violence erupted. Scholars looking at "joyful crowds" have noted how even purely celebratory occasions can turn menacing, and these strike developments illustrate similar shifts.[112]

When studying strikes, historians have persistently documented the grave issues at stake and conveyed a sense of the seriousness of the conflicts, but little has been said about activities of a playful sort. It may be that the 1886 labour demonstrations in Toronto were unusual in having such a jovial aspect, but it would be worthwhile to look closely for evidence of playfulness and its consequences in other labour confrontations. Broad public participation in demonstrations may signify both the importance of the issues and people's eagerness to join in the excitement to break the monotony of daily life.

The two categories of contentious performances evident in 1886 came at the conjuncture of an emergent culture and a residual one during a period of social transition.[113] On the one hand, the closely scripted and disciplined actions of the unionists represented the emergent culture of the new industrial era, when organized workers struck to protect and improve their situation; such purposeful behaviour was aimed at both undermining employer operations during a dispute and currying public support. Always contentious at some level, strikes and picketing were nevertheless coming to be condoned in a mass society becoming modern. On the other hand, the fluid and more spontaneous behaviour of the crowds looked backwards to practices deployed over many decades if not centuries in countless situations where community norms were transgressed. In the case of the 1886 streetcar strikes, crowd actions heightened public interest in, and concern about, the disputes, making confrontations that already directly affected the public all the more intense.

Conclusion

Toronto changed dramatically during the half-century after 1840. At the beginning of the period, the young city served as a commercial hub for the surrounding countryside, one that linked farm communities to trade with Britain. In politics, Reformers struggled to increase the power of the local executive at the governor's expense. By the 1880s, Toronto's population had soared as a result of waves of immigrants from the United Kingdom. Railways had spurred commercial connections and ended the city's seasonal dependence on its port. An industrial revolution was in full swing, bringing industrialists new power and influence and awakening a young working class to its own interests. The city's newspapers grew in number and widened their focus from politics to the coverage of local events. Throughout these transformations, people from time to time took to city streets, celebrating or demonstrating as the occasion warranted. By doing so, they conveyed both intended and unintended messages about who they were, what moved them, and their differences. On such occasions, Torontonians displayed both their loyalty to Britain and their growing national and urban pride, but also their ethno-religious, class, and gender differences, as well as hierarchies of power.

The events featured in this book underscore the centrality of religious divisions in Victorian Toronto. In 1849, Conservative leaders mobilized rank-and-file Orangemen to reinforce Tory objections to the decisions of the province's Reform government to readmit to the province rebel leader William Lyon Mackenzie and to compensate Lower Canadians who had suffered property damage during the rebellion of 1837–38. Effigy burnings added drama to nighttime protests and exposed the reluctance of civic authorities to suppress the lawbreaking of their Orange brethren. In provincial election campaigns, Conservative candidates often deployed Orangemen to intimidate rivals at meetings and at the polls, fomenting much disorder on democratic occasions. In 1860, when Torontonians welcomed the visiting Prince of Wales, some Orangemen nearly derailed the royal tour by insisting, in defiance of the colonial secretary, that their welcome include symbols of their Order. When in 1864 and 1875 Bishop Lynch encouraged Roman Catholics to assert their right to public space, they were met by the jeers, fists, and missiles of militant Protestants, which put the mayor, who was both the chief magistrate and an Orange officer, in a tight spot. It was the Orange Young Britons who stood at the forefront of disorder in the city streets during the 1870s. Throughout the period, Toronto's Orangemen enjoyed a sense of their entitlement to assert themselves in public space, and their marching tradition provided an effective means to do so.

In the ritualized violence that erupted on many occasions in Victorian Toronto, men asserted their masculine power and in so doing came into conflict with other men doing the same thing. Scuffles between Protestants and Catholics amounted to little more than a testosterone-fuelled display, however much Orangemen spoke of standing up for their principles and Catholics stood by their Church. The ritualized nature of the performances was made particularly evident when disputes focused on costumes worn in public: the right of Orangemen to don their regalia and the right of Catholic clergy to wear their vestments. The low body count amid the violence also underscores its ritual character, Matthew Sheedy's death being the exception that proves the rule.

In all the examples of expressive acts discussed in this book, class differences are revealed. Yet they were seldom the intended point of the displays, and the class identities were often masked by notables and journalists who preferred to convey the illusion of community harmony. Election procedures made class differences explicit by enfranchising only certain men of property. Nevertheless, non-electors made their presence known by voting at nomination meetings, attending candidates' meetings, and intimidating rivals at the polls. Their behaviour tested democracy and brought attention to the possibility of a wider franchise. By the time of the 1872 election, the Conservative Party was making a pitch for the votes of unionized workers and labouring men. When celebrating the suppression of the Riel resistance, the press presented Toronto as an entirely unified community, but the Volunteers the crowds honoured were known to be of a certain class of men: white-collar employees or the self-employed with the leisure time to train and the freedom to take time off work to go to the North-West. Their officers, of course, were of a still higher class of privileged white men.

Gender, too, was revealed during celebrations and demonstrations in Toronto. All such occasions put masculinities on display. The well-heeled notables, white men of property, arranged the royal visit and the welcome for the Volunteers, providing leadership that appeared natural. They asserted their power by taking charge of large public meetings, expressing the wishes of the community, and insisting on public order. Electoral candidates liked to present themselves as models of genteel masculinity well-deserving of voters' support, but at times during election campaigns, hot-headedness prevailed. Elected civic officials' assertive manliness sometimes came up for questioning, such as when the Duke of Newcastle accused the Toronto mayor of being a blackguardly liar. A mayor's authority could be challenged too by local bourgeois, as was the case when the powerful owner of the Toronto Street Railway took on Mayor Howland during the street railway strikes. During those strikes, newspapers represented the strikers as family men taking action to provide for their wives and children, while they cast lads who got involved in the crowd actions in support of the strikers as unruly ruffians.

Not all proud men could easily command authority and respect on public occasions. Witness the silencing of African Canadian men who organized in groups in the expectation of presenting their addresses of welcome to the Prince of Wales. White administrators forbade them from doing so for fear their critique of slavery in the United States would offend the American administration. The Loyal United Colored Society at least gained a place in the civic procession, even if white organizers assigned the organization the least prestigious place. Indigenous men of the province had no opportunity to present themselves publicly to the prince in Upper Canada's largest city. The colonizers had erased their history in the area.

Yet racialized people did make appearances in Victorian Toronto. African Canadian men (unlike Indigenous men) had access to the franchise on the same terms as white men, so propertied Black male voters participated in elections, their votes being enough to swing the outcomes of some campaigns. African Canadian men held their own meetings during campaigns to voice their community's support for certain candidates and opposition to others. Some Black men, probably non-electors, participated in campaigns as muscular enforcers for candidates who paid them.

Women had a much more limited role than men on all these public occasions. During celebrations, men cast women in the subordinate role of spectator. A power dynamic featured women and girls in the crowds cheering the men being honoured and the men on parade. "Ladies" – white women of the elite – gained status over other women when as spectators they appeared above the crowds on balconies or on platforms and when they attended dances elegantly dressed in their ballgowns. During protest demonstrations, women all but vanished from the scene, at least according to the press. The predominant gender ideology of the day prohibited respectable women from endangering their bodies and their femininity by becoming involved in protests. If working-class women were in attendance – and they might well have been – male journalists erased them from their accounts and constables kept them out of the police court. Racialized women were never so much as mentioned in any depiction of public displays in Toronto. Only Catholic processions included women and girls, all the faithful being welcome to walk. Girls dressed in white symbolized purity and piety when they took part in the Corpus Christi procession. When militant Protestant men attacked Catholic processions, the women and girls became entangled in the disorder. The bishop and some journalists represented the females as fragile victims of Protestant male aggression who screamed in fear and ran from the scene. Probably some were bolder than that, but the sources are respectfully silent about women throwing stones or poking people with their parasols and hatpins.

These occasions made obvious the expansion of Canadian democracy, although there were trade-offs along the way. Tory opposition to the Rebellion Losses bill marked the death of the cosy relationship between governors and the provincial Tory elite. A government having the confidence of the majority in the elected assembly got its way. We see that throughout our period, public meetings played a role in giving voice to residents and in legitimizing public decisions. Such was the case when Torontonians gathered at St Lawrence Hall to consider the costly arrangements for the royal visit, and when a city hall meeting made plans for the reception of the triumphant Volunteers. Public meetings during election campaigns aired partisan differences, and similar meetings gave militant Protestants an opportunity to condemn the Catholic archbishop and his claim on public space.

During our period, disorderly displays brought electoral reforms that gradually smoothed the rough edges of provincial electoral culture: polling stations multiplied, and taverns could no longer serve as locations for them; polling hours became regularized; guns were banned on election days; the show of hands was eliminated; the secret ballot was introduced; the electorate expanded to include some workingmen. At the same time, however, new restrictions reduced the influence of Toronto's non-electors, including unpropertied men and underage lads who had previously been active in campaigns. At nomination meetings the show of hands had provided non-electors with an opportunity to publicly register support for a candidate and give the illusion of a groundswell in his favour. Similarly, intimidation at the polls during the voice-vote era had given some non-electors a chance to intervene in the democratic process and possibly influence election results.

Colonialism is also evident in Toronto celebrations, intentionally or otherwise. The civic boosters behind the reception for the Prince of Wales saw no need to recognize the history of the place before the arrival of the Loyalists, except to use the "Red man" as a foil when touting the Toronto's progress. By contrast, colonialism triumphant was emphatically on display in 1885 when the city celebrated the suppression of the Riel resistance in the North-West. Journalists made no attempt to empathize with the situation or goals of the Métis, instead casting them as "half-breed rebels" standing in the way of Canada's advancement on the Prairies. According to the press, the heroism of the Volunteers from Toronto and elsewhere had defeated the uprising, re-established law and order, and made the frontier safe for settler colonialism.

Surviving Toronto newspapers enable us to study the city's nineteenth-century public celebrations and demonstrations. The press reported on and interpreted Toronto's displays in the streets in ways that help us reconstruct events and search for their meaning. The intense partisanship of the political journals often makes it all but impossible to determine who instigated disturbances, but by reading about an event from differently positioned journals some sense of what happened is possible. The emergence of popular journalism in the 1880s breathed new life into storytelling. By their use of language, journalists made heroes and villains out of participants, characterizations we need not accept given our distance from the events. While there is no question that newspapers reveal the values and actions of people on public occasions, it is far harder to assess the press's influence on how people behaved and the choices people made about how to vote and how to participate in public displays.

Torontonians have continued up to the present to participate in celebrations and demonstration in city streets. Only close readings of the events would permit good comparisons with the ones featured in this book. Context, of course, is vital. The expressive acts of the Victorian era vividly reveal Toronto's social hierarchies, gender conventions, and religious/ethnic relationships of that period. They provide a fine window on a period now far removed from our own time.

Notes

Introduction

1 *Globe* (Toronto), 5 May 1849.
2 *Globe*, 18 October 1849.
3 *Packet* (Bytown), 20 October 1849.
4 Annual celebrations such as Christmas and national holidays are not included here, but see, for example, *Celebrating Canada*, ed. Raymond Blake and Matthew Hayday, 2 vols. (Toronto: University of Toronto Press, 2016, 2018).
5 The best study of Canada's nineteenth-century newspapers is Paul Rutherford, *A Victorian Authority: The Daily Press in Late Nineteenth-Century Canada* (Toronto: University of Toronto Press, 1982). On the business of newspaper publishing mainly in a later period, see Minko Sotiron, *From Politics to Profits: The Commercialization of Canadian Daily Newspapers, 1890–1920* (Montreal and Kingston: McGill–Queen's University Press, 1997).
6 J.M.S. Careless, *Brown of the Globe*, 2 vols. (Toronto: Macmillan, 1959, 1963).
7 Douglas McCalla, "Beaty, James," in *Dictionary of Canadian Biography*, vol. 12, University of Toronto/Université Laval, 2003–, http://www.biographi.ca/en/bio/beaty_james_12E.html.
8 See, the *Banner* (1843–48, Reform), the *British Colonist* (1838–54, Conservative), the *Examiner* (1838–55, Reform), the *Patriot* (1834–54, Conservative), the *Mail* (1872–95, Conservative), and the *Telegram* (1876–1971, Conservative). On early Toronto newspapers, see Juliana M. Stabile, "Toronto Newspapers, 1798–1845: A Case Study in Print Culture" (PhD diss., University of Toronto, 2002); and Edith Firth, *Early Toronto Newspapers, 1793–1867* (Toronto: Baxter Publishing and Toronto Public Library, 1961).
9 See the *Mirror* (1837–65), the *Canadian Freeman* (1858–73), the *Irish Canadian* (1863–92), and the *Sentinel and Orange Protestant Advocate* (1877–96).

10 Rutherford, *A Victorian Authority*, 54–6; Thomas Lawrence Walkom, "The Daily Newspaper Industry in Ontario's Developing Capitalist Economy: Toronto and Ottawa, 1871–1911" (PhD diss., University of Toronto, 1983).
11 Russell Hann, "Brainworkers and the Knights of Labor: E.E. Sheppard, Phillips Thompson and the Toronto News, 1883–1887," in *Essays in Canadian Working-Class History*, ed. G.S. Kealey and Peter Warrian (Toronto: McClelland and Stewart, 1976), 35–57.
12 It was only in May 1889 that the *Globe* introduced an illustrated section with images based on drawings; in 1891 it introduced half-tone engravings (Rutherford, *A Victorian Authority*, 58).
13 Library and Archives Canada (hereafter LAC), "Canadian Illustrated News: Images in the News, 1869–1883," http://www.collectionscanada.gc.ca/databases/cin/001065-2010-e.html.
14 On the history of the illustrated press, see Peter W. Sinnema, *Dynamics of the Pictured Page: Representing the Nation in the Illustrated London News* (Aldershot: Ashgate, 1998); Thomas Smits, *The European Illustrated Press and the Emergence of a Transnational Visual Culture of the News, 1842–1870* (New York: Routledge, 2020); Patricia Mainardi, *Another World: Nineteenth-Century Illustrated Print Culture* (New Haven: Yale University Press, 2017); and Paul Hogarth, *Artist as Reporter* (London: Gordon Fraser Gallery, 1986).
15 George Rudé, *The Crowd in History: A Study of Popular Disturbances in France and England, 1730–1848* (New York: Wiley, 1964); *The Face of the Crowd: Studies in Revolution, Ideology, and Popular Protest: Selected Essays of George Rudé*, ed. Harvey J. Kaye (Hampstead: Harvester-Wheatsheaf, 1988); Charles Tilly, *The Vendée* (Cambridge, MA: Harvard University Press, 1964); Eric Hobsbawm, *Primitive Rebels: Studies in Archaic Forms of Social Movements in the 19th and 20th Centuries* (New York: W.W. Norton, 1965).
16 E.P. Thompson, "The Moral Economy of the Crowd in the Eighteenth Century," *Past and Present* 50 (1971): 76–136.
17 Natalie Zemon Davis, "The Rites of Violence: Religious Riot in Sixteenth-Century France," *Past and Present* 59 (1973): 51–91. See also her "Writing 'The Rites of Violence' and Afterword," *Past and Present*, Supplement 7 (2012): 8–29.
18 Charles Tilly, "Getting It Together in Burgundy, 1675–1975," *Theory and Society* 4 (1977): 479–504.
19 Charles Tilly, *Contentious Performances* (New York: Cambridge University Press, 2008); *Challenging Authority: The Historical Study of Contentious Politics*, ed. Michael Hanagan et al. (Minneapolis: University of Minnesota Press, 1998).

20 Mary Ryan, "The American Parade: Representations of the Nineteenth-Century Social Order," in *The New Cultural History*, ed. Lynn Hunt (Berkeley: University of California Press, 1989), 133, 138.
21 Mary P. Ryan, *Women in Public: Between Banners and Ballots, 1835–1880* (Baltimore: Johns Hopkins University Press, 1990); Ryan, *Civic Wars: Democracy and Public Life in the American City during the Nineteenth Century* (Berkeley: University of California Press, 1997); Brooks McNamara, *Day of Jubilee: The Great Age of Public Celebration in New York, 1788–1909* (New Brunswick: Rutgers University Press, 1997).
22 H.V. Nelles, *The Art of Nation Building: Pageantry and Spectacle in Quebec's Tercentenary Celebrations* (Toronto: University of Toronto Press, 1999); Alan Gordon, *Making Public Pasts: The Contested Terrain of Montreal's Public Memories, 1891–1930* (Montreal and Kingston: McGill–Queen's University Press, 2001); Ronald Rudin, *Founding Fathers: The Celebration of Champlain and Laval in the Streets of Quebec, 1878–1908* (Toronto: University of Toronto Press, 2003); Craig Heron and Steven Penfold, *The Workers' Festival: A History of Labour Day in Canada* (Toronto: University of Toronto Press, 2005); Steven Penfold, *A Mile of Make-Believe: A History of the Eaton's Santa Claus Parade* (Toronto: University of Toronto Press, 2016)); *Celebrating Canada*.
23 Susan Davis, *Parades and Power: Street Theater in Nineteenth-Century Philadelphia* (Philadelphia: University of Pennsylvania Press, 1985).
24 See, for example, Robert Cupido, "Public Commemoration and Ethnocultural Assertion: Winnipeg Celebrates the Diamond Jubilee of Confederation," *Urban History Review* 38 (2010): 64–74, and his "Competing Pasts, Multiple Identities: The Diamond Jubilee of Confederation and the Politics of Commemoration," in *Celebrating Canada*, 97–144.
25 Canadian examples related to this book include Peter Goheen, "Negotiating Access to Public Space in Mid-Nineteenth Century Toronto," *Journal of Historical Geography* 20 (1994): 430–49; and Goheen, "Symbols in the Streets: Parades in Victorian Urban Canada," *Urban History Review* 18 (1990): 237–43.
26 Jürgen Habermas, *The Structural Transformation of the Public Sphere* (Cambridge, MA: MIT Press, 1989); *Habermas and the Public Sphere*, ed. Craig Calhoun (Cambridge, MA: MIT Press, 1992); Pauline Johnson, *Habermas Rescuing the Public Sphere* (London: Routledge, 2006).
27 Jeffrey McNairn, *The Capacity to Judge: Public Opinion and Deliberative Democracy in Upper Canada, 1791–1854* (Toronto: University of Toronto Press, 2000).
28 Mary P. Ryan, "Gender and Public Access: Women's Politics in Nineteenth-Century America," in *Habermas and the Public Sphere*, 259–88.

29 Dan Horner, *Taking to the Streets: Crowds, Politics, and the Urban Experience in Mid-Nineteenth-Century Montreal* (Montreal and Kingston: McGill-Queen's University Press, 2020).
30 The older literature is surveyed in Scott W. See, "Nineteenth-Century Collective Violence: Toward a North American Context," *Labour/le travail* 39 (1997): 13–38. More recent studies include Ruth Bleasdale, *Rough Work: Labour on the Public Works of British North America and Canada, 1841–1887* (Toronto: University of Toronto Press, 2018); Peter Way, *Common Labour* (Cambridge: Cambridge University Press, 2009); and Dan Horner, *Taking to the Streets*.
31 Scott W. See, *Riots in New Brunswick: Orange Nativism and Social Violence in the 1840s* (Toronto: University of Toronto Press, 1993); "Aspirations and Limitations: 'Peace, Order and Good Government' and the Language of Violence and Disorder in British North America," in *Violence, Order, and Unrest: A History of British North America, 1749–1876*, ed. Elizabeth Mancke et al. (Toronto: University of Toronto Press, 2019), 17–35.
32 Cecil J. Houston and William J. Smyth, *The Sash Canada Wore: A Historical Geography of the Orange Order in Canada* (Toronto: University of Toronto Press, 1980).
33 William J. Smyth, *Toronto, the Belfast of Canada: The Orange Order and the Shaping of Municipal Culture* (Toronto: University of Toronto Press, 2018).
34 William Jenkins, *Between Raid and Rebellion: The Irish in Buffalo and Toronto, 1867–1916* (Montreal and Kingston: McGill-Queen's University Press, 2013).
35 Brian P. Clarke, *Piety and Nationalism: Lay Voluntary Associations and the Creation of an Irish Catholic Community in Toronto, 1850–1887* (Montreal and Kingston: McGill-Queen's University Press, 1993).
36 Anthony Rotundo, *American Manhood: Transformations of Masculinity from the Revolution to the Modern Era* (New York: Basic Books, 1994); George Chauncey, *Gay New York: Gender, Urban Culture, and the Making of the Gay Male World, 1890–1940* (New York: Basic Books, 1994); Robert Connell, *Masculinities* (Berkeley: University of California Press, 1995); Michael Kimmel, *Manhood in America: A Cultural History* (New York: Free Press, 1996); Michael Roper and John Tosh, eds., *Manful Assertions* (London: Routledge, 1991); John Tosh, "What Should Historians Do with Masculinity? Reflections on Nineteenth-century Britain," *History Workshop* 38 (1994) 179–202; Joy Parr, "Gender History and Historical Practice," in *Gender and History in Canada*, ed. Joy Parr and Mark Rosenfeld (Toronto: Copp Clark, 1996): 18–27; Joy Parr, The *Gender of Breadwinners: Men, Women, and Change in Two Industrial Towns, 1880–1950* (Toronto: University of Toronto Press, 1990); Lynne Marks, *Revivals and Roller Rinks: Religion, Leisure, and Identity in Late-Nineteenth-Century Small-Town Ontario* (Toronto: University of Toronto Press, 1996); Cecilia Morgan, *Public Men*

and Virtuous Women: The Gendered Languages of Religion and Politics in Upper Canada, 1791–1850 (Toronto: University of Toronto Press, 1996); Craig Heron, "Boys Will Be Boys: Working-Class Masculinities in the Age of Mass Production," *International Labor and Working Class History* 69 (2006): 6–34; "The Boys and Their Booze: Masculinities and Public Drinking in Working-class Hamilton, 1890–1946," *Canadian Historical Review* 86 (2005): 411–53; Craig Heron, *Lunch-Bucket Lives: Remaking the Workers' City* (Toronto: Between the Lines, 2015); Peter Gossage and Robert Allen Rutherdale, eds., *Making Men, Making History: Canadian Masculinities across Time and Place* (Vancouver: UBC Press, 2018).
37 Bonnie Huskins, "The Ceremonial Space of Women: Public Processions in Victorian Saint John and Halifax," in *Separate Spheres: Women's Worlds in the 19th-Century Maritimes*, ed. Janet Guildford and Suzanne Morton (Fredericton: Acadiensis Press, 1994).
38 Nelson Wiseman, *Partisan Odysseys: Canada's Political Parties* (Toronto: University of Toronto Press, 2020), 8–19.
39 Donald B. Smith, *Seen but Not Seen: Influential Canadians and the First Nations from the 1840s to Today* (Toronto: University of Toronto Press, 2020), 9–13.
40 J.M.S. Careless, *Toronto to 1918: An Illustrated History* (Toronto: James Lorimer, 1984).
41 The City of Toronto's population was reported as 14,249 in 1841; 30,775 in 1851; 44,821 in 1861; 56,092 in 1871; and 86,415 in 1881. George A. Nader, *Cities of Canada*, vol. 2 (Toronto: Macmillan, 1976), 198, 203.
42 Mark George McGowan, *Death or Canada: The Irish Famine Migration to Toronto, 1847* (Toronto: Novalis, 2009).
43 Jenkins, *Between Raid and Rebellion*, 24, 32–44.
44 *Census of Canada, 1851–1852*, 67.
45 Donald B. Smith, *Sacred Feathers: The Reverend Peter Jones (Kahkewaquonaby) and the Mississauga Indians* (Toronto: University of Toronto Press 2013), 213.
46 The manuscript census reported the Black population of Toronto in 1861 as 987. See Michael Wayne, "The Black Population of Canada West on the Eve of the American Civil War: A Reassessment Based on the Manuscript Census of 1861," *Histoire sociale/Social History* 28/56 (1995): 485.
47 *Census of the Canadas, 1860–1861* (Ottawa), 1:48–9, reports Toronto's population of people from the German states and Holland at 334; Russia and Poland, 23; and Italy and Greece, 22. On ethnicity, see Robert Harney, ed., *Gathering Place: Peoples and Neighbourhoods in Toronto, 1834–1945* (Toronto: Multicultural History Society of Ontario, 1985).
48 Douglas McCalla, *Planting the Province: The Economic History of Upper Canada, 1784–1870* (Toronto: University of Toronto Press, 1993).

49 Gregory S. Kealey, *Toronto Workers Respond to Industrial Capitalism, 1867–1891* (Toronto: University of Toronto Press, 1980).
50 Careless, *Toronto to 1918*; Peter Goheen, *Victorian Toronto, 1850 to 1900: Pattern and Process of Growth* (Chicago: University of Chicago Press, 1970).

1. Tory Rebels and a Viceregal Visit

1 J.M.S. Careless, *The Union of the Canadas: The Growth of Canadian Institutions, 1841–1857* (Toronto: McClelland and Stewart, 1967), 122 –31; Phillip A. Buckner, *The Transition to Responsible Government: British Policy in British North America, 1815–1850* (Westport: Greenwood, 1985); Barbara J. Messamore, *Canada's Governors General, 1847–1878: Biography and Constitutional Evolution* (Toronto: University of Toronto Press, 2006), ch. 4; Derek Pollard and Ged Martin, eds., *Canada 1849* (Edinburgh: Centre for Canadian Studies, 2001).
2 Daniel Horner, *Taking to the Streets: Crowds, Politics, and the Urban Experience in Mid-Nineteenth-Century Montreal* (Montreal and Kingston: McGill–Queen's University Press, 2020), ch. 6; Elinor Kyte Senior, *British Regulars in Montreal: An Imperial Garrison, 1832–1854* (Montreal and Kingston: McGill–Queen's University Press, 1981) ch. 6; Jacques Monet, "La Fontaine, Sir Louis-Hippolyte," in *Dictionary of Canadian Biography*, vol. 9, University of Toronto/Université Laval, 2003–, http://www.biographi.ca/en/bio/la_fontaine_louis_hippolyte_9E.html; Michael S. Cross and Robert Lochiel Fraser, "Baldwin, Robert," in *Dictionary of Canadian Biography*, vol. 8, University of Toronto/Université Laval, 2003, http://www.biographi.ca/en/bio/baldwin_robert_8E.html.
3 Frederick Schneid, *European Politics, 1815–1848* (Milton Park: Taylor and Francis, 2017); John K. Walton, *Chartism* (Cambridge: Cambridge University Press, 1998); W.T. Easterbrook and Hugh G.J. Aitken, *Canadian Economic History* (Toronto: University of Toronto Press, 1988).
4 Jeffrey L. McNairn, *The Capacity to Judge: Public Opinion and Deliberative Democracy in Upper Canada, 1791–1854* (Toronto: University of Toronto Press, 2000).
5 Bruce Curtis, "'The 'Most Splendid Pageant Ever Seen': Gender, the Domestic, and Condescension in Lord Durham's Political Theatre," *Canadian Historical Review* 89 (2008): 55–88; Mark Francis, *Governors and Settlers: Images of Authority in the British Colonies, 1820–1860* (Houndmills: Macmillan Academic, 1992); Peter G. Goheen, "Parading: A Lively Tradition in Early Victorian Toronto," in *Ideology and Landscape in Historical Perspective*, ed. Alan R.H. Baker and Gideon Biger (Cambridge: Cambridge University Press, 1992), 330–51; Ian Radforth, *Royal Spectacle: The 1860 Visit of the Prince of Wales to Canada and the United States* (Toronto: University of Toronto Press, 2004).

6 *Patriot* (Toronto), 26 March 1849; *British Whig* (Kingston), 4 May 1849; "Letter from Gore," *British Whig*, 25 May 1849.
7 On British nationalism, see Linda Colley, *Britons: Forging the Nation, 1707–1837* (New Haven: Yale University Press, 1992).
8 Nicole Eustace, *Passion Is the Gale: Emotion, Power, and the Coming of the American Revolution* (Williamsburg: Omohundro Institute, 2008); Kimberly K. Smith, *The Dominion of Voice: Riot, Reason, and Romance in Antebellum Politics* (Lawrence: University Press of Kansas, 1999).
9 *British Colonist* (Toronto), 6 March 1849.
10 *British Whig*, 4 May 1849.
11 *Mirror* (Toronto), 15 June 1849.
12 Donald Swainson, "Blake, William Hume," in *Dictionary of Canadian Biography*, vol. 9, University of Toronto/Université Laval, 2003–, http://www.biographi.ca/en/bio/blake_william_hume_9E.html. On duelling and the gentlemanly code, see Cecilia Morgan, "'In Search of the Phantom Misnamed Honour': Duelling in Upper Canada," *Canadian Historical Review* 76 (1995): 529–62.
13 Bryan Palmer, "Popular Radicalism and the Theatrics of Rebellion: The Hybrid Discourse of Dissent in Upper Canada in the 1830s," in *Transatlantic Subjects: Ideas, Institutions, and Social Experience in Post-Revolutionary British North America*, ed. Nancy Christie (Montreal and Kingston: McGill–Queen's University Press, 2008), 403–38.
14 *Examiner* (Toronto), 7 March 1849.
15 On Orangeism in Toronto, see William J. Smyth, *Toronto, the Belfast of Canada: The Orange Order and the Shaping of Municipal Culture* (Toronto: University of Toronto Press, 2013); William Jenkins, *Between Raid and Rebellion: The Irish in Buffalo and Toronto* (Montreal and Kingston: McGill–Queen's University Press, 2013); Gregory S. Kealey, "Orangemen and the Corporation," in *Forging a Consensus: Historical Essays on Toronto*, ed. Victor L. Russell (Toronto: University of Toronto Press, 1984), 13–34; and Peter Way, "Street Politics: Orangemen, Tories, and the 1841 Election Riot in Toronto," *British Journal of Canadian Studies* 6 (1991): 275–303.
16 The opposition leader, Sir Allan MacNab, along with William Cayley, took the petition to England. See Donald R. Beer, *Sir Allan Napier MacNab* (Hamilton: Dictionary of Hamilton Biography, 1984), 258–61. Meanwhile Francis Hincks went to England to press the government's case. See Sir Francis Hincks, *Reminiscences of His Public Life* (Montreal: W. Drysdale, 1884), 196–7; and Ged Martin, "The Canadian Rebellion Losses Bill of 1849 in British Politics," *Journal of Imperial and Commonwealth History* 6 (1977): 5–12.
17 On petitioning, see Carol Wilton, *Popular Politics and Political Culture in Upper Canada, 1800–1850* (Montreal and Kingston: McGill–Queen's

University Press, 2000); J.K. Johnson, "'Claims of Equity and Justice': Petitions and Petitioners in Upper Canada, 1815–1840," *Histoire sociale/Social History* 27/55 (1995): 219–40; and Jan Noel, *Canada Dry: Temperance Crusades before Confederation* (Toronto: University of Toronto Press, 1995), 134, 147, 150.
18 Carol Wilton, "'A Firebrand amongst the People': The Durham Meetings and Popular Politics in Upper Canada," *Canadian Historical Review* 75 (1994): 348–9.
19 Cross and Fraser, "Baldwin, Robert," 54.
20 *Pilot* (Montreal), 31 May 1849.
21 *Gazette* (Montreal), 16 May 1849.
22 Carol Wilton, "'Lawless Law': Conservative Political Violence in Upper Canada, 1818–41," *Law and History Review* 13 (1995): 111–36; Way, "Street Politics;" Kealey, "Orangemen and the Corporation"; Hereward Senior, "A Bid for Rural Ascendancy: The Upper Canadian Orangemen, 1836–1840," in *Canadian Papers in Rural History*, ed. Donald H. Akenson (Gananoque: Langdale, 1986), 5:226–34; J.K. Johnson, "Colonel James Fitzgibbon and the Suppression of Irish Riots in Upper Canada," *Ontario History* 58 (1966): 139–55; Scott W. See, "Nineteenth-Century Collective Violence: Toward a North American Context," *Labour/Le Travail* 39 (1997): 13–38.
23 See, for instance, Michael S. Cross, "Stony Monday, 1849: The Rebellion Losses Riots in Bytown," *Ontario History* 63 (1971): 177–90.
24 *Pilot*, 30 March 1849.
25 For instance, Carol Wilton reports on several effigy burnings in Upper Canada in her *Popular Politics and Political Culture in Upper Canada*, 41, 43, 74, 106, 134.
26 *Examiner*, 28 March 1849.
27 John H. Dunn and Isaac Buchanan were candidates in Toronto in the 1841 provincial election, notorious for its violence. Irving Abella, "The 'Sydenham Election' of 1841," *Canadian Historical Review* 47 (1966): 326–43; Way, "Street Politics."
28 *Patriot*, 26 March 1849.
29 *Examiner*, 28 March 1849.
30 *Examiner*, 28 March 1849; *Patriot*, 26 March 1849. See also J.M.S. Careless, *Brown of the Globe*, 2 vols. (Toronto: Macmillan, 1959, 1963), 1:89.
31 *Examiner*, 28 March 1849. Privately, Reformers made much the same point about the Tory bias of Toronto city officials and militia officers. George Ridout wrote to Robert Baldwin soon after that riot: "I cannot help thinking that these worthies winked at if they did not actually encourage an invite to violence and outrage." Toronto Reference Library (hereafter TRL), Robert Baldwin Papers, A66/11, G. Ridout to Robert Baldwin, 28 March 1849.

32 Michael S. Cross, "'The Laws Are Like Cobwebs': Popular Resistance to Authority in Mid-Nineteenth Century British North America," in *Law in a Colonial Society: The Nova Scotia Experience*, ed. Peter Waite, Sandra Oxner, and Thomas Barnes (Toronto: Carswell, 1984), 103–23; Wilton, "'Lawless Law.'"
33 *Patriot*, 26 March 1849. Writing privately to Baldwin, a local Reformer worried that the preparations would not be enough, given that people expected various effigies to be burned and "houses [had been] threatened to be fired." Afterwards, however, another Reformer reported to Baldwin that "comparative quiet" had prevailed, thanks to the show of force. TRL, Robert Baldwin Papers, A71/43, J. Small to Robert Baldwin, 23 March 1849; A71/43, G. Ridout to Robert Baldwin, 28 March 1849; A66/11, J. Small (Toronto) to Robert Baldwin, 23 March 1849. "Canadian Rifles" refers to a British army regiment then stationed in Toronto and formally known as the Royal Canadian Rifle Regiment.
34 Smith, *Dominion of Voice*, 76. On the troubled history of the professionalization of Toronto's police force, see Nicholas Rogers, "Serving Toronto the Good," in *Forging a Consensus*, 116–40.
35 *Examiner*, 28 March 1849.
36 *Canadian Free Press*, 8 May 1849.
37 See TPL, Robert Baldwin Papers, A66/97, D. Robb (Napanee) to R B, 16 June 1849, where Robb, a Reformer, refers to "the 'Effigy Agents' at Napanee" when describing attempts to charge those responsible for effigy burning.
38 Nicholas Rogers, "Burning Tom Paine: Loyalism and Counter-Revolution in Britain, 1792–1793," *Histoire sociale/Social History* 32/64 (1999): 139–71; Frank O'Gorman, "The Paine Burnings of 1792–1993," *Past and Present* 193 (2006): 111–56; Alan Booth, "Popular Loyalism and Public Violence in the North-West of England, 1790–1800," *Social History* 8 (1983): 295–313.
39 *Globe*, 5 May 1849.
40 O'Gorman, "The Paine Burnings," 132–3.
41 On charivaris in Canada, see Allan Greer, "From Folklore to Revolution: Charivaris and the Lower Canadian Rebellion of 1837," *Social History* 15 (1990): 25–43; Bryan Palmer, *Cultures of Darkness: Night Travels in the Histories of Transgression* (New York: Monthly Review, 2000), 23–47; and Bryan D. Palmer, "Discordant Music: Charivaris and White-Capping in Nineteenth-Century North America," *Labour/Le Travailleur* 3 (1978): 5–62.
42 *Globe*, 5 May 1849.
43 *Globe*, 5 May 1849; *Examiner*, 16 May 1849. Wilton provides a historical context in her "'Lawless Law.'"
44 *Examiner*, 2 May 1849.
45 Cited in *Packet* (Bytown), 26 May 1849.

46 *Examiner*, 16 May 1849.
47 Radforth, *Royal Spectacle*; Francis, *Governors and Settlers*, ch. 2; Curtis, "The 'Most Splendid Pageant Ever Seen.'"
48 Elgin to Grey, 3 June 1849, Arthur G. Doughty, *The Elgin–Grey Papers*, 4 vols (Ottawa, 1937), 1:361.
49 Francis, *Governors and Settlers*, 251–2.
50 Elgin to Grey, 3 June 1849, *Elgin–Grey Papers*, 1:361.
51 *Gazette*, 10 October 1849.
52 *British American* (Woodstock), 21 July 1849.
53 Curtis, "The 'Most Splendid Pageant Ever Seen,'" 88.
54 Broadsheet reproduced in *Mirror*, 24 August 1849, and in the *Elgin–Grey Papers*, 2:462.
55 Enclosed in Elgin to Grey, 23 September 1849, *Elgin–Grey Papers*, 2:475–6.
56 *Globe*, 26 July 1849; John Charles Dent, *Last Forty Years: Canada Since the Union of 1841* (Toronto: G. Virtue, 1881), reproduces a long letter of 8 September 1849 from Baldwin to "an intimate friend in Toronto," 1:177–8.
57 *Transcript* (Montreal) and *Gazette*, cited by *Bathurst Courier* (Perth), 24 August 1849.
58 Elgin to Grey, 19 October 1849, *Elgin–Grey Papers* 2:523.
59 *Packet* (Bytown), 20 October 1849; *Punch* (London) n.d., reprinted in *Mirror*, 24 August 1849; *Gazette*, 16 October 1849.
60 *Globe*, 18 October 1849.
61 *British American*, 6 October 1849. Elgin enclosed copies of many addresses and replies in his letters to Grey; see *Elgin–Grey Papers*, 2:483–516.
62 W.H. Blake to Robert Baldwin, 18 September 1849, A34/32, Robert Baldwin Papers, TRL; Elgin to Grey, 25 October 1849, *Elgin–Grey Papers*, 2:525.
63 *Gazette*, 10 October 1849; *Bathurst Courier*, 12 October 1849; *British American*, 6 October 1849; *Globe*, 6 October 1849; *British Colonist*, 10 October 1849.
64 *Gazette*, 4 October 1849; *British Colonist*, 12 October 1849.
65 *Mirror*, 12 October 1849.
66 *Mirror*, 12 October 1849; *Courier* (Montreal), reprinted in *Mirror*, 19 October 1849.
67 The occupations were reported as labourer, tailor, shoemaker, carter, tinsmith, confectioner, tavern keeper (*Globe*, 11 October 1849). See also Way, "Street Politics," 298.
68 Kealey, "Orangemen and the Corporation," 60; *Examiner*, 17 October 1849.
69 On the capital's move from Montreal, see David B. Knight, *A Capital for Canada: Conflict and Compromise in the Nineteenth Century* (Chicago: University of Chicago, Department of Geography, 1977), ch. 5.

70 Elgin to Grey, 7 October 1849, *Elgin–Grey Papers*, 2:518.
71 Charles Tilly, *Contentious Performances* (Cambridge: Cambridge University Press, 2008), 14–15.

2. The Press and Election Culture

1 On the 1834 and 1836 elections, see Carol Wilton, *Popular Politics and Political Culture in Upper Canada, 1800–1850* (Montreal and Kingston: McGill-Queen's University Press, 2000), 156–63, 179–83; Sean T. Cadigan, "Paternalism and Politics: Sir Francis Bond Head, the Orange Order, and the Election of 1836," *Canadian Historical Review* 72 (1991): 319–47; Graeme Hazlewood Patterson, "Studies in Elections and Public Opinion in Upper Canada" (PhD diss., University of Toronto, 1969).
2 Irving Martin Abella, "The 'Sydenham Election' of 1841," *Canadian Historical Review* 47 (1966): 326–43.
3 Paul G. Cornell, *The Alignment of Political Groups in Canada* (Toronto: University of Toronto Press, 1962); Gordon T. Stewart, *The Origins of Canadian Politics: A Comparative Approach* (Vancouver: UBC Press, 1986).
4 Until Confederation, provincial elections were, predictably, the purview of the provincial government. In 1867, Dominion elections became a Dominion responsibility under Ottawa's control.
5 Charles Tilly, *Contentious Performances* (Cambridge: Cambridge University Press, 2008). See also Christian Borch, *Politics of Crowds: An Alternative Sociology* (Cambridge: Cambridge University Press, 2012).
6 J.M.S. Careless, *Brown of the Globe*, 2 vols. (Toronto: Macmillan, 1959, 1963).
7 Douglas McCalla, "Beaty, James," in *Dictionary of Canadian Biography*, vol. 12, University of Toronto/Université Laval, 2003–, http://www.biographi.ca/en/bio/beaty_james_12E.html.
8 Other Toronto newspapers read for the duration of parliamentary election campaigns are the *Banner* (Reform), *British Colonist* (Conservative), *Canadian Freeman* (Irish Catholic, Reform to 1860, Conservative subsequently), *Examiner* (Reform), *Mirror* (Irish Catholic, Reform), and *Patriot* (Conservative). Additional newspapers (*Commercial Herald, Independent,* and *North American*) were consulted, but scattered surviving issues had no coverage of electioneering. Nor did the *Christian Guardian* cover the details of election campaigns. On Toronto newspapers, see Juliana M. Stabile, "Toronto Newspapers, 1798–1845: A Case Study in Print Culture" (PhD diss., University of Toronto, 2002); and Edith Firth, *Early Toronto Newspapers, 1793–1867* (Toronto: Baxter Publishing and Toronto Public Library, 1961).
9 On women's keen involvement in elections, see Bettina Bradbury, "Women at the Hustings: Gender, Citizenship, and the Montreal

By-Elections of 1832," in *Rethinking Canada: The Promise of Women's History*, 5th ed., ed. Mona Gleason and Adele Perry (Toronto: Oxford University Press, 2006), 73–94; and Mary P. Ryan, *Women in Public: Between Banners and Ballots, 1825–1880* (Baltimore: Johns Hopkins University Press, 1990).

10 But see Michael S. Cross, *A Biography of Robert Baldwin: The Morning-Star of Memory* (Toronto: Oxford University Press, 2012), 128–9, 164–5, 233–4; and Ged Martin, *Favourite Son? John A. Macdonald and the Voters of Kingston, 1841–1891* (Kingston: Kingston Historical Society, 2010).

11 Scott W. See, "Polling Crowds and Patronage: New Brunswick's 'Fighting Election' of 1842–3," *Canadian Historical Review* 72 (1991): 127–56.

12 Dan Horner, *Taking to the Streets: Crowds, Politics, and the Urban Experience in Mid-Nineteenth-Century Montreal* (Montreal and Kingston: McGill–Queen's University Press, 2020), 122–34.

13 Colin Grittner, "Of Bludgeons and Ballots: Political Violence, Municipal Enfranchisement, and Local Governance in Mid-Nineteenth-Century Montreal," in *Violence, Order, and Unrest: A History of British North America, 1749–1876*, ed. Elizabeth Mancke et al. (Toronto: University of Toronto Press, 2019), 312–35.

14 George Emery, *Elections in Oxford County, 1837–1875: A Case Study of Democracy in Canada West and Early Ontario* (Toronto: University of Toronto Press, 2012).

15 Duncan Koerber, "Style over Substance: Newspaper Coverage of Early Election Campaigns in Canada, 1820–1841," *Canadian Journal of Communication* 36 (2011): 435–53.

16 Frank O'Gorman, "Campaign Rituals and Ceremonies: The Social Meaning of Elections in England, 1780–1860," *Past and Present* 135 (1992): 79–115; see also his *Voters, Patrons, and Parties; The Unreformed Electoral System of Hanoverian England, 1734–1832* (Oxford: Clarendon Press, 1989); James Vernon, *Politics and the People: A Study in English Political Culture, c. 1851–1867* (Cambridge: Cambridge University Press, 1993), 80–102; and Michael E. McGerr, *The Decline of Popular Politics: The American North, 1865–1928* (New York and Oxford: Oxford University Press, 1986). See also Mary P. Ryan, *Civic Wars: Democracy and Public Life in the American City during the Nineteenth Century* (Berkeley: University of California Press, 1997), 94–180.

17 William J. Smyth, *Toronto, the Belfast of Canada: The Orange Order and the Shaping of Municipal Culture* (Toronto: University of Toronto Press, 2015); Gregory S. Kealey, "Orangemen and the Corporation: The Politics of Class during the Union of the Canadas," and Barry Dyster, "Captain Bob and the Noble Ward," in *Forging a Consensus: Historical Essays on Toronto*, ed. Victor L. Russell (Toronto: University of Toronto Press, 1984), 13–34, 87–115.

18 For examples, see Emery, *Elections in Oxford*, 28, 91; and Martin, *Favourite Son*, 28.
19 *North American* (Toronto), 4 December 1851.
20 *Globe*, 10 December 1857; Careless, *Brown of the Globe*, 1:243–4.
21 *Globe*, 9 December 1857.
22 *Leader*, 5 December 1857; *Globe*, 7 December 1857.
23 *Leader*, 14 January 1874; *Globe*, 23 January 1874.
24 *Banner* (Toronto), 24 December 1847. Such posturing was typical of addresses of the era. Vernon, *Politics and the People*, 80–1.
25 *Globe*, 17 December 1857.
26 *Leader*, 5 July 1861.
27 *Consolidated Elections Act*, SC 1849 (12 Vict), c. 27.
28 Vernon, *Politics and the People*, 89.
29 Ged Martin makes a similar point in *Favourite Son*, 31. Emery cites newspaper reports of non-voters, including boys, participating in the show of hands; see, *Elections in Oxford*, 95–6, 116.
30 *Amendment to Elections Act*, SC 1866 (29 Vict), c. 13 (Province of Canada).
31 The Hon. A.A. Dorion when introducing the 1874 electoral reforms. Canada, *House of Commons Debates* (21 April 1874), 160.
32 Until 1874, the high qualification of £500, the unpaid position of a member of Provincial Parliament, and the costs of campaigning and living in the capital (when not Toronto) ensured that only the well-to-do stood for office. Emery, *Elections in Oxford*, 14–15.
33 *Consolidated Elections Act*, c. 27; Emery, *Elections in Oxford County*, 16.
34 *Globe*, 29 June 1861.
35 *Leader*, 2 July 1861.
36 *Banner*, 24 December 1847; *Examiner*, 2 December 1851.
37 *Globe*, 15 June 1863; *Leader*, 23 January 1874; *Globe*, 22 January 1874. Hecklers were said to have disrupted George Brown's 1857 nomination in North Oxford. Emery, *Elections in Oxford*, 94.
38 *Globe*, 15 June 1863.
39 O'Gorman, "Campaign Rituals," 86–8.
40 Vernon, *Politics and the People*, 87.
41 On ward meetings in Kingston, see Martin, *Favourite Son*, 69.
42 Julia Roberts, *In Mixed Company: Taverns and Public Life in Upper Canada* (Vancouver: UBC Press, 2009), 86–8.
43 *Leader*, 1 December 1857; *Globe*, 18 December 1857.
44 *Leader*, 22 June 1861.
45 *Leader*, 21, 22, 17 June and 2 July 1861; *Globe*, 3 and 4 July 1861.
46 *Examiner*, 16 December 1851.
47 *Globe*, 17 August 1858.

48 Donald Swainson, "Cameron, John Hillyard," in *Dictionary of Canadian Biography*, vol. 10, University of Toronto/Université Laval, 2003–, http://www.biographi.ca/en/bio/cameron_john_hillyard_10E.html.
49 On stereotypes, see William Jenkins, "Poverty and Place: Documenting and Representing Toronto's Catholic Irish, 1845–1890," in *At the Anvil: Essays in Honour of William J. Smyth*, ed. Patrick J. Duffy and William Nolan (Dublin: Geography Publications, 2014), 477–511.
50 *Globe*, 15 June 1863.
51 *Mirror*, 14 July 1854.
52 *Globe*, 19 and 21 December 1857; *Leader*, 21 December 1857.
53 *Globe*, 17 August 1858.
54 The mayor was obliged to call public meetings, preside over them, and ensure order under the terms of Reform legislation. *An Act to provide for the calling and orderly holding of Public Meetings*, 1843, 7 Vict., c. 7 (Province of Canada).
55 *Leader*, 10 December 1857; *Globe*, 9 and 10 December 1857.
56 *Globe*, 20 and 29 June 1861; *Leader*, 20 June 1861; David A. Wilson, *Thomas D'Arcy McGee*, vol. 2, *The Extreme Moderate, 1857–1868* (Montreal and Kingston: McGill–Queen's University Press, 2013), 124–5.
57 *Banner*, 30 December 1847.
58 *Leader*, 5 July 1861.
59 On Witton, see Bryan D. Palmer, *A Culture in Conflict: Skilled Workers and Industrial Capitalism in Hamilton, Ontario, 1860–1919* (Montreal and Kingston: McGill–Queen's University Press, 1979), 145–9. On courting working-class votes in the 1872 campaign, see Gregory S. Kealey, *Toronto Workers Respond to Industrial Capitalism, 1867–1892* (Toronto: University of Toronto Press, 1980), 135–8.
60 *Leader*, 17 August 1872.
61 Cross, *A Biography of Robert Baldwin*, 53–4, 128.
62 *An Act to Provide for the Freedom of Elections*, 1842, 6 Vict. c. 1 (Province of Canada). Polling was reduced to one day in 1871 for Dominion elections. See Emery, *Elections in Oxford County*, 136–7.
63 D.G.G. Kerr, "The 1867 Elections in Ontario," *Canadian Historical Review* 51 (1970): 379–80.
64 *Consolidated Elections Act*, 1849, 12 Vict., c. 27 (Province of Canada). On the importance of taverns as public space, see Roberts, *In Mixed Company*, 56–76.
65 *Act to extend the Elective Franchise, and better to define the qualification of Voters*, 1853, 16 Vict., c. 153 (Province of Canada); *An Act to define the Elective Franchise, to provide for the Registration of Voters, and for other purposes therein mentioned*, 1858, 22 Vict., c. 82 (Province of Canada); John Garner, *The Franchise and Politics in British North America, 1877–1867* (Toronto:

University of Toronto Press, 1969), 108–13; Kerr, "The 1867 Elections," 372–7.
66 *Globe*, 19 December 1851.
67 *Leader*, 22 December 1857.
68 *Patriot*, 10 December 1851. A "plumper" is a vote given exclusively to one candidate in ridings where voting for more than one candidate is possible.
69 Emery cites 1857 examples from South Oxford; *Elections in Oxford County*, 100–1.
70 *Globe*, 22 December 1857.
71 *Leader*, 5 July 1861. Garner, *The Franchise and Politics*, 235n33, says that 1858 legislation required a voter to make these sworn declarations.
72 *Globe*, 22 December 1857.
73 *Leader*, 23 December 1857.
74 William Jenkins, "Patrolmen and Peelers: Immigration, Urban Culture, and 'The Irish Police' in Canada and the United States," *Canadian Journal of Irish Studies* 28/29 (2002): 10–29.
75 *An Act to Provide for the Freedom of Elections*, 1842, 6 Vict., c. 1 (Province of Canada); Blake R. Brown, *Arming and Disarming: A History of Gun Control in Canada* (Toronto: Osgoode Society, 2012), 25–6.
76 *Mirror*, 20 March 1841.
77 *Globe*, 22 December 1857.
78 *Globe*, 21 December 1857.
79 *Banner*, 31 [30?] December 1847; *Leader*, 28 August 1858 and 8 July 1861.
80 *Leader*, 5 July 1861.
81 *Patriot*, 3 March 1841; *Journals of the Legislative Assembly of the Province of Canada*, vol. 13, App. N. (Quebec: R. Campbell, 1855); vol. 16 (Toronto: R. Campbell, 1858); Elections Canada, *History of Federal Ridings since 1867*, https://lop.parl.ca/About/Parliament/FederalRidingsHistory/HFER.asp.
82 *Mirror*, 9 April 1841.
83 Abella, "'Sydenham Election,'" 337–8.
84 Garner, *Franchise and Politics*.
85 *Globe*, 8 July 1861.
86 Allan Greer, "Historical Roots of Canadian Democracy." *Journal of Canadian Studies* 34 (1999): 7–26.
87 *Leader*, 11 July 1861.
88 Garner, *Franchise and Politics*, 108; *Leader*, 16 September 1878.
89 Emery, *Elections in Oxford*, 99–100, 115–16.
90 Cross, *Biography of Robert Baldwin*, 172.
91 *Leader*, 30 August 1858; 24 June 1863.
92 *North American*, 5 July and 2 August 1854; *Globe*, 27 April 1864.

93 *An Act for the more effectual prevention of corrupt practices at Elections*, 1860, 23 Vict., c. 17 (Province of Canada).
94 Garner, in *Franchise and Politics*, 202, reports that fewer than 10 per cent of contests were contested, but in the hotly fought 1857 campaign the percentage rose to 27 per cent.
95 Province of Canada, *Debates of the Legislative Assembly* (June 28, 1841) 1:156–7, 291 (Petition of Henry Sherwood).
96 Emery, *Elections in Oxford*, 170–1; Garner, *Franchise and Politics*, 210–13; Renaud Séguin, "Pour une nouvelle synthèse sur les processus électoraux du XIXe siècle Québecois," *Journal of the Canadian Historical Association* 16 (2005): 75–100.
97 *British Colonist*, 19 January 1857.
98 Peter G. Goheen, "Symbols in the Streets: Parades in Victorian Urban Canada," *Urban History Review* 18 (1990): 237–43; Craig Heron and Steve Penfold, *The Workers' Festival: Labour Day Parades in Canada* (Toronto: University of Toronto Press, 2005); Ian Radforth, *Royal Spectacle: The 1860 Visit of the Prince of Wales to Canada and the United States* (Toronto: University of Toronto Press, 2004); Brooks McNamara, *Day of Jubilee: The Great Age of Public Celebrations in New York, 1788–1909* (New Brunswick: Rutgers University Press, 1997); Ryan, *Civic Wars*, 58–93.
99 *Leader*, 8 July 1861; *Globe*, 8 July 1861.
100 *Leader*, 24 June 1863; *Globe*, 24 June 1863.
101 *Globe*, 26 June 1863.
102 *Globe*, 30 January 1874; see also police court testimony, *Globe*, 5 February 1874.
103 *Patriot*, 16 December 1851; *British Colonist*, 16 December 1851.
104 Peter Way, "Street Politics: Orangemen, Tories, and the 1841 Election Riot in Toronto," *British Journal of Canadian Studies* 6 (1991): 275–303.
105 *An Act to Provide for the Freedom of Elections*, 1842, 6 Vict., c. 1.
106 Cross, *Biography of Robert Baldwin*. 142–6.
107 *An Act Respecting Elections of Members of the House of Commons*, SC 1874 (37 Vict), c. 9.
108 Canada, *House of Commons Debates* (21 April 1874): 161–2 (A.A. Dorion). See also Peter B. Waite, *Canada, 1874–1896: Arduous Destiny* (Toronto: McClelland and Stewart, 1974), 24–5.
109 Canada, *House of Commons Debates* (21 April 1874): 166 (J.H. Cameron); *Nation* (Toronto), 22 January 1875.
110 McGerr, *Decline of Popular Politics*, 94–180.
111 Nancy Bouchier, "Idealized Middle-Class Sport for a Young Nation: Lacrosse in Nineteenth-Century Ontario Towns, 1871–1891," *Journal of Canadian Studies* 29 (1994): 89–111.

3. A Prince in Town

1 *Times* (London), 24 July 1860.
2 Ian Radforth, *Royal Spectacle: The 1860 Visit of the Prince of Wales to Canada and the United States* (Toronto: University of Toronto Press, 2004), ch. 2.
3 Nathaniel August Woods, *The Prince of Wales in Canada and the United States* (London: Bradbury and Evans, 1861); Kinahan Cornwallis, *Royalty in the New World: or, the Visit of the Prince of Wales to America* (New York: Doolady, 1860); A British Canadian [Henry James Morgan], *The Tour of H.R.H. the Prince of Wales through British America and the United States* (Montreal: John Lovell, 1860); Robert Cellem, *Visit of His Royal Highness the Prince of Wales to the British North American Provinces and United States in the Year 1860* (Toronto: Henry Rowsell, 1861).
4 Illustrated coverage is found in *Illustrated London News*; *Illustrated Times* (New York); *Frank-Leslie's Illustrated Newspaper* (New York); and *New-York Illustrated News*.
5 *Globe* (Toronto), and *Leader* (Toronto), 7, 21, and 29 June 1860.
6 Michael P. Breen, "Addressing la ville des dieux: Entry Ceremonies and Urban Audiences in Seventeenth-century Dijon," *Journal of Social History* 38 (2004): 341–64.
7 *Globe*, 21 June 1860.
8 On national societies on parade in Montreal, see Gillian I. Reich, "Claiming the Streets: Negotiating National Identities in Montreal's Parades, 1840–1880," in *Celebrating Canada*, ed. Raymond Blake and Matthew Hayday, 2 vols. (Toronto: University of Toronto Press, 2016, 2018), 1:33–40.
9 Mary P. Ryan, *Civic Wars: Democracy and Public Life in the American City during the Nineteenth Century* (Berkeley: University of California Press, 1997), 59.
10 M. James, "Ritual, Drama, and the Social Body in the Late Medieval English Town," *Past and Present* 98 (1983): 3–29; Roy Strong, *Art and Power: Renaissance Festivals, 1450–1650* (Berkeley: University of California Press, 1984); Lawrence Bryant, *The King and the City in the Parisian Royal Entry Ceremony: Politics, Ritual, and Art in the Renaissance* (Geneva: Librairie Droz, 1986); Michael McCormick, *Eternal Victory: Triumphal Rulership in Late Antiquity, Byzantium, and the Early Medieval West* (Cambridge: Cambridge University Press, 1986); David Jütte, "Entering a City," *Urban History* 41 (2014): 204–27.
11 On arch-building in the nineteenth century, see Mark Francis, *Governors and Settlers: Images of Authority in the British Colonies, 1820–60* (London: Macmillan, 1992), 31–4; Reich, "Claiming the Streets," 1:46; and David Waldstreicher, *In the Midst of Perpetual Fetes: The Making of American Nationalism, 1774–1820* (Chapel Hill: University of North Carolina Press and the Omohundro Institute, 1997).

12 *Globe*, 8 September 1860.
13 *Globe*, 7 September 1860.
14 Francis, *Governors and Settlers*, 31–4.
15 Morgan, *Tour of H.R.H.*, 249–50.
16 *Globe*, 8 September 1860; Morgan, *Tour of H.R.H.*, 244–5.
17 Michael Wayne, "The Black Population of Canada West on the Eve of the American Civil War: A Reassessment Based on the Manuscript Census of 1861," in *A Nation of Immigrants: Women, Workers, and Communities in Canadian History, 1840–1960s*, ed. Franca Iacovetta with Paula Draper and Robert Ventresca (Toronto: University of Toronto Press, 1998), 58–61.
18 *Globe*, 11 August 1860.
19 The addresses can be found in LAC, RG 7 G23, Office of the Governor General, vol. 1.
20 LAC, RG 7 G23, vol. 1, draft of reply from the governor general to A.R. Green, 8 September 1860.
21 On black newspapers, see Jane Rhodes, *Mary Ann Shadd Cary: The Black Press and Protest in the Nineteenth Century* (Bloomington: Indiana University Press, 1998), 249–50.
22 Victoria Freeman, "Toronto Has No History! Indigeneity, Settler Colonialism, and Historical Memory in Canada's Largest City, *Urban History Review* 38 (2010): 21–35.
23 Oxford University (OU hereafter), Bodleian Library (BL herafter), Acland Family Papers, d. 12, Henry Acland to Sarah Acland, 2 and 21 September 1860.
24 Trudy Nicks, "Dr Oronhyatekha's History Lessons: Reading Museum Collections as Texts," in *Reading beyond Words: Contexts for Native History*, ed. Jennifer S.H. Brown and Elizabeth Vibert (Peterborough: Broadview Press, 1996), 483–508; Gayle M. Comeau-Vasilopoulos, "Oronhyatekha," in *Dictionary of Canadian Biography*, vol. 13, University of Toronto/Université Laval, 2003–, http://www.biographi.ca/en/bio/oronhyatekha_13E.html.
25 Contexts for such a friendship are provided in Cecilia Morgan, *Travelling through Empire: Indigenous Voyages from Early Canada* (Montreal and Kingston: McGill–Queen's University Press, 2017).
26 LAC, RG 10, Records of the Department of Indian Affairs, vol. 545, Bartlett Letterbook, W.R. Bartlett to the Rev. Allen Salt, 27 July 1860.
27 Radforth, *Royal Spectacle*, 222–32.
28 J.R. Miller, "Petitioning the Great White Mother: First Nations' Organizations and Lobbying in London," in *Reflections on Native–Newcomer Relations* (Toronto: University of Toronto Press, 2017), 217–41.
29 David Cressy, *Bonfire and Bells: National Memory and the Protestant Calendar in Elizabethan and Stuart England* (London: Weidenfeld and Nicolson, 1989), 18–24.

30 Mary P. Ryan, *Women in Public: Between Banners and Ballots, 1835–1880* (Baltimore: Johns Hopkins University Press, 1991); Bonnie Huskins, "The Ceremonial Space of Women: Public Processions in Victorian Saint John and Halifax," in *Separate Spheres: Women's Worlds in the 19th-Century Maritimes*, ed. Janet Guildford and Suzanne Morton (Fredericton: Acadiensis Press, 1994).
31 *Globe*, 22, 23, 24, 25, and 29 August 1860.
32 *New York Times*, 10 September 1860; Ian Malcolm, "Robert Sutherland: The First Black Lawyer in Canada?," *Law Society Gazette* 26 (1992): 183–5.
33 *Globe*, 5 September 1860.
34 Alfred Sandham, *Medals Commemorative of the Visit of H.R.H. the Prince of Wales to Montreal in 1860* (Montreal: Privately printed, 1871); *Globe*, 3 and 5 September 1860.
35 "Sentinel" qtd in Cellem, *Visit of His Royal Highness*, 247.
36 *Globe*, 8 August 1860; Woods, *Prince of Wales in Canada and the United States*, 204–5.
37 LAC, MG 24-A-34, R2459-0-3-E, Henry Pelham Fiennes Pelham-Clinton, 5th Duke of Newcastle Collection (microform) [hereafter Newcastle Collection], Newcastle to Queen Victoria, 12 September 1860; Royal Archives (hereafter RA), VIC A/467/33, General Bruce to the prince consort, 11 September 1860; RA, VIC/Add A 3/19, Bertie to Mama, 11 September 1860.
38 William J. Smyth, *Toronto, The Belfast of Canada: The Orange Order and the Shaping of Municipal Culture* (Toronto: University of Toronto Press, 2015), ch. 4.
39 Cecil. J. Houston and William J. Smyth, *The Sash Canada Wore: A Historical Geography of the Orange Order in Canada* (Toronto: University of Toronto Press, 1980); Gregory S. Kealey, "The Orange Order in Toronto: Religious Riot and the Working Class," in *Essays in Canadian Working-Class History*, ed. G.S. Kealey and Peter Warrian (Toronto: McClelland and Stewart, 1976), 13–34; William Jenkins, *Between Raid and Rebellion: The Irish in Buffalo and Toronto, 1867–1916* (Montreal and Kingston: McGill–Queen's University Press, 2013).
40 On Orangeism's marching tradition, see Dominic Bryan, *Orange Parades: The Politics of Ritual, Tradition and Control* (London: Pluto, 2000); T.G. Fraser, *The Irish Parading Tradition: Following the Drum* (New York: St Martin's Press, 2000).
41 Michael Cottrell, "St Patrick's Day Parades in Nineteenth-Century Toronto: A Study of Immigrant Adjustment and Elite Control," in *A Nation of Immigrants*, 35–54; Rosalyn Trigger, "Irish Politics on Parade: The Clergy, National Societies, and St Patrick's Day Processions in Nineteenth-Century Montreal and Toronto," *Histoire sociale/Social History* 37/74 (2004): 159–99; Reich, "Claiming the Streets," 48–50.

42 Radforth, *Royal Spectacle*, 169–70; Ian Radforth, "Orangemen and the Crown," in *The Orange Order in Canada*, ed. David A. Wilson (Dublin: Four Courts Press, 2007), 78–80.
43 *Globe*, 31 August 1860.
44 Radforth, *Royal Spectacle*, 173.
45 *Globe*, 31 August 1860.
46 *Globe*, 20, 23, 28, 30, and 31 August 1860.
47 Radforth, "Orangemen and the Crown," 69–88.
48 *Globe*, 5 September 1860. Some people thought that the duke must be a Roman Catholic because of his opposition to Orangeism, but he was a High Church Anglican. See F. Darrell Munsell, *The Unfortunate Duke: Fifth Duke of Newcastle, 1811–1864* (Columbia: University of Missouri Press, 1985), 14.
49 LAC, MG 26 A, John A. Macdonald Papers, v. 297, Memorandum of Brockville meeting enclosed in Alexander Campbell to John A. Macdonald, 30 September 1860, 136165–8.
50 Radforth, *Royal Visit*, 177–8; Ged Martin, *Favourite Son? John A. Macdonald and the Voters of Kingston, 1841–1891* (Kingston: Kingston Historical Society, 2010), 56–8.
51 Radforth, *Royal Spectacle*, 178–86.
52 Macdonald's co-premier, George-Étienne Cartier, continued to accompany the prince during John A.'s absence, which lasted throughout the Toronto visit. See Martin, *Favourite Son*, 58.
53 Morgan, *The Tour of H.R.H.*, 149.
54 RA, Vic Add, A/3/19, Bertie to Mama, 11 September 1860.
55 *Globe*, 8 September 1860. On the symbolism of Orange arches, banners, and so on, see Neil Jarman, *Material Conflicts: Parade and Visual Displays in Northern Ireland* (Oxford and New York: Berg, 1997).
56 *Globe*, 6 September 1860.
57 Radforth, *Royal Spectacle*, 191–2; Trigger, "Irish Politics on Parade," 159–99.
58 OU, BL, MS Add d. 12, Acland Family Papers, Henry Acland to Sarah Acland, 11 September 1860.
59 Radforth, *Royal Spectacle*, 193.
60 *Times* (New York), 10 September 1860; Toronto Reference Library, Baldwin Room, Larrett Smith Diaries, 9 September 1860.
61 *Le Canadien* (Quebec), 21 September 1860.
62 LAC, Newcastle Collection, reel A-307, Newcastle to Palmerston, 12 September 1860.
63 Radforth, *Royal Spectacle*, 195–6; Woods, *The Prince of Wales in Canada*, 219.
64 LAC, Newcastle Collection, reel A-307, Newcastle to Palmerston, 12 September 1860.

65 Radforth, *Royal Spectacle*, 197–203; Martin, *Favourite Son*, 55–66.
66 *Globe*, 17 September 1860; *Leader*, 13 September 1860; *Le Courrier du Quebec* (Quebec), 7 September 1860; *Irish-American* (New York), 15 September 1860.
67 *Globe*, 8 September 1860.
68 *Globe*, 13 November 1860.

4. Religious Processions and Disorder

1 Resolution of Toronto District Orange Lodge, *Mail* (Toronto), 2 October 1875.
2 For alternative interpretations of these conflicts, see Martin J. Garvin, "The Jubilee Riots in Toronto, 1875," Canadian Catholic Historical Association, *Report* 26 (1959): 93–107; "Catholic-Protestant Relations in Ontario, 1864–1875" (MA thesis, University of Toronto, 1962); Mark McGowan, "'We endure what we cannot cure': John Joseph Lynch and Roman Catholic–Protestant Relations in Toronto, 1864–1875," Canadian Society of Church History, *Papers* 18 (1984): 89–111; Brian Clarke, "Religious Riot as Pastime: Orange Young Britons, Parades, and Public Life in Victorian Toronto," in *The Orange Order in Canada*, ed. David A. Wilson (Dublin: Four Courts Press, 2007), 109–27; Timothy Edgar Strauch, "Walking for God and Raising Hell: The Jubilee Riots, The Orange Order, and the Preservation of Protestantism in Toronto, 1875" (MA thesis, Queen's University, 1999); and Peter W. Goheen, "Symbols in the Streets: Parades in Victorian Canada," *Urban History Review* 18 (1990): 237–43.
3 Ronald Rudin, "Marching and Memory in Early Twentieth-Century Quebec: La Fête-Dieu, la Saint-Jean-Baptiste, and le Monument Laval," *Journal of the Canadian Historical Association* 10 (1999): 209–35; Dan Horner, *Taking to the Streets: Crowds, Politics, and the Urban Experience in Mid-Nineteenth-Century Montreal* (Montreal and Kingston: McGill–Queen's University Press, 2020), 162–71.
4 Susan E. Houston and Alison Prentice, *Schooling and Scholars in Nineteenth-Century Ontario* (Toronto: University of Toronto Press, 1988), 273–96; A.I. Silver, "Ontario's Alleged Fanaticism in the Riel Affair," *Canadian Historical Review* 69 (1988): 21–50; A.I. Silver, *The French-Canadian Idea of Confederation, 1864–1900* (Toronto: University of Toronto Press, 1982).
5 William Jenkins, *Between Raid and Rebellion: The Irish in Buffalo and Toronto, 1867–1916* (Montreal and Kingston: McGill–Queen's University Press, 2013), 24, 32–44.
6 Roberto Perin, *The Many Rooms of This House: Diversity and Toronto's Places of Worship Since 1840* (Toronto: University of Toronto Press, 2017), 16–17.

7 Ian McKay, "The Liberal Order Framework: A Prospectus for a Reconnaissance of Canadian History," *Canadian Historical Review* 81 (2000): 617–51.
8 Charles W. Humphries, "Lynch, John Joseph," in *Dictionary of Canadian Biography*, vol. 11, University of Toronto/Université Laval, 2003–, http://www.biographi.ca/en/bio/lynch_john_joseph_11E.html; Gerald J. Stortz, "John Joseph Lynch, Archbishop of Toronto: A Biographical Study of Religious, Political, and Social Commitment" (PhD diss., University of Guelph, 1980); Roberto Perin, *Rome in Canada: The Vatican and Canadian Affairs in the Late Victorian Age* (Toronto: University of Toronto Press, 1990), 20–4; Michael J. Cottrell, "Political Leadership and Party Allegiance among Irish Catholics in Victorian Toronto," in *Catholics at the "Gathering Place": Historical Essays on the Archdiocese of Toronto, 1841–1999*, ed. Mark George McGowan and Brian P. Clarke (Toronto: Canadian Catholic Historical Association, 1993), 53–68.
9 *Canadian Freeman* (Toronto), 26 May 1864.
10 The delegation was unusual in that Corpus Christi celebrations triggered no delegations or demonstrations in 1863, 1865 and 1866 (see *Canadian Freeman*, 22 June 1863, 22 June 1865, and 7 June 1866). On Medcalf, see Barrie Dyster, "Medcalf, Francis Henry," in *Dictionary of Canadian Biography*, vol. 10, University of Toronto/Université Laval, 2003–, http://www.biographi.ca/en/bio/medcalf_francis_henry_10E.html.
11 Correspondence tabled at city council on 30 May 1864 and printed in *Globe* (Toronto), 31 May 1864. See also *Canadian Freeman*, 2 June 1864.
12 *Globe*, 30 May 1864; *Irish Canadian* (Toronto), 2 June 1864.
13 *Irish Canadian*, 1 June 1864. On the *Irish Canadian*, see Mark McGowan, "Boyle, Patrick," in *Dictionary of Canadian Biography*, vol. 13, University of Toronto/Université Laval, 2003–, http://www.biographi.ca/en/bio/boyle_patrick_13E.html; and Gerald J. Stortz, "The Irish Catholic Press in Toronto, 1887–1892," *Canadian Journal of Communications* 10 (1983–4): 27–46.
14 *Canadian Freeman*, 2 June 1864.
15 *Globe*, 30 May 1864.
16 Archives of the Roman Catholic Archdiocese of Toronto (ARCAT hereafter), Lynch Papers, AG 01.016, Lynch to Lord Monck, 3 June 1864; AG 01.05, Lynch to Étienne-PaschalTaché, 3 June 1864; AG 01.07, Denis Godley to Lynch, 6 June 1864; AG 01.08, J.A. Macdonald to Lynch, 14 June 1864.
17 *Canadian Freeman*, 2 June 1864.
18 Guy Fawkes Day celebrates the successful suppression of a 1605 plot by Fawkes and other Catholics to blow up Parliament and the Protestant king.

19 *Globe*, 10 November 1864.
20 *Leader* (Toronto), 7 and 8 November 1864; *Globe*, 9 November 1864.
21 *Canadian Freeman*, 10 November 1864; Lynch's statement appears in *Globe*, 12 November 1864.
22 Requisition, *Mail*, 27 September 1875.
23 George Knox to the editor of the *Globe*, 4 October 1875.
24 *Leader*, 27 September 1875; *Mail*, 27 September 1875.
25 *Globe*, 28 September 1875; *Mail*, 27 September 1875; report on Council meeting discussion, *Mail*, 28 September 1875.
26 *Mail*, 2 October 1875.
27 *Mail*, 2 October 1875. On conflicts within the Orange Order, see Cecil J. Houston and William J. Smyth, *The Sash Canada Wore: A Historical Geography of the Orange Order in Canada* (Toronto: University of Toronto Press, 1980), 147–9; and David A. Wilson, "'Orange influences of the right kind': Thomas D'Arcy McGee, the Orange Order, and the New Nationality," in *The Orange Order in Canada*, 89–108.
28 *Mail*, 4 October 1875; Lynch circular, 2 October 1875, printed in *Mail*, 4 October 1874; ARCAT, Lynch Papers, AG 02.01, F.H. Medcalf to Lynch, 2 October 1875; *Irish Canadian*, 20 October 1875.
29 *Leader*, 1 October 1875.
30 LAC, MG 24 B40, R2634-0-9-E, C2345-7, George Brown fonds, George Brown to Anne Brown, 4 October 1875.
31 *Leader*, 4 October 1875; Bruce W. Hodgins and Paul W. White, "Macdonald (Sandfield), Donald Alexander," in *Dictionary of Canadian Biography*, vol. 12, University of Toronto/Université Laval, 2003–, http://www.biographi.ca/en/bio/macdonald_donald_alexander_12E.html.
32 *Irish Canadian*, 13 October 1875.
33 Court testimony reported in *Globe*, 14 January 1876.
34 *Globe*, 4 and 6 October 1875. On the police force's thrice-weekly drilling in preparation for street disturbances, see Peter Vronsky, "History of the Toronto Police, 1859–1875, Part 3: Toronto Police in 1859–1875, The Militarization of the Constables," www.petervronsky.org/crime/cph3.htm; and ARCAT, Lynch Papers, AG 02.04, Lynch to A. MacNabb, 5 October 1875; and AG 02.02,"Report on meeting at De La Salle Institute, October 6, 1875."
35 "Harrison Benchbook," January 1876, ctd. in Strauch, "Walking for God," 73.
36 The occupations of the fourteen accused were: labourer (five), cabman (two), dairyman, carpenter, grocery clerk, ropemaker, train brakeman, shopkeeper, and tailor. (Strauch, "Walking for God," 64.)
37 Strauch, "Walking for God," chs. 3 and 4.

38 *Leader*, 27 September 1875; *Globe*, 28 September 1875; *British American Presbyterian*, 1 October 1875.
39 *Irish Canadian*, 1 June 1864; 29 September and 6 October 1875; *Globe*, 5 October 1875.
40 *Leader*, 2 October 1875; *Canadian Freeman*, 2 June 1864; *Mail*, 28 September 1875; *Intelligencer*, ctd. in *Leader*, 5 October 1875.
41 *Globe*, 5 October 1875.
42 Clarke, "Religious Riot as Pastime," 111–25.
43 *Irish Canadian*, 13 October 1875.
44 *Irish Canadian*, 13 and 20 October 1875; see also Lynch's remarks to Premier Taché, 3 June 1864, ARCAT, AG 01.05 Lynch Papers.
45 *Nation*, 1 and 15 October 1875.
46 Michael Cottrell, "St Patrick's Day Parades in Nineteenth-Century Toronto: A Study of Immigrant Adjustment and Elite Control," in *A Nation of Immigrants: Women, Workers, and Communities in Canadian History, 1840–1960s*, ed. Franca Iacovetta with Paula Draper and Robert Ventresca (Toronto: University of Toronto Press, 1998), 35–54; 44; see also Brian Clarke, *Piety and Nationalism: Lay Voluntary Associations and the Creation of an Irish-Catholic Community in Toronto, 1850–1895* (Montreal and Kingston: McGill–Queen's University Press, 1993), ch. 8.
47 *Leader*, 27 September 1875; *Mail*, 28 September 1875; *Leader*, 4 October 1875.
48 Clarke, *Piety and Nationalism*. On ultramontanism, see also Perin, *Rome in Canada*; and Mary Heimann, *Catholic Devotion in Victorian England* (Oxford: Clarendon, 1995).
49 Heimann, *Catholic Devotion*, 35–6; Ann Taves, *The Household of Faith: Roman Catholic Devotions in Mid-Nineteenth-Century America* (Notre Dame: University of Notre Dame Press, 1986), 28–30.
50 Taves, *Household of Faith*, 27; Mark George McGowan, *The Waning of the Green: Catholics, the Irish, and Identity in Toronto, 1887–1922* (Montreal and Kingston: McGill–Queen's University Press, 1999) 101.
51 Stortz, "John Joseph Lynch"; Humphries, "Lynch."
52 McGowan, "'We endure,'" 99–102; Jenkins, *Between Raid and Rebellion*, 109–10.
53 John Joseph Lynch, *Questions and Objections Concerning Catholic Doctrine and Practices* (Toronto: W. Warwick, 1877); Thomas Fenwick, *Archbishop Lynch's "Answers to questions and objections concerning Catholic doctrine and practice"* (Toronto: Presbyterian Print and Publishing Company, 1890). On deliberative democracy, see Jeffery L. McNairn, *The Capacity to Judge: Deliberative Democracy and Public Opinion in Upper Canada, 1791–1854* (Toronto: University of Toronto Press, 2000).
54 Taves, *Household of Faith*, 133.

55 Privately, Lynch was not sure the treaty extended beyond Quebec to Toronto; nor were authorities. See ARCAT, Lynch Papers, AG 01.05, Lynch to Étienne-Paschal Taché, 3 June 1864; AG 01.08, Macdonald to Lynch, 14 June 1864. Though Lynch did not make the argument, he might have contended that Catholic rights derived as well from the Quebec Act (1774), which applied to the old Province of Quebec, which included the region that would later become Upper Canada and then Ontario.
56 E.A. Heaman, "Rights Talk and the Liberal Order Framework," in *Liberalism and Hegemony: Debating the Canadian Liberal Revolution*, ed. Jean-François Constant and Michel Ducharme (Toronto: University of Toronto Press, 2009), 162–3. Tensions between liberalism and the collective rights of a Catholic institution in Quebec are discussed in J.I. Little, "Charities, Manufactures, and Taxes: The Montreal Sisters of Providence Spruce Gum Syrup Case, 1876–78," *Canadian Historical Review* 95, no. 1 (2014): 54–77.
57 Houston and Prentice, *Schooling and Scholars*, 273–96.
58 Jean-Roch Rioux, "Guibord, Joseph," in *Dictionary of Canadian Biography*, vol. 9, University of Toronto/Université Laval, 2003–, http://www.biographi.ca/en/bio/guibord_joseph_9E.html; Susan Mann Trofimenkoff, *The Dream of Nation: A Social and Intellectual History of Quebec* (Toronto: Gage, 1983), 115–30.
59 Stortz, "John Joseph Lynch," 138; *Globe*, 14, 15, and 29 September 1875; *Globe*, 14 September 1875; see also *Nation*, 1 October 1875.
60 *Christian Guardian* (Toronto), 6 October 1875; *Cookstown Advocate*, reprinted in *Leader*, 9 October 1875.
61 *Globe*, 4 October 1875.
62 *Globe*, 20 January 1876; Carole B. Stelmack, "Harrison, Robert Alexander," in *Dictionary of Canadian Biography*, vol. 10, University of Toronto/Université Laval, 2003, http://www.biographi.ca/en/bio/harrison_robert_alexander_10E.html; Strauch, "Walking for God," ch. 3; Peter N. Oliver, "Introduction," *The Conventional Man: The Diaries of Ontario Chief Justice Robert A. Harrison, 1858–1878*, ed. Peter N. Oliver (Toronto: University of Toronto Press, 2003); R. Blake Brown, "'Stars and Shamrocks Will Be Sown': The Fenian State Trials, 1866–7," in *Canadian State Trials, vol. 3: Political Trials and Security Measures, 1840–1914*, ed. Barry Wright and Susan Binnie (Toronto: University of Toronto Press, 2009), 45–84.
63 I have found no Anglican sources on either dispute. It is likely that Toronto's Anglican evangelicals, many of Irish origin, opposed the processions and that High churchmen did not. See Alan L. Hayes "Repairing the Walls: Church Reform and Social Reform, 1867–1939," in *By Grace Co-workers: Building the Anglican Diocese of Toronto, 1780–1989*, ed. Alan L. Hayes (Toronto: Anglican Book Centre, 1989), 43–96.

64 *Christian Guardian*, 20 October 1875; *Mail*, 6 October 1875.
65 *Christian Guardian*, 29 September 1875; *British American Presbyterian* (Toronto), 15 October 1875.
66 Paul Laverdure, *Sunday in Canada: The Rise and Fall of the Lord's Day* (Yorkton: Gravelbooks, 2004).
67 *Christian Guardian*, 20 October 1875.
68 *Globe*, 4 October 1875; LAC, MG 24–B40, George Brown fonds, C2345–7, George Brown to Anne Brown, 4 October 1875.
69 Synopsis of Robb's sermon, *Globe*, 4 October 1875.
70 1829, 10 George IV, c. 7, clause 26 (repealed 1926) (United Kingdom).
71 D.G. Paz, *Popular Anti-Catholicism in Mid-Victorian England* (Stanford: Stanford University Press, 1992), 238–9; G.I.T. Machin, *Politics and the Churches in Great Britain, 1832–1868* (Oxford: Clarendon, 1977), 254–6.
72 *Canadian Freeman*, 22 June 1865; Stortz, "John Joseph Lynch," 219.
73 Lynch, *Questions and Objections*, 13.
74 J.R. Miller, "Anti-Catholic Thought in Victorian Canada," *Canadian Historical Review* 64 (1985): 488.
75 John R. Dichtl, *Frontiers of Faith: Bringing Catholicism to the West in the Early Republic* (Lexington: University Press of Kentucky, 2008), 155–6.
76 *Christian Guardian*, 20 October 1875.
77 *British American Presbyterian*, 15 October 1875.
78 *Christian Guardian*, 3 November 1875; *British American Presbyterian*, letter to the editor, 29 September 1875; editorial, 15 October 1875.
79 *Canadian Freeman*, 22 June 1865; ARCAT, AA 11.09, Lynch, "Pastoral," 4 March 1874.
80 Clarke, "Religious Riot as Pastime," 120–1; Jenkins, *From Raid to Rebellion*, 193–219.

5. Colonialism Triumphant: Celebrating the Suppression of the North-West Resistance of 1885

1 *Mail* (Toronto), 28 March 1885.
2 *Mail*, 28 March 1885. On Otter, the Infantry School, and the Toronto militia, see Desmond Morton, *The Canadian General: Sir William Otter* (Toronto: Hakkert, 1974).
3 *Globe* (Toronto), 30 March 1885.
4 *Mail*, 28 March 1885.
5 *Telegram* (Toronto), 29 March 1885.
6 *World* (Toronto), 29 March 1885.
7 See, for example, George F.C. Stanley, *The Birth of Western Canada: A History of the Riel Rebellions*, reprint (Toronto: University of Toronto Press, 1992); Bob Beal and Rod MacLeod, *Prairie Fire: The 1885 North-West*

Rebellion (Edmonton: Hurtig, 1984); Desmond Morton, *The Last War Drum: The North West Campaign of 1885* (Toronto: Hakkert, 1972); Thomas Flanagan, *Riel and the Rebellion: 1885 Reconsidered*, 2nd ed. (Toronto: University of Toronto Press, 2000); J.M. Bumsted, *Louis Riel v. Canada: The Making of a Rebel* (Winnipeg: Great Plains, 2001); Maggie Siggins, *Riel: A Life of Revolution* (Toronto: HarperCollins, 1994); George Woodcock, *Gabriel Dumont: The Metis Chief and His Lost World* (Edmonton: Hurtig, 1975); and Walter Hildebrandt, *The Battle of Batoche: British Small Warfare and the Entrenched Metis*, 2nd ed. (Vancouver: Talon Books, 2012).

8 Desmond Morton dates Canada's "moment of militarism" to the campaign at the beginning of the twentieth century. See his "The Cadet Movement in the Moment of Canadian Militarism," *Journal of Canadian Studies* 13 (1978): 56–68.

9 Russell Hann, "Brainworkers and the Knights of Labor: E.E. Sheppard, Phillips Thompson, and the Toronto News, 1883–1887," in *Essays in Canadian Working-Class History*, ed. G.S. Kealey and Peter Warrian (Toronto: McClelland and Stewart, 1976), 35–57.

10 By contrast, in Halifax critics said that Nova Scotians had no enthusiasm for sending militiamen to a distant conflict that had nothing to do with them. Stanley attributes this hostility to "repealers," who still hoped Nova Scotia might withdraw from Confederation. See George F.G. Stanley, "New Brunswick and Nova Scotia and the North-West Rebellion, 1885," in *The Developing West: Essays on Canadian History in Honor of Lewis H. Thomas*, ed. John E. Foster (Edmonton: University of Alberta Press, 1983), 71–100.

11 On the expansion of settler colonialism in an earlier period and other regions of Canada, see John G. Reid, "Empire, Settler Colonialism, and the Rise of Violence in Indigenous Dispossession in British North America, 1749–1830," in *Violence, Order, and Unrest: A History of British North America, 1749–1876*, ed. Elizabeth Mancke et al. (Toronto: University of Toronto Press, 2019), 117–34.

12 For varied perspectives on the causes and meaning of the resistance movements of 1869–1870 and 1885, see Gerald Friesen, *The Canadian Prairies: A History* (Toronto: University of Toronto Press, 1984), 220–31; Bumsted, *Louis Riel v. Canada*; Flanagan, *Riel and the Rebellion*; and Gerhard Ens, *Homeland to Hinterland: The Changing Worlds of the Red River Metis in the Nineteenth Century* (Toronto: University of Toronto Press, 1996).

13 Diane P. Payment, *The Free People – Li Gens Libres: A History of the Metis Community of Batoche, Saskatchewan* (Calgary: University of Calgary Press, 2009), 8–11; Alan McCullough, "Parks Canada and the 1885 Rebellion/Uprising/Resistance," *Prairie Forum* 27 (2002): 161–98.

14 Blair Stonechild and Bill Waiser, *Loyal till Death: Indians and the North-West Rebellion* (Calgary: Fifth House, 1997).

15 J.M.S. Careless, *Toronto to 1918: An Illustrated History* (Toronto: J. Lorimer, 1984), ch. 4.
16 J.M.S. Careless, "The First Hurrah: Toronto's Semi-Centennial of 1884," in *Forging a Consensus: Historical Essays on Toronto*, ed. Victor L. Russell (Toronto: University of Toronto Press, 1984), 141–54. See also Victoria Freeman, "'Toronto Has No History!': Indigeneity, Settler Colonialism, and Historical Memory in Canada's Largest City," *Urban History Review* 38 (2010): 21–35; and Todd Stubbs, "Patriotic Masculinity and Mutual Benefit Fraternalism in Urban English Canada: The Sons of England, 1874–1900," *Histoire sociale/Social History*, 45/89 (2012): 25–49.
17 On British nationalism, see Linda Colley, *Britons: Forging the Nation, 1707–1837* (New Haven: Yale University Press, 2009).
18 *Dominion Churchman* (Toronto), 6 August 1885. In fact, Catholic clergy had broken with Riel, who at this time saw himself as a prophet. See Stanley, *Birth of Western Canada*, 316–17.
19 On racial discourse in the period, see Douglas Lorimer, "From Victorian Values to White Virtues: Assimilation and Exclusion in British Racial Discourse, c. 1870–1914," in *Rediscovering the British World*, ed. Phillip Buckner and R. Douglas Francis (Calgary: University of Calgary Press, 2005), 109–34; and Paula Hastings, "'Our Glorious Anglo-Saxon Race Shall Ever Fill Earth's Highest Place': The *Anglo-Saxon* and the Construction of Identity in Late Nineteenth-Century Canada," in *Canada and the British World: Culture, Migration, and Identity*, ed. Phillip Buckner and R. Douglas Francis (Vancouver: UBC Press, 2006), 92–109.
20 *Globe*, 7 April 1885.
21 *Telegram*, 30 May 1885.
22 Morton, *Last War Drum*, 6–49; Desmond Morton, *A Military History of Canada*, 5th ed. (Toronto: McClelland and Stewart, 2007), 93–107; J.L. Granatstein, *Canada's Army: Waging War and Keeping the Peace* (Toronto: University of Toronto, 2002), 28–32. Canada's *Militia Act* required the force to be commanded by a senior officer in the British army.
23 James Wood, *Militia Myths: Ideas of the Canadian Citizen Soldier, 1896–1921* (Vancouver: UBC Press, 2010), 29–31. See also Mike O'Brien, "Manhood and the Militia Myth: Masculinity, Class, and Militarism in Ontario, 1902–1914," *Labour/Le travail* 42 (1998): 115–41; Mark Moss, *Manliness and Militarism: Educating Young Boys in Ontario for War* (Toronto: Oxford University Press, 2001); and K.B. Wamsley, "Cultural Signification and National Ideologies: Rifle-Shooting in Late Nineteenth-Century Canada," *Social History* 20 (1995): 63–72. Desmond Morton notes that when William Otter first joined the Queen's Own in 1861 his uniform cost him a month of his salary as a clerk with the Canada Company. See Desmond Morton, "Otter, Sir William Dillon," in *Dictionary of Canadian Biography*, vol. 15,

University of Toronto/Université Laval, 2003, http://www.biographi.ca/en/bio/otter_william_dillon_15E.html.
24 In fact, there is no good study of the composition of the Canadian militia, but see O'Brien, "Manhood and the Militia Myth," 124–27; Morton, *Military History of Canada*, ch. 3; Gillian Poulter, *Becoming Native in a Foreign Land: Sport, Visual Culture, and Identity in Montreal, 1840–85* (Vancouver: UBC Press, 2009), 209; and Carman Miller, *Painting the Map Red: Canada and the South African War, 1899–1902* (Montreal and Kingston: Canadian War Museum and McGill–Queen's University Press, 1993), 58–60.
25 Royal Archives, Cambridge Papers, General Middleton to Duke of Cambridge, 6 May 1885, ctd. in Morton, *Last War Drum*, 69; General Middleton to A. Caron, Minister of Militia, 26 June 1885, in *Telegrams of the North-West Campaign 1885*, ed. Desmond Morton and Reginald H. Roy (Toronto: Champlain Society, 1972), 361.
26 *Mail*, 27 July 1885.
27 Ctd. by Desmond Morton, "Middleton, Sir Fredrick Dawson," in *Dictionary of Canadian Biography*, vol. 12, University of Toronto/Université Laval, 2003, http://www.biographi.ca/en/bio/middleton_frederick_dobson_12E.html; R.S. Cassels, "The Diary of R.S. Cassels," in *The Reminiscences of a Bungle: And Two Other Northwest Rebellion Diaries*, ed. R.C. Macleod (Edmonton: University of Alberta Press, 1983), 235.
28 *Mail*, 27 April 1885.
29 Morton, *Last War Drum*, 34.
30 *World*, 29 March 1885; *Globe*, 30 March 1885.
31 In Quebec City during the tercentenary celebrations, French Canadians appeared in large numbers to see local troops. See H.V. Nelles, *The Art of Nation-Building: Pageantry and Spectacle at Quebec's Tercentenary* (Toronto: University of Toronto Press, 1999), 203–6; Ronald Rudin, *Founding Fathers: The Celebration of Champlain and Laval in the Streets of Quebec, 1878–1908* (Toronto: University of Toronto Press, 2003), 197–8.
32 Access to Toronto's public space for celebratory purposes is discussed in Peter G. Goheen, "Negotiating Access to Public Space in Mid-Nineteenth Century Toronto," *Journal of Historical Geography* 20 (1994): 430–49, and "The Assertion of Middle-Class Claims to Public Space in Late Victorian Toronto," *Journal of Historical Geography* 29 (2003): 73–92.
33 *World*, 29 March 1885.
34 *Leader*, 16 and 17 May 1870.
35 Granatstein, *Canada's Army*, 28.
36 *Telegram*, 30 March 1885.
37 *Mail*, 31 March 1885.
38 *Mail*, 31 March 1885.
39 *News* (Toronto), 30 March 1885.

40 *Irish Canadian* (Toronto), 2 April 1885. On the *Irish Canadian*, see Gerald J. Stortz, "The Irish Catholic Press in Toronto, 1874–1887," Canadian Catholic Historical Association, *Study Sessions* 47 (1980): 27–46; and Mark C. McGowan, *The Waning of the Green: Catholics, the Irish, and Identity in Toronto, 1887–1922* (Montreal and Kingston: McGill–Queen's University Press, 1999), 187–90.
41 *Mail*, 31 March 1885.
42 *Telegram*, 30 March 1885.
43 *World*, 31 March 1885; *Globe*, 31 March 1885.
44 *Mail*, 31 March 1885; *World*, 31 March 1885; *News*, 31 March 1885; *Globe*, 30 March 1885; *Varsity* (Toronto), 4 April 1885. The Civil War song popular among Northerners had "Jeff Davis," president of the Confederacy, hanging from a sour apple tree.
45 *Illustrated War News* (Toronto), 4 April 1885.
46 *Varsity*, 4 April 1885; *Globe*, 30 March 1885.
47 The spontaneity more closely resembled urban crowds reacting to news of the outbreak of war in 1914 rather than the carefully planned send-offs of the first contingent; see Robert Rutherdale, "Canada's August Festival: Communitas, Liminality, and Social Memory," *Canadian Historical Review* 77 (1996): 221–50.
48 Granatstein, *Canada's Army*, 32; Morton, *Last War Drum*, 67–70, 73–95, 104–8.
49 Sarah A. Carter, *Capturing Women: The Manipulation of Cultural Imagery in Canada's Prairie West* (Montreal and Kingston: McGill–Queen's University Press, 1997), 48–157.
50 *Mail*, 31 March 1885.
51 *Telegram*, 25 April 1885. Newspapers also contracted with militiamen (some from their own staffs) to send home stories from the front. See *La Patrie* (Montreal), 2 April 1885.
52 Pte. ____ to A. Caron, 2 April 1885, in *Telegrams of the North-West Campaign*, 89–90.
53 *The Sentinel and Orange and Protestant Advocate* (Toronto), 25 March 1888. Apart from passing this motion, the Orange Order did not take a public role in Toronto's celebrations of the militiamen.
54 *Globe*, 3 April 1885.
55 *Mail*, 25 April 1885.
56 *News*, 5 May 1885.
57 *Illustrated War News*, 9 May 1885.
58 Altogether the militia suffered 26 dead and 103 wounded (Granatstein, *Canada's Army*, 32). Firm numbers of losses on the other side are unavailable.
59 *Globe*, 2 June 1885.

60 *News*, 21 and 27 May, 1, 5, and 27 June 1885.
61 *Globe*, 26 June 1885.
62 Report of the meeting of the reception committee, *Mail*, 30 June 1885.
63 Report of the meeting of the reception committee, *Mail*, 13 July 1885. The station occupied the site of the 1916 station that is now an LCBO liquor store.
64 Report of the meeting of the reception committee, *Mail*, 18 July 1885.
65 *Mail*, 28 July 1885.
66 *News*, 12 July 12 1885.
67 *Mail*, 20 July 1885.
68 *Globe*, 21 July 1885.
69 *Telegram*, 24 July 1885; *World*, 24 July 1885.
70 *Mail*, 23 July 1885; *Irish Canadian*, 23 July 1885.
71 *Illustrated War News*, 25 July 1885.
72 The significance of arches in public display is discussed in Ian Radforth, *Royal Spectacle: The 1860 Visit of the Prince of Wales to Canada and the United States* (Toronto: University of Toronto Press, 2004), 58–69.
73 *World*, 23 July 1885.
74 *World*, 23 July 1885.
75 See reports of the meetings called by Le Club National in the *Gazette* (Montreal), 22 April and 9 June 1885.
76 *Mail*, 24 July 1885.
77 See, for instance, ads in the *World*: P. Patterson and Son offering Volunteers revolvers at "less than cost"; P. Jamieson drawing attention to his war on clothing prices with the heading "War! War! War!" (6 April 1885); W. McDowall's pitch to Volunteers for leather belts and repeating rifles (7 April 1885); and P. Burns's offer to families of Volunteers of special rates on fuel (11 April 1885).
78 *Mail*, 23 July 1885.
79 *Globe*, 24 July 1885.
80 *Globe*, 24 July 1885.
81 *Christian Guardian* (Toronto), 29 July 1885, 9.
82 Newspapers took the trouble to name every individual who had a ticket of entry to the station. See, for example, *Mail*, 24 July 1885.
83 *Globe*, 24 July 1885.
84 *Globe*, 24 July 1885.
85 The Toronto dailies and the *Times of London* lionized Howard, and Torontonians honoured him with a reception and banquet (*News*, 24 July 1885; *Mail*, 25 July 1885). Howard's contribution was doubted by General Middleton, however; see *Telegrams of the North-West Campaign*, 361. The *Irish Canadian*, following the lead of the *Palladium of Labor*, insisted that Howard was a mere mercenary (*Irish Canadian*, 4 June 1885).

86 George T. Denison, *Soldiering in Canada: Recollections and Experiences*, 2nd ed. (Toronto: G.N. Morang), 839.
87 *Globe*, 24 July 1885.
88 *News*, 24 July 1885.
89 *Globe*, 24 July 1885.
90 *Mail*, 24 July 1885.
91 *Irish Canadian*, 18 June 1885.
92 *Mail*, 27 July 1885; *The Trip Hammer* (a publication of the employees of Massey Manufacturing in Toronto), August 1885; *The Trader* (a Toronto publication for jewellers and hardware merchants), August 1885. Such feelings have been analysed as examples of *communitas* in the case of Toronto's response to news of the outbreak of war in August 1914; see Rutherdale, "August Festivals."
93 Nelles, *Art of Nation-Building*, 199.
94 Cassels, "Diary," 234–5.
95 On the Baptist press in this regard, see Gordon L. Heath, "Traitor, Half-Breeds, Savages, and Heroes: Canadian Baptist Newspapers and Constructions of Riel and the Events of 1885," in *Baptists and Public Life in Canada*, ed. Gordon L. Heath and Paul R. Wilson (Eugene: Pickwick, 2012), 203. On the religious rhetoric associated with the South African War, see Gordon L. Heath, *A War with a Silver Lining: Canadian Protestant Churches and the South African War, 1899–1902* (Montreal and Kingston: McGill–Queen's University Press, 2009); on the First World War, see Jonathan F. Vance, *Death So Noble: Memory, Meaning, and the First World War* (Vancouver: UBC Press, 1997), ch. 2.
96 *Telegram*, 11 July 1885; *News*, 11 July 1885; John Warkentin, *Creating Memory: A Guide to Outdoor Public Sculpture in Toronto* (Toronto: Becker Associates, 2010), 67; the inscription from Horace can be translated as "It is sweet and right to die for your country."
97 See https://www.metisnation.org/news/louis-riel-day-2019-video.
98 Mary P. Ryan, *Civic Wars: Democracy and Public Life in the American City during the Nineteenth Century* (Berkeley: University of California Press, 1997).
99 Radforth, *Royal Spectacle*, 123–7; Craig Heron and Steve Penfold, *The Workers' Festival: A History of Labour Day in Canada* (Toronto: University of Toronto Press, 2005), 45.
100 *Palladium of Labor*, 8 August 1885.
101 Stanley, "New Brunswick and Nova Scotia," 82–4; the *Globe* described receptions in Winnipeg (17 July 1885), Montreal, and Ottawa (21 July 1885).
102 *Gazette* (Montreal), 3 April and 21 July 1885; *La Presse* (Montreal), 2 and 3 April 1885, and "Extra," 20, 21, and 24 July 1885; *L'Étendard* (Montreal), 4 April, 21 and 22 July 1885.

103 *La Patrie* (Montreal), 6 April 1885; *Gazette*, 7 April 1885.
104 *La Patrie*, 21 and 23 April 1885.
105 *Globe*, 24 July 1885.
106 *Mail*, 25 July 1885.

6. Boys, Young Men, and Disorder

1 Paul Craven, "Law and Ideology: The Toronto Police Court, 1850–80," in *Essays in the History of Canadian Law*, vol. 2, ed. David H. Flaherty (Toronto: Osgoode Society and University of Toronto Press, 1983), 248–307; and William Jenkins, "Poverty and Place: Documenting and Representing Toronto's Catholic Irish, 1845–1890," in *At the Anvil: Essays in Honour of William J. Smyth*, ed. Patrick J. Duffy and William Nolan (Dublin: Geography Publications, 2014), 477–511.
2 Craig Heron, "The Boys and Their Booze: Masculinities and Public Drinking in Working-Class Hamilton, 1890–1946," *Canadian Historical Review* 86 (2005): 416.
3 See Scott W. See, "Aspirations and Limitations: 'Peace, Order and Good Government' and the Language of Violence and Disorder in British North America," in *Violence, Order, and Unrest: A History of British North America, 1749–1876*, ed. Elizabeth Mancke et al. (Toronto: University of Toronto Press, 2019), 17–35.
4 Tamara Myers, *Caught: Montreal's Modern Girls and the Law, 1869–1945* (Toronto: University of Toronto Press, 2006), 7.
5 Natalie Zemon Davis, "The Rites of Violence," in her *Society and Culture in Early Modern France: Eight Essays* (Stanford: Stanford University Press, 1975), 183.
6 *Globe* (Toronto), 5 May 1849; *Examiner* (Toronto), 28 March 1849; *Globe*, 5 May 1849.
7 Cecil J. Houston and William J. Smyth, *The Sash Canada Wore: A Historical Geography of the Orange Order in Canada* (Toronto: University of Toronto Press, 1980); and Gregory S. Kealey, "The Orange Order in Toronto: Religious Riot and the Working Class," in *Essays in Canadian Working-Class History*, ed. Gregory S. Kealey and Peter Warrian (Toronto: McClelland and Stewart, 1976), 13–34.
8 *Leader* (Toronto), 16 July 1855.
9 *Leader*, 16 and 18 July 1855; *Globe*, 24 July 1855.
10 "The Circus Riot: The Investigation by the City Council," *Globe*, 24 July 1855.
11 Gregory S. Kealey, "The Orangemen and the Corporation," in *Forging a Consensus: Historical Essays on Toronto*, ed. Victor L. Russell (Toronto: University of Toronto Press and City of Toronto Sesquicentennial Board, 1984),

42–86; Brian Clarke, "Religious Riot as Pastime: Orange Young Britons, Parades, and Public Life in Victorian Toronto," in *The Orange Order in Canada*, ed. David A. Wilson (Dublin: Four Courts Press, 2007), 109–27; William J. Smyth, *Toronto, the Belfast of Canada: The Orange Order and the Shaping of Municipal Culture* (Toronto: University of Toronto Press, 2015), 47–50; Michael Cottrell, "St Patrick's Day Parades in Nineteenth-Century Toronto: A Study of Immigrant Adjustment and Elite Control," *Histoire sociale/Social History* 25/49 (1992): 57–73; Rosalyn Trigger, "Irish Politics on Parade: The Clergy, National Societies, and St Patrick's Day Processions in Nineteenth-Century Montreal and Toronto," *Histoire sociale/Social History* 37/74 (2004): 59–99.

12 *Globe*, 24 April 1858.
13 Ian Radforth, "Collective Rights, Liberal Discourse, and Public Order: The Clash over Catholic Processions in Mid-Victorian Toronto," *Canadian Historical Review* 95 (2014): 511–44.
14 For a study of recent rioting that documents such motivations, see Laura Naegler, "The Ritual of Insurrection and the 'Thrill-Seeking Youth': An Instant Ethnography of Inner-City Riots in Germany," in *Riot, Unrest, and Protest on the Global Stage*, ed. Paul Pritchard and Francis Pakes (Basingstoke: Palgrave Macmillan, 2014), 151–69.
15 *Globe*, 5 October 1875.
16 *Irish Canadian* (Toronto), 29 September 1875.
17 David Mills, *The Idea of Loyalty in Upper Canada, 1785–1850* (Montreal and Kingston: McGill–Queen's University Press, 2014).
18 Ian Radforth, "Orangemen and the Crown," in Wilson, *Orange Order in Canada*, 69–88.
19 Keith Walden, "Respectable Hooligans: Male Toronto College Students Celebrate Hallowe'en, 1884–1910," *Canadian Historical Review* 68 (1987): 1–34.
20 On play, see E. Anthony Rotundo, *American Manhood: Transformations in Masculinity from the Revolution to the Modern Era* (New York: Basic Books, 1993), 35–7; and David Nassau, *Children of the City: At Work and at Play* (Garden City: Anchor Press, 1985).
21 *News* (Toronto), 27 May 1886.
22 *Globe*, 11 October 1853.
23 *Globe*, 29 May 1854.
24 *Globe*, 6 February 1856; 7, 9 April and 15 June 1858; 16 November 1858; 24 May, 22 June, 15 August, and 19 September 1859; 27 April, 9 May, 18 June, and 2 October 1860; 1 April 1861.
25 *Globe*, 24 July 1856 (arrests), 1 August 1856 (police court charges), and 30 October 1856 (trial).
26 *Globe*, 1, 2, 6, 8, 9, 12, 14, 15, 18, 19, 20, 22, 26, and 30 April 1861; 1 May 1861; 3, 4, and 9 October 1861; 2, 17, and 31 December 1861; 7, 9, and 11 January 1862.

27 *Globe*, 11 March 1862; Jennifer L. Bonnell, *Reclaiming the Don: An Environmental History of Toronto's Don River Valley* (Toronto: University of Toronto Press, 2014), 90–7.
28 *Leader*, 3, 4, 6, 8, and 10 January 1855; Barrie Dyster, "Captain Bob and the Noble Ward: Neighbourhood and Provincial Politics in Nineteenth-Century Toronto," in *Forging a Consensus*, 98–100.
29 *Globe*, 14 March 1855.
30 *Globe*, 30 October 1858, testimony at the fall assizes.
31 *Globe*, 2 July 1859, commemorating the Battle of Aughrim (1691), a significant Williamite victory in Ireland.
32 City of Toronto Archives (hereafter CTA), Reports of the Chief Constable to Toronto City Council, appended annually to City Council Minutes, 1862–75.
33 CTA, City Council Minutes for 1860, App. XVI, 44, By-law No. 310.
34 Craig Heron maintains that males were not part of saloon life until their late teens; see *his Booze: A Distilled History* (Toronto: Between the Lines, 2003), 113–15.
35 *Globe*, 27 February 1854; Jenkins discusses some similar evidence of children's gangs in "Poverty and Place," 493.
36 *Globe*, 21 December 1865.
37 *Globe*, 27 December 1865.
38 *Globe*, 11 and 12 October 1860.
39 Clarke, "Religious Riot as Pastime."
40 *Globe*, 15 August 1877.
41 *Globe*, 16 August 1876.
42 *Globe*, 27 July 1871.
43 *Globe*, 3 September 1870.
44 Jenkins, "Poverty and Place."
45 *Globe*, 21 September 1870.
46 *Globe*, 5 July 1869; *Irish Canadian* (Toronto), 7 July 1869.
47 *Globe*, 1 January 1875.
48 *Globe*, 21 September 1870.
49 George Emery, *Elections in Oxford County, 1837–1975: A Case Study of Democracy in Canada West and Early Ontario* (Toronto: University of Toronto Press, 2012), 40; see also ch. 2 above.
50 Smyth, *Toronto, the Belfast of Canada*, 99.
51 See ch. 5 above.
52 Dennis Ryan and Kevin Wamsley, "A Grand Game of Hurling and Football: Sport and Irish Nationalism in Old Toronto," *Canadian Journal of Irish Studies* 30 (2004): 21–31.
53 Nicholas Rogers, "Serving Toronto the Good: The Development of the City Police Force, 1834–84," in *Forging a Consensus*, 120–1.
54 *Crime and Punishment in Canada*, http://www.petervronsky.org/crime/cph5.htm.

55 CTA, Minutes of the Toronto City Council for 1864, Report of the Chief Constable for 1863, 9.
56 See, for example, *Globe*, 14 July 1862, 18 March 1864.
57 Susan E. Houston, "The Victorian Origins of Juvenile Delinquency: A Canadian Experience," *History of Education Quarterly* 12 (1972): 245–80; Bryan Hogeveen, "'The Evils with Which We Are Called to Grapple': Elite Reformers, Eugenicists, Environmental Psychologists, and the Construction of Toronto's Working-Class Boy Problem, 1860–1930," *Labour/Le travail* 55 (2005): 37–68.
58 Alison Prentice, *The School Promoters: Education and Social Class in Mid-Nineteenth Century Upper Canada* (Toronto: McClelland and Stewart, 1977), 133–4.
59 Susan E. Houston and Alison Prentice, *Schooling and Scholars in Nineteenth-Century Ontario* (Toronto: University of Toronto Press, 1998), 307.
60 Charlotte Neff, "The Ontario Industrial Schools Act of 1874," *Canadian Journal of Family Law* 12 (1994–5): 171–208. In 1887 the Victoria Industrial School was opened in nearby Mimico. See Paul W. Bennett, "Taming 'Bad Boys' of the 'Dangerous Class': Child Rescue and Restraint at the Victoria Industrial School, 1887–1935," *Histoire sociale/Social History* 21/41 (1988): 71–96.
61 This work was undertaken from 1853 by the Toronto Protestant Orphans' Home. See Charlotte Neff, "The Role of Protestant Children's Homes in Nineteenth-Century Ontario: Child Rescue or Family Support?," *Journal of Family History* 34 (2009): 62–5.
62 Houston, "Victorian Origins of Juvenile Delinquency."
63 *Globe*, 20 January 1877, where Professor Daniel Wilson paraphrases the police chief.
64 Robert M. Mennel, *Thorns and Thistles: Juvenile Delinquents in the United States, 1825–1940* (Hanover: University Press of New England, 1973), 53–5.
65 *Globe*, 19 and 27 September 1859; Charlotte Neff, "Role of Protestant Children's Homes," 51. On the Toronto Girls' Home founded in 1859, and care provided earlier by the Public Nursery, see Neff, "Role of Protestant Children's Homes," 65–8.
66 *Globe*, 28 October 1862, Annual Meeting of the Toronto Boys' Home.
67 Province of Canada, Sessional Papers 1862, No. 19, Second Annual Report of the Board of Inspectors of Asylums, Prisons, etc. 1861, Separate Report of Mr E.A. Meredeth, 17.
68 Susan Elizabeth Houston, "The Impetus to Reform: Urban Crime, Poverty, and Ignorance in Ontario, 1850–1875" (PhD diss., Ontario Institute for Studies in Education, 1974), 395–6.
69 Neff, "Role of the Protestant Children's Home," 72–4.

70 Neff, "Role of the Protestant Children's Home," 76; Houston, "Impetus to Reform," 298–9.
71 Houston, "Impetus to Reform," 299.
72 Neff, "Role of the Protestant Children's Homes"; Charlotte Neff, "Government Approaches to Child Neglect and Mistreatment in Nineteenth-Century Ontario," *Histoire social/Social History* 41/81 (2008): 165–214.
73 On the Newsboys Lodging House in New York established in 1854, see David E. Whisnant, "Selling the Gospel News, or: the Strange Career of Jimmy Brown the Newsboy," *Journal of Social History* 5 (1972): 269–309.
74 Brian Clarke, *Piety and Nationalism: Lay Voluntary Associations and the Creation of an Irish Catholic Community in Toronto, 1850–1895* (Montreal and Kingston: McGill–Queen's University Press, 1993).
75 *Globe*, 24 October 1868.
76 Elizabeth Hulse, "'A Long and Happy Life': Daniel Wilson with Family and Friends," in *Thinking with Both Hands: Sir Daniel Wilson in the Old World and the New*, ed. Marinell Ash (Toronto: University of Toronto Press, 1999), 262–3.
77 *Globe*, 18 April 1873, Report of Annual Meeting, News-Boys Home.
78 On the self-fashioning of street children, see Thomas J. Gilfoyle, "Street-Rats and Gutter-Snipes: Child Pickpockets and Street Culture in New York City, 1850–1900," *Journal of Social History* 37 (2004): 853–62; and Heather Shore, "Cross Coves, Buzzers, and General Sorts of Prigs: Juvenile Crime and the Criminal 'Underworld' in the Early Nineteenth Century," *British Journal of Criminology* 39 (1999): 10–24.

7. Strikers and Their Supporters

1 *World* (Toronto), 12 March 1886.
2 For a recent study of spectacle in an earlier Canadian strike, see Dan Horner, "Solemn Processions and Terrifying Violence: Spectacle, Authority, and Citizenship during the Lachine Canal Strike of 1843," *Urban History Review* 38 (2010): 36–47.
3 Gregory S. Kealey, *Toronto Workers Respond to Industrial Capitalism, 1867–1892* (Toronto: University of Toronto Press, 1980), 199–211; Desmond Morton, *Mayor Howland: The Citizens' Candidate* (Toronto: Hakkert, 1973); Eric Tucker, "The Faces of Coercion: The Legal Regulation of Labor Conflict in Ontario, 1880–1889," *Law and History Review* 12 (1994): 277–339; Eric Tucker, "Who's Running the Road? Street Railway Strikes and the Problem of Constructing a Liberal Capitalist Order in Canada, 1886–1914," *Law and Social Inquiry* 35 (2010): 451–85; Eric Tucker, "Street Railway Strikes, Collective Violence, and the Canadian State, 1886–1914"

in *Canadian State Trials*, vol. 3: *Political Trials and Security Measures, 1840–1914*, ed. Barry Wright and Susan Binnie (Toronto: University of Toronto Press, 2009), 257–93.
4 Charles Tilly, *Contentious Performances* (Cambridge: Cambridge University Press, 2008). See also Christian Borch, *Politics of Crowds: An Alternative Sociology* (Cambridge: Cambridge University Press, 2012); *Challenging Authority: The Historical Study of Contentious Politics*, ed. Michael Hanagan, Leslie Page Moch, and Wayne te Brake (Minneapolis: University of Minnesota Press, 1998).
5 E.P. Thompson, "The Moral Economy of the English Crowd in the Eighteenth Century," *Past and Present* 50 (1976): 76–136; Tilly, *Contentious Performances*, 62–72.
6 Street railways and modernity are discussed in Christopher Armstrong and H.V. Nelles, *Monopoly's Moment: The Organization and Regulation of Canadian Utilities, 1830–1930* (Toronto: University of Toronto Press, 1988), 34–55. Modernity in Toronto is explored more widely in Keith Walden, *Becoming Modern in Toronto: The Industrial Exhibition and the Shaping of Modern Culture* (Toronto: University of Toronto Press, 1997).
7 The only other sources that touch on street events are court records, and these provide only terse depictions of what happened. Tucker has made good use of court records in "Faces of Coercion." The labour press had almost nothing to say about the strike. Even *Palladium of Labor*, which was highly supportive of the Knights of Labor in Ontario, did not report on the events of the dispute.
8 Paul Rutherford, *A Victorian Authority: The Daily Press in Late Nineteenth-Century Canada* (Toronto: University of Toronto Press, 1982). At pages 238–9, Rutherford provides some reported circulation figures for Toronto dailies in 1880: *Globe* 57,000; *Mail* 69,558; *Telegram* 14,000; *World* 11,500; and in 1883, *News* 31,500.
9 On the support of the *News* for the Knights of Labor, see Russell G. Hann, "Brainworkers and the Knights of Labor: E.E. Sheppard, Phillips Thompson, and the Toronto News, 1883–1887," ed. G.S. Kealey and Peter Warrian (Toronto: McClelland and Stewart 1976), 35–57.
10 Weekly newspapers did not contain similar detailed coverage, though Toronto weeklies as diverse as the *Week*, *Palladium of Labor*, and *Monetary Times* briefly commented on issues raised by them.
11 Jürgen Habermas, *The Structural Transformation of the Public Sphere* (Cambridge, MA: MIT Press, 1993); Jeffrey L. McNairn, *The Capacity to Judge: Public Opinion and Deliberative Democracy in Upper Canada, 1791–1854* (Toronto: University of Toronto Press, 2000), ch. 3; Duncan Koerber, "Style over Substance: Newspaper Coverage of Early Election Campaigns in Canada, 1820–1841," *Canadian Journal of Communication* 36 (2011): 435–53.

12 *Telegram* (Toronto), 9 May 1886.
13 Bryan Palmer, "'Give Us the Road and We Will Run It': The Social and Cultural Matrix of an Emerging Labour Movement," in *Essays in Canadian Working-Class History*, 106–24; Bryan D. Palmer, *A Culture in Conflict: Skilled Workers and Industrial Capitalism in Hamilton, Ontario, 1860–1914* (Montreal and Kingston: McGill-Queen's University Press, 1979), 209–16; Craig Heron, *Lunch-Bucket Lives: Remaking the Workers' City* (Toronto: Between the Lines, 2015), 221–6; Patricia Roy, "The British Columbia Electrical Railway and Its Employees," *BC Studies* 16 (1972–3): 3–24; Robert H. Babcock, "The Saint John Street Railwaymen's Strike and Riot, 1914," *Acadiensis* 11 (1982): 3–27; Jonathan Hildebrand, "Class, Community, and Urban Consciousness: The Winnipeg Street Railway, 1906–1910," *Manitoba History* 60 (2009): 2–13; Scott Molloy, *Trolley Wars: Streetcar Workers on the Line* (Washington, D.C.: Smithsonian Institute Press, 1996); Robert Babcock, "'Will You Walk? Yes, We'll Walk': Popular Support for a Street Railway Strike in Portland, Maine," *Labor History* 35 (1994): 372–98; Harold E. Cox, "The Wilkes-Barre Street Railway Strike of 1905," *Pennsylvania Magazine of History* 94 (1970): 75–94.
14 Armstrong and Nelles, *Monopoly's Moment*, 34–55.
15 *Globe*, 4 April 1885. See also https://canadiana.ca. *Rules and Regulations for Drivers & Conductors of the Toronto Street Railway Co.* (Toronto: Bell, 1880).
16 Kealey, *Toronto Workers*, 175–9. See also Gregory S. Kealey and Bryan D. Palmer, *Dreaming of What Might Be: The Knights of Labor in Ontario, 1880–1990* (Toronto: New Hogtown Press, 1987), 56–111.
17 Kealey and Palmer, *Dreaming*, 56–111.
18 Armstrong and Nelles, *Monopoly's Moment*, 53.
19 Christopher Armstrong and H.V. Nelles, *The Revenge of the Methodist Bicycle Company: Sunday Streetcars and Municipal Reform in Toronto, 1888–1897* (Toronto: Oxford University Press, [1977] 2011), 30–1; *Globe*, 26 January and 14 November 1885.
20 *Globe*, 9 April and 10 July 1885 (line extensions); 5 March 1886 (Sunday service); 20 September 1886 (women).
21 *Globe*, 9 December 1885.
22 Mark McGowan, "Smith, Sir Frank," in *Dictionary of Canadian Biography*, vol. 13, University of Toronto/Université Laval, 2003–, http://www.biographi.ca/en/bio/smith_frank_13E.html.
23 Whether French Canadian strikebreakers from Montreal were actually arranged for by Smith was a matter of dispute. See *News* charges, 11 March 1886; Smith's denials, *World*, 13 March 1886.
24 Kealey, *Toronto Workers*, 91–2, 233. Striking printers defeated the ironclad and, in a contentious performance, burned the contract in the *Mail* offices on 3 February 1886 (*Toronto Workers*, 235).

25 The name and number of the assembly is not mentioned by the press, and Kealey lists it as "?" (*Toronto Workers*, 196).
26 *News* (Toronto), 10 March 1886; *World*, 11 March 1886.
27 *Mail* (Toronto), 11 March 1886.
28 *News*, 11 March 1886.
29 *World*, 12 March 1886.
30 Tucker, "Faces of Coercion," passim.
31 *Telegram*, 11 March 1886.
32 *Mail*, 11 March 1886.
33 *News*, 10 March 1886.
34 *Telegram*, 11 March 1886.
35 *Mail*, 11 March 1886.
36 *Mail*, 11 March 1886.
37 *News*, 10 March 1886.
38 *News*, 10 March 1886.
39 *Mail*, 11 March 1886.
40 *News*, 10 March 1886.
41 *World*, 11 March 1886.
42 *World*, 11 March 1886; *Mail*, 11 March 1886.
43 *Monetary Times* (Toronto), 19 May 1886.
44 Kealey, *Toronto Workers*, 203–4. In part, Kealey echoes an analysis made in David Frank, "Trouble in Toronto: The Street Railway Lockout and Strike, 1886," unpublished paper, 1972.
45 For a study of recent rioting that documents such motivations, see Laura Naegler, "The Ritual of Insurrection and the 'Thrill-Seeking Youth': An Instant Ethnography of Inner-City Riots in Germany," in *Riot, Unrest, and Protest on the Global Stage*, ed. Paul Pritchard and Francis Pakes (Basingstoke: Palgrave Macmillan, 2014), 151–69.
46 *News*, 10 March 1886; *Globe*, 12 March 1886; *Mail*, 12 March 1886; *World*, 11 March 1886.
47 Heron, *Lunch-Bucket Lives*, 224–5.
48 Craig Heron, "The Boys and Their Booze: Masculinities and Public Drinking in Working-Class Hamilton, 1890–1946," *Canadian Historical Review* 86 (2005): 416.
49 *Palladium of Labor*, 8 April 1886. Thompson was writing under his pen name "Enjolras."
50 *World*, 12 March 1886.
51 *Mail*, 11 March 1886.
52 On masculinity and the Ontario working class, see also Christina Burr, *Spreading the Light: Work and Labour Reform in Late-Nineteenth Century Toronto* (Toronto: University of Toronto Press, 1999); Joy Parr, *The Gender of Breadwinners: Women, Men, and Change in Two Industrial Towns, 1880–1950* (Toronto: University of Toronto Press, 1990).

53 *News*, 11 March 1886; *Mail*, 11 March 1886.
54 The stable staff did mostly walk out; the animals were cared for by a skeleton staff (*World*, 11 March 1886).
55 *Mail*, 11 March 1886.
56 *Mail*, 11 March 1886.
57 Ron Sawatsky, "Howland, William Holmes," in *Dictionary of Canadian Biography*, vol. 12, University of Toronto/Université Laval, 2003–, http://www.biographi.ca/en/bio/howland_william_holmes_12E.html.
58 *News*, 11 March 1886.
59 *Mail*, 20 May 1886.
60 *Telegram*, 11 March 1886.
61 *World*, 12 March 1886.
62 *World*, 12 March 1886.
63 *Globe*, 12 March 1886.
64 *News*, 11 March 1886.
65 *Globe*, 12 March 1886.
66 *Telegram*, 13 March 1886.
67 *Globe*, 12 March 1886.
68 *Telegram*, 12 March 1886.
69 *Mail*, 13 March 1886.
70 *World*, 13 March 1886.
71 *Telegram*, 12 March 1886.
72 *Telegram*, 12 March 1886.
73 *Telegram*, 12 March 1886.
74 *Telegram*, 12 March 1886.
75 Tucker, "Faces of Coercion," 299.
76 Norman Knowles, "Denison, George Taylor," in *Dictionary of Canadian Biography* vol. 15, University of Toronto/Université Laval, 2003–, http://www.biographi.ca/en/bio/denison_george_taylor_1839_1925_15E.html. See also Gene Howard Homel, "Denison's Law: Criminal Justice and the Police Court in Toronto, 1877–1921," *Ontario History* 73 (1980): 171–86.
77 Tucker, "Faces of Coercion," 300.
78 *Palladium of Labor*, 3 April 1886.
79 *Palladium of Labor*, 3 April 1886.
80 *Mail*, 13 March 1886.
81 *Mail*, 13 March 1886.
82 *World*, 10 May 1886; *Globe*, 10 and 11 May 1886.
83 "Statement of the Executive Committee of the Strikers," *Telegram*, 10 May 1886.
84 *News*, 10 May 1886.
85 *Globe*, 10 May 1886.
86 *Mail*, 8 May 1886.
87 *News*, 8 May 1886.

88 *News*, 8 May 1886.
89 *Telegram*, 12 May 1886.
90 *Mail*, 20 May 1886.
91 Kealey, *Toronto Workers*, 205; Tucker, "Faces of Coercion," 302.
92 *Globe*, 15 May 1886, prints a copy of the requisition and names and addresses of its signatories.
93 *Globe*, 20 May 1886.
94 *Telegram*, 18 May 1886; *News*, 20 May 1886.
95 *Mail*, 17 May 1886.
96 *News*, 10 May 1886.
97 *Globe*, 12 May 1886; *Telegram*, 13 May 1886.
98 *World*, 22 May 1886.
99 *Mail*, 17 May 1886.
100 *Mail*, 22 May 1886.
101 *Telegram*, 12 May 1886; *Mail*, 17 May 1886.
102 Kealey and Palmer, *Dreaming*, 366–7; on New York, see Mayor Howland's comments, *Telegram*, 10 May 1886.
103 *Telegram*, 13 May 1886.
104 *Mail*, 26 May 1886.
105 *Mail*, 26 May 1886.
106 *Mail*, 26 May 1886.
107 Kealey and Palmer, *Dreaming*, 124–6; "Anti Blatherskite" to editor of the *Globe*, 21 May 1886.
108 Morton, *Mayor Howland*, 55.
109 Armstrong and Nelles, *Revenge*, 33–4.
110 Tucker, "Who's Running the Road," 459, 462.
111 *News*, 21 May 1886.
112 J. Lofland, "Crowd Joys," *Urban Life* 10 (1982): 355–81. The term "playful crowd" has been used in a study of amusement parks: Gary S. Cross and John K. Walton, *The Playful Crowd: Pleasure Places in the Twentieth Century* (New York: Columbia University Press, 2005).
113 The terms "emergent" and "residual," which Kealey applies in *Toronto Workers*, 65, come from Raymond Williams, "Base and Super-Structure in Marxist Cultural Theory," *New Left Review* 82 (1973): 3–16.

Index

Page numbers in italics denote illustrations.

9th Voltigeurs (Québec), 112, 122
10th Royal Grenadiers: battles and casualties, 119, 120, 126; mobilization for North-West Campaign, 107, *114*, 116; return to Toronto, 122, 124, 125
65th Carabiniers Mont-Royal (Montreal), 112, 131

Acland, Henry, 63, 70, 80
Act of Union (1840), 11–12, 39, 45
Act to Restrain Party Processions in Certain Cases (1843), 146, 151
addresses (orations), 18, 33–4, 36, 39, 43, 67–70, 72
African Canadians, 13, 49, 66, 69–70, 179
Albert Edward, Prince of Wales' state visit: overview of, 5, 7, 62–3; addresses (orations) for, 67–70, 72; arch-building for, 67, *68*, 74–6, 79–82, *80*, 83; balls (dances), 73, 81; Cobourg arrival, 78–9; illuminations for, 72–3; Indigenous participation in, 71–2; Kingston arrival, 78; merchandise and services on offer for, 73; press coverage, 7, 63–4; in Toronto, 65–7, 73–4, 79–81, 83, 180; transparencies for, 72, 79, 80. *See also* "the Orange difficulty"
Allan, George William, 136–7, 149
Allward, Walter, 129
"The American Parade" (M.P. Ryan), 9
Anishinabeg people, 12, 71
annexation movement, 16
Anti-Slavery Society of Canada, 49
arch-building: for Lord Elgin's tour, 5, 18, 29, 34; for Prince of Wales' state visit, 67, *68*, 74–6, 79–82, *80*, 83; for returning Volunteers, 122. *See also* "the Orange difficulty"
Autumn Jubilee. *See* Jubilee riots

Baldwin, Robert: Rebellion Losses bill controversy, 15, 16, 23, 24, 30–2, 190n31; reform legislation, 51, 53, 59
Banner (Toronto), 45, 50
Barry, Michael, 140–1
Batoche, Battle of, 119, 120, 124, 132
Beard, Robert, 27
Beaty, James, 40
Bethune, Donald, 43, 45

Blake, William Hume, 21, 24
Boulton (electoral candidate), 52, 58
boys and young men: Brook's Bush Gang, 140–1; circus riot, 136–7; college students, 139; discouraging violence among, 146–7; drunkenness and larceny, 143; instigating violence and disorder, 6, 134–5, 137, 142, 150–1; in the March Toronto Street Railway strike, 139–40, 152, 153, 160–1, 163–4, 166–7; in the May Toronto Street Railway strike, 140, 171, 172, 174, 175–6; social reform strategies for, 147–50, 151; in Toronto police court, 141–4. *See also* Jubilee riots; Orange Young Britons; violence and rowdy behaviour; Young Irishmen's Benevolent Association
Breen, Michael P., 65–6
bribery, 38, 55, 59
British American (Woodstock), 30
British American Presbyterian (Toronto), 94, 100–1, 103
British Colonist (Toronto), 49, 53, 55, 58
British Relief Act (1829), 102
British Whig (Kingston), 19, 21
Brook's Bush Gang, 140–1
Brown, George: campaigns, news reports on, 42–3, 45, 47, 48, 49–50, 52, 53; election victories, 54, 55; as *Globe* publisher, 7, 25, 40, 101, 105; on Prince of Wales' state visit, 76–7

"C Company" Infantry School, 107
Cameron, John Hillyard, 48, 49, 59, 81
Canada, Dominion of, 13
Canada East. *See* Lower Canada (Canada East)
Canada West. *See* Upper Canada (Canada West)
Canadian Freeman (Toronto), 88, 89, 103
Canadian Illustrated News (Toronto), 8, 137
Canadian Pacific Railway (CPR), 107, 115, 121
Le Canadien (Québec), 81
canvassing, 43–4
The Capacity to Judge (McNairn), 10
Captain Carter's Colored Corps, 122
Careless, J.M.S., 110
Caron, Adolphe, 112
Carter, Sarah, 119
Cartier, George-Étienne, 12, 76
Cassels, Dick, 112, 128
Catholic Church. *See* ethno-religious conflict; Irish Catholics in Toronto; Roman Catholic processions
celebrations and demonstrations in Victorian Toronto: approach to, overview of, and conclusions on, 3–7, 177–81; context for discussion, 11–14; sources and historiography, 7–11. *See also* Albert Edward, Prince of Wales' state visit; boys and young men; contentious performances; Elgin, Eighth Earl of (James Bruce); ethno-religious conflict; newspapers; North-West Campaign press coverage; political expression, acts of; processions and parades; Rebellion Losses bill controversy; Roman Catholic processions; Toronto Street Railway Company; Toronto Street Railway strikes; violence and rowdy behaviour; Volunteers (volunteer militia)
Charbonnel, Bishop, 75
charivari, 27

children's homes, 149–50
Christian Guardian (Toronto), 100–1, 103, 124
circus riot, 136–7
Civic Wars (M.P. Ryan), 9
Clarke, Brian: *Piety and Nationalism*, 11; "Religious Riot as Pastime," 95–6
class: college students, 139; and elections, 58, 178; identities, 4, 178; of men tried, post–Jubilee Riots, 94, 205n36; stratification in Toronto, 14; working class in the press, 95, 104, 180. *See also* Toronto Street Railway strikes
colonialism, 6, 13, 181
Confederation (1867), 12, 13, 14
Conservative Party (Tories): formation of, 12, 39; relationship with governor, 16, 34, 35, 180; "Tory rebels," 5, 15. *See also* election culture; Elgin, Eighth Earl of (James Bruce); *Leader* (Toronto); Rebellion Losses bill controversy
contentious performances: around elections, 40, 46, 50, 59; around strikes, 9, 153–4, 171–2, 175–6; Rebellion Losses bill and, 36; ritualistic, limited nature of, 9, 160, 178. *See also* political expression, acts of
Cooke's Presbyterian Church, 98, 101
Corpus Christi celebration (1864), 5–6, 87–9, 94, 105, 204n10
Corrupt Practices Prevention Act (1860), 55, 60
Courier (Montreal), 35
Le Courrier du Canada (Québec), 82–3
Crawford, John, 45, 46, 47, 50, 54, 56
Credit River, 12, 13, 70
crowd actions: as contentious performances, 9, 153–4, 175–6; during Toronto Street Railway March strike, 152, 153–6, 160–2, 163, 164, 169–70, 175–6; during Toronto Street Railway May strike, 171
Cut Knife Hill, Battle of, 119, 124

Davis, Natalie Zemon, 9, 135
debates. *See* public debates
democracy, deliberative, 10, 18, 26, 36, 37. *See also* muscular conservatism
demonstrations. *See* political expression, acts of; riots
Denison, George Taylor, 126, 169, 172–3
Dewdney, Edgar, 111
Dominion Churchman (Toronto), 110
Don River, 12, 13, 140–1
Draper, Francis Collier, 159, 166, 167, 168, 169
Durham report, 23

effigy-burnings, 3, 15, 23–4, 26–9, 36. *See also* riots
election culture: approach to and overview of discussion, 38–42; addresses (orations), 39, 43; bribery, 38, 55, 59; campaign posters, 52; campaigns as contentious events, 5, 38–9; candidate selection, 42–3; canvassing, 43–4; changes under Dominion parliament, 39, 193n4; class and, 58, 178; election results, 54–5, 198n94; election writ, 44; heckling, 39, 41, 42, 46, 48, 49, 59; nominations, 39, 44–6, 195n32; non-voters, 44, 48, 61, 180–1; plumpers, 52, 197n68; polling, 5, 38, 44–5, 51–4; reforms, 39, 51, 53, 55, 59, 60–1, 180; requisitions,

42–3; treating, 44, 46–7, 51, 55, 59; victory processions, 5, 40, 56–9, 57. *See also* intimidation; political parties; public meetings; violence and rowdy behaviour; voting methods
electoral (voter) lists, 51, 54–5
Elgin, Eighth Earl of (James Bruce): 1849 Governor's Tour, 3, 5, 15, 18, 29–30, 32–6, 67; burned in effigy, 3, 15, 26–7; newspaper depictions of, *17*, *31*; petitions for recall, 22–3, 36; Rebellion Losses bill, signing of, 16, 21; responsible government, support for, 15, 16, 18, 23, 30
Emery, George, 41
ethno-religious conflict: civil vs. Church authority as factor in, 99; Corpus Christi celebration (1864), 5–6, 87–9, 94, 105, 204n10; intolerance of Catholic rituals and vestments, 85–6, 87–8, 90, 96–7, 102–3, 105, 178; narrative of Protestant male aggression, 96, 104, 180; Protestant response to Lynch's lectures, 97–8; religious conflict in Ireland as factor in, 6, 86, 103; tolerance, calls for, 86, 100–3. *See also* Jubilee riots; marching traditions; "the Orange difficulty"; Roman Catholic processions
evangelicals, Protestant, 100–1, 102, 103, 105, 137, 207n63
Examiner (Toronto): on anti-Mackenzie rioters, 24, 26, 136; on failures of the authorities, 25, 28, 29; on nominations, 45–6, 48

Fenianism (Irish republicanism), 89, 91, 95, 97, 105
First Nations, 12, 70–2, *71*, 109, 179

Fish Creek, Battle of, 119
Fitch, William Charles, 120
Fleming, Sandford, 67
Fox, W.W., 81
fraternal organizations. *See* Hibernians; Orange Order; Orange Young Britons; Young Irishmen's Benevolent Association
free houses, 45
Freedom of Elections Act (1842), 53, 146, 151
Freeman, Victoria, 70
French Canadians: North-West Campaign and, 112, 131–2; political alliances with, 12, 21, 37; portrayed as threat, 19, 21, 36–7; Rebellion Losses compensation, 4–5, 16

Gazette (Québec), 32
gender. *See* masculinity; women and girls
girls. *See* women and girls
Globe (Toronto): on anti-Mackenzie rioters, 136; calls for tolerance, 100, 105, 106; campaign coverage, 40, 42–3, 45, 46, 47–8, 49–50, 51–2; on crime and street violence, 134, 135–6, 140, 143, 144; on election results, 54, 55; on Elgin effigy burning, 3, 27–8; on the Guibord affair, 99; introduction of illustrations, 184n12; letter to editor on Jubilee riot, 96, 104; on North-West Campaign, 116, 117, 120, 123, 124, 126; on Orange Young Britons, 95, 138, 145; on "the Orange difficulty," 76, 79, 82; on Prince of Wales' state visit, 63–4, 67, 73, 74, 83; on Riel and the Métis, 107, 109, 110; support for Rebellion Losses bill, 25; on

Toronto Street Railway strikes, 154, 156, 163, 166; on victory processions, 56; violence against offices of, 57; as voice of Reform, 7
Glorious Twelfth (12 July), 75, 136, 137, 142
Gowan, Ogle, 30, 91
Grey, Third Earl of (Henry George Grey), 32, 35
Grittner, Colin, 41
Guibord, Joseph, 99
Guy Fawkes Day, 26, 89, 204n18

Habermas, Jürgen: *The Structural Transformation of the Public Sphere*, 9–10
Hagarty, James, 143
Halifax provisional battalion, 122
Hamilton streetcar strike (1906), 163
Harrison, Robert Alexander, 94, 100
Head, Edmund, 63, *64*, 75, 77
Heaman, E.A., 98
heckling, 39, 41, 42, 46, 48, 49, 59
Herald (New York), 64
Heron, Craig, 135
Hibernians, 89–90, 91, 96, 97 104
High Tories, 12
Hobsbawm, Eric, 8
Horner, Dan: *Taking to the Streets*, 10, 41
House of Industry, 148
Houston, Cecil J.: *The Sash Canada Wore*, 10
Howard, Captain, 126, 213n85
Howland, William, 152, 153, 166, 169, 170, 171, 172, 179
hustings, 44

illuminations, 72–3
Illustrated War News (Toronto), 8, 117, 120, 123
Indigenous peoples, 12, 70–2, *71*, 109, 179

Industrial School Act (1874), 148, 151
Intelligencer (Belleville), 95
intimidation: at the polls, 5, 22, 39, 40–1, 59, 61, 181; prevention of, 54, 55, 146, 151
Irish Canadian (Toronto): on the North-West Campaign, 116, 123, 126; on Orange Young Britons, 138, 145; on Roman Catholic processions, 87, 91, 94–5, 96
Irish Catholics in Toronto: historic right to practise religion, 98–9, 207n55; newspapers for, 8; organized sports, 146–7; population in Toronto, 13, 14; tensions with Protestants, 5–6, 7, 10–11, 85–6, 134. *See also* ethno-religious conflict; riots; Roman Catholic processions; violence and rowdy behaviour
Irish republicanism (Fenianism), 89, 91, 95, 97, 105
Irish-American (New York), 83
Iroquois people, 12

Jarvis, William Botsford, 45, 58, 66
Jenkins, William, 10–11, 145
journalism. *See* newspapers
Jubilee riots: assigning blame for, 94–8, 134, 137, 205n36; events, 5–6, 90–4, *93*, 138
Jury, Alfred, 169

"K" Company, 117, *128*, 128–9
Kealey, Gregory S., 35
Kingston (Upper Canada), 32, 77–8
Knights of Labor: Toronto Street Railway strikes, role in, 164, 169, 170, 172, 173, 174, 175; union organizing by, 153, 157, 158–9
Koerber, Duncan, 41

labour disputes. *See* Toronto Street Railway Company; Toronto Street Railway strikes; unionism
Ladies Volunteer Supply Committee, 120, 124
LaFontaine, Louis-Hippolyte, 15, 16, 19
Langevin, Hector-Louis, 76
laws, selective enforcement of, 25–6, 29, 89, 105, 135, 138–9. *See also* bribery; public order
Leader (Toronto): campaign coverage, 40, 42–4, 45, 46, 47–8, 49–50, 51–2; Conservative Party and, 7; on election results, 54–5; on the Jubilee riots, 95, 97; on the need for public order, 94; on the Prince of Wales' state visit, 63–4; on victory processions, 56
Lower Canada (Canada East), 11–12, 15–16, 19, 77, 82–3. *See also* Albert Edward, Prince of Wales' state visit; Rebellion Losses bill controversy
Loyal United Colored Society, 66, 179
Loyalists, 12–13
Lutherans, 102
Lynch, John Joseph: actions during Jubilee riots, 90, 91, 92; blamed for procession violence, 96–7, 104; as chief Catholic defender in Toronto, 97–8; on collective rights and religious practise, 86, 89, 98–9, 106; on conversions, 103; Corpus Christi celebration (1864), 87–9, *88*; defense of Hibernians' march, 89–90; on the Guibord affair, 99; ultramontanism of, 86, 97, 98, 106; on vestments and religious symbols, 102

Macdonald, Donald Alexander, 92
Macdonald, John A.: alliance with George-Étienne Cartier, 12; challenging W.H. Blake to a duel, 21; electioneering, 50–1; Knights of Labor and, 172; North-West Campaign, 107, 111–12; Prince of Wales' state visit, 76, 77, 78, 82, 83–4; response to Bishop Lynch, 89
Mackenzie, Kenneth, 94
Mackenzie, William Lyon, 24–6, 135–6, 177
MacNab, Allan, 34
Mail (Toronto): on causes of the North-West conflict, 109; ironclad agreements, use of, 158; on Lord Elgin's tour, 33; on March strike, 160, 161, 162, 163, 165, 167, 169; on May strike, 174; on mobilization for North-West Campaign, 107, 112, 116, 117; on North-West Campaign and return from, 119, 120, 122, 123, 126–7, 129, 132; on Prince of Wales' state visit, 82; on Protestant-Catholic violence, 95, 97; Toronto Street Railway strikes, unsympathetic view of, 154, 159
Maloney, Matthew, 159, 166
Manitoba Act, 115
Manning, Alexander, 121, 124–5, 129
The Many Rooms of This House (Perin), 86
marching traditions, 75, 83, 85, 89–90, 96, 178
Martin, Peter, 70–1, *71*
masculine behaviours: aggression vs. restraint, in the press, 38, 47, 53–4, 60–1; of election crowds and candidates, 38, 39–40, 45, 46, 50, 58, 179; marching traditions, 75, 83, 85, 89–90, 96, 178; as muscular conservatism, 18, 33, 36,

37, 58–9; narrative of Protestant male aggression, 96, 104, 180; public drunkenness, 45, 61; use of military metaphors, 52. *See also* ethno-religious conflict; heckling; intimidation; treating; violence and rowdy behaviour
masculine identities, 11, 134
masculinity: aggression as, 153, 164; of Black people, in the press, 49; boys and, 134, 151, 164; gentlemanly versions of, 39, 43, 179; manly duty, understandings of, 113; of militia, 111, 119, 131; of non-violent striking men, 164, 175; organized sports and, 146–7
Mason, James, 126
McDougall, Judge, 152
McGerr, Michael E., 41, 60
McIntosh, John, 24
McNairn, Jeffrey: *The Capacity to Judge*, 10; on public debate, 18
Medcalf, Francis Henry, 87, 89, 90, 91
Métis people, 109, 110, 112, 129, 131, 181
Metropolitan Methodist Church, 92, *93*
Middleton, Frederick Dobson, 111, 112
Midland battalion, 122
militarism, 108, 117, 129, 209n8
militia. *See* Volunteers (volunteer militia)
Mirror (Toronto), 21, 35, 48–9, 54
Mississauga people, 12, 13, 70, 72
Mohawk people, 33. *See also* Oronhyatekha ("Burning Cloud" or Peter Martin)
Monetary Times (Toronto), 162
Monklands, 29–30
Montgomery, John, 25
Montreal: 65th Carabiniers Mont-Royal, 112, 131; as capital city, 16, 32; Guibord affair, 99; newspapers, 35, 131–2; political violence in, 5, 10, 16, 26, 29, 32, 41; religious controversies in, 86; Shamrocks lacrosse team, 147; St Andrews Society, 33; Victoria Bridge, 63
Moor, Thomas, 120
"The Moral Economy of the Crowd in the Eighteenth Century" (Thompson), 8–9
Moran, Edward, 168
Mowat, Oliver, 91
Mulvey, John, 56
Murphy, Michael, 50, 97
muscular conservatism, 18, 33, 36, 37, 58–9. *See also* democracy, deliberative
Myers, Tamara, 135

Nasmith, John, 73
Nation (Toronto), 59, 96
Neff, Charlotte, 149
Nelles, H.V., 127–8
New York Times, 81
Newcastle, Fifth Duke of (Henry Pelham Fiennes Pelham-Clinton): Orangemen, conflict with, 77–82, 179, 202n48; role as political advisor to Prince of Wales, 63, *64*, 67–8, 70, 72, 74
News (Toronto): on March strike, 160, 161, 162, 163, 165, 166, 168; on May strike, 170, 171, 172, 175; on North-West Campaign, 108, 116, 117, 121, 123, 129, 131; "penny daily" style and audience, 8; Toronto Street Railway strikes, sympathetic view of, 154, 159
News-boys' Lodging Home, 150
newspapers: campaign coverage, partisan nature of, 5, 38–9, 40, 42, 59, 60; censuring of rowdy

behaviour, 38, 50; growth and evolution of, 7–8, 177, 181; illustrations in, 8, 184n12; Lord Elgin's tour, partisan reporting on, 30, *31*, 32, 33, 35; 22 March 1849 riot, partisan reporting on, 23–6, 27–9; on masculine aggression vs. restraint, 38, 47, 53–4, 60–1; on the Métis, 110; on Prince of Wales' state visit, 63–4; Rebellion Losses bill, partisan reporting on, 19–22, *20*, 23–4; on religious expression in public space, 105–6; on street violence, 104–5; on "the Orange difficulty," 82–3; on Toronto Street Railway strikes, 153, 154–6, 159, 179, 220n10. *See also Globe* (Toronto); *Leader* (Toronto); *Mail* (Toronto); North-West Campaign press coverage; *Telegram* (Toronto); *World* (Toronto); *specific names of other newspapers*

nominations, 39, 44–6, 195n32

North-West Campaign press coverage: accuracy of depictions, 132; embedded reporters, 119; in Halifax, 209n10; home front reporting, 119–20; homecoming preparations, 123–4; in Montreal, approach to, 131–2; in Toronto, approach to, 130–1, 132–3; Volunteer reporters, 212n51; on Volunteers' mobilization, 107–10, 112–13, 114, *118*; on Volunteers' return, 124–9. *See also* 9th Voltigeurs (Québec); 10th Royal Grenadiers; 65th Carabiniers Mont-Royal (Montreal); Halifax provisional battalion; "K" Company; Midland battalion; newspapers; Queen's Own Rifles (QOR); Riel, Louis; Volunteers (volunteer militia)

Northwest Rebellion Monument, 129, *130*

O'Donoghue, Daniel J., 157
O'Donohoe, John, 43, 57
O'Gorman, Frank, 41, 46
Oneida people, 33, 72
O'Neill (electoral candidate), 52, 58
"the Orange difficulty": George Brown's rousing of Protestants, 76–7; Orangemen-Catholics arch-building conflict, 74–6, 178; Orangemen-Duke of Newcastle conflict, 77–82, 179, 202n48; repercussions, 83–4

Orange Order: Cameron, John Hillyard, 48, 81; campaign of self-discipline, 146, 151; claiming public space, 5, 75, 83, 178; class and, 22, 58, 94, 104; elections and, 42–3, 61; Elgin effigy-burning, 3, 35; Glorious Twelfth (12 July), 75, 136, 137, 142; Guy Fawkes Day, 26, 89, 204n18; Lodges, influence of, 10, 22, 32, 138–9; male bonding, 75, 95–6, 104, 144; newspapers, 8; post-election riot (1841), 58–9; recruitment of rowdies, 50, 177–8. *See also* Corpus Christi celebration (1864); Jubilee riots; marching traditions; "the Orange difficulty"; riots; violence and rowdy behaviour

Orange Young Britons: campaign of self discipline, 146, 151; circus riot, 136; criticism of, in the press, 145; in the Jubilee riots, 90, 94–5, 137–8; male bonding, 95–6, 104, 144; street violence, 101, 105, 144–5,

178. *See also* boys and young men; violence and rowdy behaviour
Orange-Green conflict. *See* ethno-religious conflict; Irish Catholics in Toronto; Orange Order
Order of Foresters, 70
Oronhyatekha ("Burning Cloud" or Peter Martin), 70–1, *71*
Ottawa, 13
Otter, William, 107, 113, 115

Palladium of Labor (Hamilton), 131, 164, 169
Palmer, Bryan D., 22
parades. *See* processions and parades
Parliament, Canadian, 16, 39, 60
Patriot (Toronto), 19, 24, 25, 52, 58
Penetanguishene reformatory, 149, 173
"penny dailies," 8
Perin, Roberto: *The Many Rooms of This House*, 86
petitions, 22–3, 36
Piety and Nationalism (Clarke), 11
Pius IX (pope), 89, 97
police: partisanship and bias, 53, 135, 139, 147; reforms, 147, 151; selective enforcement of laws, 25–6, 29, 89, 105, 135, 138–9; Toronto police court, 141–4, 169; unexpected defense of Catholics, 92–4. *See also* Toronto Street Railway strikes
political expression, acts of: addresses (orations), 18, 33–4, 36, 39, 43, 67–70, 72; arch-building for Lord Elgin's tour, 5, 18, 29, 34; arch-building for state visit, 67, *68*, 74–6, 79–82, *80*, 83; arch-building for Volunteers, 122;

effigy-burnings, 3, 15, 23–4, 26–9, 36; fire alarm bell ringing, 25, 34–5, 88; illuminations, 72–3; muscular conservatism and, 18, 33, 36, 37, 58–9; petitions, 22–3, 36; public debates, 18–22; rioting, 26; transparencies, 50, 72, 79, 80. *See also* election culture; marching traditions; processions and parades; riots; violence and rowdy behaviour
political parties, 12, 39. *See also* Conservative Party (Tories); Reform Party (later Liberal Party)
political violence. *See* violence and rowdy behaviour
polling, 5, 38, 44–5, 51–4, 181. *See also* intimidation; voting methods
"Polling Crowds and Patronage" (See), 40–1
Presbyterian Church of Canada, 68–9
press. *See* newspapers
Prince of Wales. *See* Albert Edward, Prince of Wales' state visit
processions and parades: Act to Restrain Party Processions in Certain Cases (1843), 146, 151; military, 113, 125–6; popular, 127–8; for Prince of Wales' state visit, 65–7, 83; as public rituals/celebrations, 9, 18; victors' post-election, 5, 40, 56–9, *57*. *See also* marching traditions; "the Orange difficulty"; Roman Catholic processions
Protestant-Catholic tensions. *See* ethno-religious conflict; Fenianism (Irish republicanism); Hibernians; Irish Catholics in Toronto; marching traditions; Orange

Order; Orange Young Britons; Roman Catholic processions; Young Irishmen's Benevolent Association

public debates, 18–22

public meetings, 21–2, 46–51, 196n54. *See also* heckling; newspapers; treating; violence and rowdy behaviour

public order: calls for, post-riots, 94; concerns about maintaining, 6, 151, 169; efforts to establish in Toronto, 146–7, 151; religious practises and, 85–6, 94, 104; understandings of, 35

public space, 4, 5, 9–10, 75, 83, 103, 178

Punch in Canada, 30, *31*, 33

Québec (city), 13, 26, 35, 76–7, 86, 112, 122, 211n31. See also *Le Canadien* (Québec); *Le Courrier du Canada* (Québec); *Gazette* (Québec)

Queen's Own Rifles (QOR), 107, *114*, 116, 119, 122, 124–5, *125*. *See also* "K" Company

Rebellion Losses bill controversy, 3, 4–5, 15–16, 18–21, 36–7, 177. *See also* Conservative Party (Tories); Elgin, Eighth Earl of (James Bruce)

Red River uprising, 109, 114, 115

Reform Party (later Liberal Party), 12, 21, 39. See also *Globe* (Toronto); Rebellion Losses bill controversy

Reid, Samuel, 141

religion. *See* ethno-religious conflict

"Religious Riot as Pastime" (Clarke), 95–6

requisitions, 42–3

responsible government, 12, 15, 16, 18, 23, 30, 37

Reynolds, Richard, 46

Ridout, George Percival, 52, 58, 72, 190n31

Riel, Louis, 6, 109, 112, 121, 123, 129, 132. See also *Globe* (Toronto); *Mail* (Toronto); North-West Campaign press coverage

rights, collective vs. individual, 98–9

riots: assigning blame for, 94–8, 134; circus riot, 136–7; Corpus Christi celebration (1864), 5–6, 87–9, 94, 105, 204n10; Guibord affair in Montreal (1875), 99; Jubilee (*see* Jubilee riots); 22 March 1849, over Mackenzie's return, 24–6, 135–6; post-election (1841), 58–9. See also effigy-burnings; Orange Young Britons; political expression, acts of; violence and rowdy behaviour

rituals. *See* contentious performances; political expression, acts of; processions and parades

Robb, James Gardiner, 98, 101

Robinson, John Beverley (1791–1863), 28–9

Robinson, John Beverley (1820–1896), 43, 52

Rolph, John, 25

Roman Catholic Church, 75

Roman Catholic processions, 87, 88, 96, 97, 102, 103. *See also* Corpus Christi celebration (1864); ethno-religious conflict; Jubilee riots; women and girls

Rudé, George, 8

Ryan, Dennis, 147

Ryan, Mary P.: on "ceremonial citizenship," 66; *Civic Wars*, 9, 131; on publicness, 10; "The American Parade," 9

Ryerson, Egerton, 69

Sabbatarianism, 101, 137
Sarnia, 71–2
The Sash Canada Wore (Houston; Smyth), 10
schools, separate, 99
Scott, Thomas, 109, 146
secret ballot, 39, 59, 60, 180
See, Scott W.: "Polling Crowds and Patronage," 40–1; research, 10
Sewell, Isaiah, 140–1
Sheedy, Matthew, 137, 178
Sherwood, Henry, 52, 58
Simcoe, John Graves, 13
Smith, Frank: anti-unionism, 158–9, 165, 170, 172; conflict with Mayor Howland, 166, 179; response to strikers, 167, 169, 174–5, 176. *See also* Toronto Street Railway Company; Toronto Street Railway strikes
Smyth, William J.: *The Sash Canada Wore*, 10
sports, organized, 146–7, 151
St Andrews Society, 33
St James (Anglican) Cathedral, 79, 81
St Mary's Church, 91–2
St Michael's Cathedral, 76, 87, 90, 91
St Nicholas Home, 150
St Patrick's Church, 90
St Patrick's Day (17 March), 75, 137
Stanton, Robert, 45
street demonstrations. *See* political expression, acts of; processions and parades; public space
strikes. *See* Knights of Labor; Toronto Street Railway strikes; unionism
The Structural Transformation of the Public Sphere (Habermas), 9–10
Sutherland, Robert, 73
Sydenham, First Baron (Charles Poulett Thomson), 39, 54

Taché, Étienne-Paschal, 89
Taking to the Streets (Horner), 10, 41
Taves, Ann, 98
Telegram (Toronto): on the North-West Campaign and monument, 108, 110, 115, 123, 129; on Toronto Street Railway strikes, 154, 155, 160, 168, 172
Thompson, E.P.: "The Moral Economy of the Crowd in the Eighteenth Century," 8–9
Thompson, T. Phillips, 164, 169
Tilly, Charles, 8, 9, 36
Times (London), 63, 64, 74, 82
Times (New York), 73
Tories. *See* Conservative Party (Tories)
Toronto: in 1880s, characteristics of, 109–10, 177; as capital city, 13, 32, 35, 65; industrialization and stratification, 13–14; origins, 12–13; population, 13, 187n41, 187n46. *See also* newspapers
Toronto Boys' Home, 149, 150
Toronto Lacrosse Club, 147
Toronto Street Railway Company: employees and working conditions, 156–7; ironclad agreements, use of, 153, 158, 159, 164, 165, 170; public attitudes toward, 6–7, 157–8, 162–3. *See also* Smith, Frank; Toronto Street Railway strikes
Toronto Street Railway strikes: bus cooperative, 173–4, 175; crowd actions during March strike, 152, 153–6, 160–2, 163, 164, 169–70, 175–6; crowds, and May strike, 171; March strike, police response to, 139, 159, 161, 162, 165, 166–9; March strike settlement, 169–70; May street demonstration, 173–4;

May strike, police response to, 170–1; strike-breakers, 153, 158, 163, 167, 173; strikers' stance against violence, 164, 170, 171–2. *See also* boys and young men; Knights of Labor; Toronto Street Railway Company

Toronto Trades and Labour Council, 173

Toronto Volunteers Reception Committee, 121

"Tory rebels," 5, 15

transparencies, 50, 72, 79, 80

treating, 44, 46–7, 51, 55, 59

Treaty of Paris (1763), 87

Tribune (New York), 64

ultramontanism, 11, 86, 97, 98, 99, 106. *See also* Lynch, John Joseph

unionism, 6–7, 14, 157

United Province of Canada, 11–12, 13, 39

University of Toronto, 34, 117

Upper Canada (Canada West), 10, 11–12, 15–16, 18, 77, 82–3. *See also* Albert Edward, Prince of Wales' state visit; Rebellion Losses bill controversy

Varsity (University of Toronto student newspaper), 117

Vernon, James, 41, 44, 46

Victoria, Queen, 13, 62, 63, 68

violence and rowdy behaviour: bullying behaviours, 22, 48, 53, 58, 101, 139; of college students, 139; effigy-burnings, 3, 15, 23–4, 26–9, 36; fire alarm bell ringing, 25, 34–5, 88; heckling, 39, 41, 42, 46, 48, 49, 59; Hibernian, 89–90, 96; murder of Samuel Reid, 141; at polling places, 5, 38, 52–3; in public meetings, 47, 48, 49–50; ritualized, 39–40, 92, 139, 160, 178; spontaneous, in city streets, 140; strategies for diffusing, 146–50; Toronto police court, 141–4, 169; at victory processions, 56, 58–9. *See also* boys and young men; ethno-religious conflict; laws, selective enforcement of; Orange Order; Orange Young Britons; riots; Roman Catholic processions; Toronto Street Railway strikes; Young Irishmen's Benevolent Association

voice-vote system, 39, 51, 181

Volunteers (volunteer militia): active service, lack of, 108, 112; activities in support of the troops, 119–20, 212n53; "C Company" Infantry School, 107; casualties and funerals, 120, 212n58; creation of and recruitment for, 111–12, 178, 210n22; mobilization and send-off, 113–17, 212n47; Northwest Rebellion Monument, 129, *130*; preparations for return of, 123–4, 180; reception in Toronto, 124–9, *127*. *See also* North-West Campaign press coverage

voters' (electoral) lists, 51, 54–5

voting methods: secret ballot, 39, 59, 60, 180; show of hands, 44–5, 180; voice-vote, 39, 51, 181. *See also* election culture; polling

Walden, Keith, 139

Walsh, John, 76

Wamsley, Kevin, 147

Way, Peter, 58

William III, King (William of Orange), 79–80, *80*

Wilson, Adam, 65, 76, 79–80, 179

Wilson, Daniel, 150
Witton, Henry Buckham, 50
Wolseley, Garnet, 114, 115
women and girls: Brook's Bush Gang, 140–1; canvassers, 43–4; Corpus Christi celebration (1864), 87, 88, 89, 104, 180; gender conventions and public roles, 11, 66, 67, 179–80; journalists' erasures of, 11, 40, 163, 180; Jubilee riots and, 91–2, 104; narrative of Protestant male aggression, 96, 104, 180; and the North-West Campaign, *114*, 116, 119, 120; racialized, 180; and reformers, 135; in Toronto police court, 143; Toronto Street Railway strikes and, 162, 163, 167, 168, 171, 173

Woods, Nathaniel August, 64

World (Toronto): on the North-West Campaign, 108, 113, 114, 116, 117, 123; "penny daily" style and audience, 8; on Toronto Street Railway strikes, 154, 163, 164, 166

YMCA (Young Men's Christian Association), 96

Young Irishmen's Benevolent Association, 144, 145

www.ingramcontent.com/pod-product-compliance
Lightning Source LLC
Chambersburg PA
CBHW020404080526
44584CB00014B/1164